Skills Training in
Degree Programmes

Skills Training in Research Degree Programmes: Politics and Practice

Edited by
Richard Hinchcliffe,
Tony Bromley and
Steve Hutchinson

Open University Press

Open University Press
McGraw-Hill Education
McGraw-Hill House
Shoppenhangers Road
Maidenhead
Berkshire
England
SL6 2QL

email: enquiries@openup.co.uk
world wide web: www.openup.co.uk

and Two Penn Plaza, New York, NY 10121-2289, USA

First published 2007   **1005301914**

Copyright © Hinchcliffe, Bromley and Hutchinson, 2007

A catalogue record of this book is available from the British Library

ISBN-13: 978-0-33-522148-6 (pb) 978-0-33-522147-9 (hb)
ISBN-10: 0-33-522148-3 (pb) 0-33-522147-5 (hb)

Library of Congress Cataloging-in-Publication Data
CIP data applied for

Typeset by Exeter Premedia Services Private Ltd., Chennai, India
Printed in Poland EU by OZGraf S. A. www.polskabook.pl

The **McGraw-Hill** Companies

*This book is dedicated to Sir Gareth Roberts and to research students
everywhere – past, present and future.*

Contents

Foreword

Gareth Roberts

The training of postgraduate research students within the structure of a research degree programme is a controversial and difficult issue for many academics and for the institutions within which they work. So it should be. I say this because when colleagues grapple with the issue of research training, they are compelled to think about what it *means* to do a PhD. This can be a thorny process. Perhaps it occurs whenever the training appears to supervisor, research student or both as being peripheral to the research project itself, or perhaps it occurs because of the pressures of time on the duration of the project. These factors are not mutually exclusive; but together they concentrate the mind on what the process of a PhD is about rather than the content of the thesis. The product that the PhD student creates is not the thesis – vital though it is to their subject area through the creation of original knowledge; rather, the product of their study is the development of themselves.

I have been instrumental in making sure that universities engage with training researchers to meet the needs of the economy, the research environment and the career and personal development needs of the researchers themselves. In the Roberts report, which I completed for the Treasury in 2003, I recommended that research students should attend at least six weeks of training – mainly in transferable skills – over the period of registration for their research. The research councils addressed this specification and now research council funded research students bring with them a 'purse' of nearly a thousand pounds per year to help their institution with the provision of these skills. Since then, institutions of all kinds have joined those who had, in the 1990s, already created training programmes to offer a range of sessions, courses, workshops and opportunities to researchers to raise their skills beyond the previous threshold of research attributes.

For the research student whose thoughts only chime with the complexities of Linear Collider Physics or Chaucerian semantics, the idea of engaging with transferable skills training can be difficult. The exposure to the culture of academic research – a concentrated, full-on investigation into a small but distinct and original area of the subject – may predispose the early career researcher into downgrading the training experience. Training, particularly in transferable skills, may appear to be anything from quaint to condescending to an interesting diversion or a necessary evil that has to be undergone before the real study is completed. Perhaps it appears as a distraction from the main event, as if the ushers who have just sat you in a seat for the principal performance are now dragging you off to a sideshow that you neither understand nor care about.

While this analogy clearly has its limits, it is worth pursuing a little further in order to orientate the reader towards some of the educational conceptions being discussed in this book. Firstly, the skills training 'sideshow', where researchers may undergo the skills development listed by the research councils such as 'personal development' or 'career management', may not initially appear to be of interest to the individual being trained. This is ironic, as this is the person who is doing the research, the 'self' who at the end of it all is awarded the research degree with much ceremony and hand-shaking. Secondly, the reluctance of many full-fledged academics themselves to engage with the skills development that is required for their own career illustrates an interesting but dangerous dynamic within the structure of higher education everywhere. It is interesting because this failure to engage with skills development does not necessarily stop them from climbing to top academic and research related positions – the need to fill these positions with those familiar with the subject area is paramount. Yet it is dangerous because once in these 'gatekeeper' positions they can undervalue the importance of skills development within early career researchers and staff whilst perpetuating the myth that training and development are only for those individuals who want to work outside academia. 'I'm going to be an academic so I don't require any of this skills training', is a phrase I have heard mentioned by students in their naivety and replayed to me by skills practitioners who encounter this attitude all too frequently. This seriously affects the sustainability of the research community as I illustrated in *SET for Success* where evidence from a host of employers showed that 'postgraduate education does not lead them to develop the transferable skills and knowledge required by R&D employers' (Roberts 2002). It will be a long haul in terms of turning around these attitudes. At the 2006 UK GRAD Conference 'Profiting from Postgraduate Talent', Rosie Sotillo, Head of Graduate Development, Barclays Global Investors, informed the conference that they no longer sought PhD recruits from Britain with the necessary high computational and mathematical skills but instead preferred American research graduates. This is not because UK research graduates did not have these specialist skills in abundance, but because in Barclays' experience similarly talented American research graduates had greater maturity and were less likely to come with a negative attitude towards business needs.

The reality check that greets most, if not all, research graduates is that finding a job, being able to transfer skills and securing a position commensurate with subject knowledge and ability is a difficult proposition. Research suggests that far fewer than half of all PhDs find a job in higher education as lecturers or researchers – a goal which may have been their aim during their studies (Shinton 2004).[1] Those who do become members of an academic staff may then be surprised at the skills required in order to thrive in such an environment where they are expected to balance teaching, administration, research and perhaps have a family and a rewarding social life. A further and perhaps related set of research students find that during their studies the solitary experience of being responsible for the creation of their own research is something that they are not adequately prepared for. We have seen a percentage of non-completions significant enough to be of serious concern, and while many of these may have personally benefited from the experience it will nevertheless be considered by many to be a waste of time, money and resources for both the individual and the economy. Research students have access to the generic skills training provision now implemented in virtually every higher education institution in the country, which is incidentally now being copied and replicated furiously in many European and American institutions. Courses address the skill needs for both career development and successful submission. They facilitate not just good thesis writing or how to write a CV but also how to be assertive and confident with other colleagues such as supervisors, heads of department and vice chancellors and fellow research students themselves.

By far, the majority of research students and their supervisors appreciate the need for wider training and what it entails.

Skills development for all early career researchers – PhD students, postdoctoral researchers and academic staff already in position – is a duty to our profession. We owe it to future generations of researchers to provide them with a rich heritage of opportunity not just as custodians of our respective subject areas but also as contributors to an economy that sustains universities, research establishments and exciting and well-rewarding careers in every industrial sector – public and private. Invariably, this will not be possible by producing ever more detailed discussion on the habits of the fruit fly or the intricacies of nanoparticulate dispersions, but rather by the development of a range of essential generic skills such as teamwork, good communication, project and career management and personal effectiveness itself. I notice that the Joint Skills Statement by the Research Councils lists 'a willingness and ability to learn and acquire knowledge', along with 'flexibility, open-mindedness and self-awareness'. For many researchers habituated to the cultures of their respective departments and subject traditions these may seem to be common sense but in the extraordinarily diverse and competitive world we now live in, a commitment to a lifelong learning of these skills makes a significant difference – not just to the individuals concerned but to all who benefit from their talent.

I commend this book to you. It informs on the research training practices currently to be found in a variety of our institutions and it describes good practice, obstacles to success and lessons learnt in equal measure.

It attempts to identify, describe and demystify the current research training initiatives while looking to the future of the PhD, its structure and the professional practices that sustain it. I look forward to the second edition in order to keep track of this fast-changing and exciting area of expertise.

Professor Sir Gareth Roberts was Visiting Professor of Science Policy at the Saïd Business School and President of Wolfson College, University of Oxford.

Note

1   *What Do PhDs Do?* was based on first destination data and does not include later career destinations. A longitudinal survey is in the process of being commissioned.

Preface

It was Thomas Kuhn (1962) who raised the idea of science having 'paradigms'. Paradigms are ideas within a subject area that appear to stand the test of time, are held dear by the profession and are rarely questioned. However, there are moments in time when evidence gathers to make a particular paradigm look a little less robust and as more evidence gathers, this leads to eventual breakdown.

This book chronicles the early stages of a paradigm change in the PhD from a 'traditional' purely research model to one including research and personal and professional training and development. The evidence which suggests the necessity of this change is broad, but it has four key strands:

- The academic role is very different now from what it was 10 or 20 years ago, with more significant demands in all areas of teaching and learning, research and administration. If the academic role has changed, then the 'training' for the role of being a research student must change to reflect this.
- The Roberts report (Roberts 2002) summarizes that 'skills acquired by PhD graduates do not serve their long-term needs. Currently, PhDs do not prepare people adequately for careers in business or academia'.
- Data on the careers paths of PhD graduates (Shinton 2004) show that around half leave research altogether and only a quarter pursue an academic career. Therefore, the notion that the PhD experience is training for academia does not hold.
- Finally, given the changes in the academic role, it is clear that new skills, attributes, techniques and behaviours need to be nurtured in the next generation of academics to meet the challenges to academia in the twenty-first century.

This book covers these issues in three sections. Part 1 considers the politics and cultural changes behind the paradigm shift, probes what employers are looking for and closely examines issues in the PhD qualification itself.

Part 2 considers how the skills training and development agenda has been implemented in practice across the UK's higher education institutions. The section raises a host of practical issues and illustrates how three specific institutions have addressed the issues in their own context.

Finally, Part 3 looks to the future and what the PhD might look like. This section covers the changing role of the supervisor, how the PhD might look in the future and the influence of Europe.

This is an exciting time of change in doctoral study. For the first time, this book brings together the views and experience of many of the key figures in skills training and development in the UK to provide a resource for a broad range of people involved in the skills training and development agenda across the higher education sector.

Contributors

Dr Esat Alpay (Imperial College London)
Dr Charlie Ball (Graduate Prospects)
Dr Simon Beecroft (University of Sheffield)
Professor Tim Birtwistle (Leeds Metropolitan University)
Dr Tony Bromley (University of Leeds)
Professor Howard Green (Staffordshire University)
Dr Ged Hall (University of Nottingham)
Dr Richard Hinchcliffe (University of Liverpool)
Dr Steve Hutchinson (Independent Consultant)
Peter Lewis (University of Nottingham)
Professor Alistair McCulloch (Edge Hill University)
Professor Chris Park (Lancaster University).
Professor Stuart Powell (University of Hertfordshire)
Imelda Race (University of East Anglia)
Dr Julie Reeves (University of Manchester)
Professor Al Richardson (Royal Institute and Cranfield University)
Dr Sara Shinton (Shinton Consulting)
Clair Souter (University of Leeds)
Dr Peter Stokes (University of Central Lancashire)
Dr Judi Sture (University of Bradford)
Elaine Walsh (Imperial College London)

Disclaimer

The views expressed in each chapter are the personal views of the authors and should not be assumed to represent the views of the body or institution to which they are affiliated.

Abbreviations and Acronyms

AHRC	Arts and Humanities Research Council
CIPD	Chartered Institute of Personnel and Development
CPD	continuing professional development
CROS	Careers in Research Online Survey
DfES	Department for Education and Skills (before 2001 the Department for Education and Employment)
EFQ	European Framework of Qualifications
EHEA	European Higher Education Area
EMPRESS	(Report) Employers' Perceptions of Research Staff and Students
EPSRC	Engineering and Physical Sciences Research Council
ERA	European Research Area
ESIB	European Student Union Body
ESRC	Economic and Social Research Council
EUA	European University Association
FEC	full economic cost
GTA	graduate teaching assistant
HE	higher education
HEFCE	Higher Education Funding Council for England
HEI	higher education institution
HESA	Higher Education Statistics Agency
JSS	Joint Skills Statement (Joint Statement of Skills Training Requirements of Research Postgraduates)
KT	Knowledge Transfer
LNA	learning needs analysis (usually referred to as training needs analysis (TNA))
MBTI	Myers–Briggs Type Indicator
NPC	National Postgraduate Committee
NWUA	North-West University Association
OECD	Overseas Economic Development Agency
OST	Office of Science and Technology
PDP	personal development planning
PG	postgraduate
PGR	postgraduate researcher

PREQ	Postgraduate Research Experience Questionnaire (Australian)
PRES	Postgraduate Research Evaluation Survey
QAA	Quality Assurance Agency (for Higher Education)
RAE	research assessment exercise
RCUK	Research Councils UK
RDP	research degree programme
RTU	Research Training Unit (from Sheffield University)
SKIPI	Skills Perception Inventory (from University of East Anglia)
SOLSTICE	Supporting Online Learning for Students and Teachers in Continuing Education
THES	Times Higher (Educational Supplement)
TNA	training needs analysis
UKCGE	UK Council for Graduate Education
UK GRAD	The role of the UK GRAD Programme is to support the academic sector to embed personal and professional skills development into research degree programmes.
WDPD	*What Do Postgraduates Do?* (title of often-cited Postgraduate Careers Report)

Part 1
Politics

1

Can Generic Skills Training Change Academic Culture?

Richard Hinchcliffe

Introduction

Postgraduate research training in generic skills still creates divisions amongst university lecturing staff even though provision of such training has been growing steadily in all kinds of universities and across different subject areas for at least a decade. Such formal training takes place outside the traditional supervisor/apprentice relationship and is often part of a programme of skills training that many, perhaps the majority of, research students now undergo. Regardless of whether this training is either compulsory or voluntary, outright opposition or plain glum indifference to it is encountered by all transferable skills practitioners within academia. Many of the other contributors in this book, such as Imelda Race, Julie Reeves and Simon Beecroft, all comment on the prevalence of opposition amongst what may sometimes be a significant minority of colleagues. Anecdotal evidence as to the make-up of this opposition, however, suggests that it is the ability to shout loudest that makes the difference, as those who protest may frequently be senior academics or those who have served their time working with colleagues who distrust change. In turn, this may well indicate that more recent generations of academics are less likely to be anti-generic skills training and that those who have experienced generic research skills training as research students may be even more favourably inclined. In this chapter, I suggest that the generic skills or transferable skills initiative within doctoral training confronts current academic culture and, whether intentionally or not, is set to change it by subtly altering the character make-up of those who enter the profession. I conclude that such changes, if managed correctly, should strengthen the role of academics in society by making them more responsive to the external markets for knowledge professionals. In this regard, I agree with Barnett (2000: 411) who states that '[n]ew, even more challenging roles are opening up for [universities], roles that still enable us to see continuities with its earlier self-understandings built around personal growth, societal enlightenment and the promotion of critical forms of understanding.'

A supervisor's antipathy towards skills training should be no surprise given the structural changes occurring within higher education (HE). Generic skills training is seen by some as symptomatic of the erosion of the authority of the academic in a world of ever proliferating knowledge – part of a 'dumbing down' process that many see as inevitable now that universities have been given the task of educating over 75 per cent more students since 1988/1989 (HEFCE 2001). Research student numbers have also risen as graduates attempt to raise their profile and institutions seek extra manpower. In order to assist and further develop the skills agenda for researchers, supervisors are required to embrace new practices, inform their research students of the breadth and depth of skills opportunities and offer the hand of partnership to groups of skills practitioners whom they may distrust as having no experience of supervision, having never met them and knowing nothing about their syllabus. Thus, bridge-building between trainers and supervisors will go a long way towards embedding generic skills in research degree programmes.

As commentators have noted since the 1960s, managerialism has slowly asserted itself within HE as the role of the university changes and becomes more complex so as to best meet the needs of the national and world economy. Managerialist procedures seek to impose change rather than seek consensus through informal or, in the case of academia, collegiate structures. They do this in order that the institution or the sector as a whole can make rapid changes in the face of market pressure. The Roberts report *SET for Success* (2002), and the consequent increase in the supply of generic skills training to research students, is a classic example of this market pressure. Collegiate processes where a consensus of 'common room' practices used to patrol the boundaries and corridors of HE have now been dispersed to the margins. What is slowly replacing that structure is a more market-orientated response. This implies that universities can no longer assume that they are part of an establishment that industry and government will always heed and respect as the highest instrument of learning practice and pedagogic expertise. Their authority, like every structural entity within the postmodern realm, must be subject to change. Peter Jarvis comments that 'Higher Education is ... part of the superstructure and it matters not how hard academics argue for their independence, they will be forced to respond to the infrastructural social pressures that shape the world as a whole' (Jarvis 2000: 45). Ownership of knowledge has proliferated amongst a wide variety of individuals and groups and has become disaggregated to the point where universities are now competing with everything from the Internet to the corporation 'university' to the networked knowledge base of professionals (Barnett 2000). These developments threaten to further decouple HE from the position it previously enjoyed as being the sole trainer of highly educated individuals in order to restock an elite workforce within the civil service, large corporations, law and, of course, academia itself. As student numbers in the UK have grown from 8 to 10 per cent of school leavers in the 1960s to close to 50 per cent today, that clientele has also broadened. These changes have fundamentally affected both the way institutions service their students and the relationship between supervisor and early career researcher. The current skills initiative within research degree programmes is therefore a part of HE's response to these global changes. It appears as a greater threat to the traditionalists who are perhaps more at home with the collegiate tradition because it is directed precisely at those who will renew the profession – young doctoral researchers. 'Younger academics have not yet been tainted by the old ways. We should support and encourage them', notes an unattributed academic manager in Will Archer's report on the crisis within human resources in HE (Archer 2005: 19).

Even though there may be many more colleagues in favour of what might be loosely termed the 'Roberts initiative' as there are ranged against it, the divide over training for research students in generic skills goes to the heart of what it means to do a research degree and, given that a PhD is a passport to an academic career, to what it means to be an academic in the twenty-first century. It is possible for colleagues to reposition their epistemological stance towards research skills *and* maintain their stance on what it means to be an academic in the traditional sense of a university, but the wider considerations of the social, economic and political market for knowledge and expertise must be taken into account. Postdoctoral workers from all disciplines should repay the world for giving them the potential for higher earning; but we need them also to have all the skills at their disposal to help solve the urgent problems that beset the world today.

Academic culture: what is it?

If you work in HE, it is reasonable to assume that you know of numerous anecdotes, reportage, stories, myths and legends regarding either individual academics or academic character types. As in any profession or calling, these stories give us insight into what it means to be a part of such a subset of society and also what it may look like from the outside. One example of research looking at how academic culture might perceive itself is the work of Blaxter et al. (1998), who have analysed three forms of account: academic novels; the professional media, such as the *Times Higher Education Supplement*; and 'How to Guides', the practical texts that explain to novice academics what to expect and how to cope with the core activities of academic life. Blaxter et al. have an interesting comment on this latter material, which they claim is mainly concerned with teaching. This interest in teaching, they say, 'is not surprising' as it is a 'core academic task'. However, they comment that this is 'somewhat in contradiction, [as] it is also a task in which novice and experienced academics may have little interest or motivation' (Blaxter et al. 1998: 308–9). For most people, and I suggest this is also true of those in the profession, the notion that there is little interest in teaching is surely paradoxical for a profession in which teaching is a core activity. However, the authors go on to indicate that a further element of reflexive scrutiny is lacking as '[f]or many academics an interest in researching higher education would either be seen as navel gazing or simply bizarre' (Blaxter et al. 1998: 313).

One way round the impasse of trying to get academics to look at themselves is to fictionalize the lives of lecturers and allow them a voyeuristic experience of seeing stereotypical characters engaging with stereotypical institutional structures and forces. Thus, in novels such as Malcolm Bradbury's (1975) *The History Man* and David Lodge's (1989) *Nice Work*, characters that supposedly typify the average British university are seen to be lacking in a range of skills, attributes and behaviours that have come to typify the common view of the academic. These colleagues are typically identified as distant, disengaged or so concentrated on their work as to make normal social intercourse either difficult and anxiety inducing, or to be so disconnected as to create a range of misunderstandings resulting in tragicomic circumstances for all involved. At one level, *Nice Work* centres on the antipathies that a female arts academic and a male manager of a heavy engineering works have for each other's professions. The lecturer has deep misgivings about the dirty masculine commercial world while the manager suspects the academic world of English literature to be a waste of time. Asked as part of the university's 'outreach' work to shadow each other's job, they learn mutual respect and readers sense the possibilities and potential to be gained from interactions between previously perceived disparate subject areas.

Blaxter et al. note that the preoccupation of the campus novel is with 'class, gender and race' and that '[t]hese concerns should not be surprising, of course, given the centrality of hierarchy and status to academic life, and its function in enablement of individual betterment' (Blaxter et al. 1998: 302–3). Oxford and Cambridge are quoted as being the setting for 71 per cent of 204 campus novels between 1945 and 1988, indicating the dominance of those institutions in setting the cultural perception of academics. On this basis, elitism and class consciousness would appear to dominate the view of academic culture from the outside. Lecturers themselves, however, may also be persuaded by their continual interaction and maintenance of the examination system that an elitist outlook is a reasonable approach to make in terms of judging oneself and those around you. Course marking and degree classifications allow individuals, employers and other educationalists to make decisions relating to roles and capabilities. The dominant use of Oxford and Cambridge in the campus novel is clearly a reflection on how ingrained this elitism is.

Both Bradbury's and Lodge's novels rely on the premise that typical academic mannerisms produce communication difficulties either because the academic character does not have the skill to communicate properly or because those of their colleagues who do are seen to be at a distinct advantage over those who do not. The character of Henry Beamish in

Bradbury's *The History Man*, for instance, is seen to be bumptious and accident prone not just physically but also in terms of how he is easily manipulated by Howard Kirk, the radical 'History Man' sociologist, whose rhetorical skills enable him to outflank all the other characters and indeed the University of 'Watermouth' itself (Bradbury 1975). It is arguable whether the instance of poor communication skills is a burden that academia has to bear above any other professional grouping – medical doctors, for instance, are also subject to this stereotyping; however, research graduates are expected to have a number of communication attributes. The Joint Skills Statement (JSS) of the Research Councils (RCUK 2001a) points out the need for the ability to write clearly, construct coherent arguments, defend research outcomes, contribute to the public understanding of one's research field and support the learning of others. Listening skills, interestingly, are contained within the section on networking and teamworking as if they are considered tools for career advancement rather than aids to communication. There is no mention within the JSS, however, of the level of skill to be attained – just that individuals should have them. One of the most damning reports concerning the communication skills of academics was contained in a report by the Institute of Employment Studies to the Engineering and Physical Sciences Research Council (EPSRC) on 'Employers' Views of Postgraduate Physicists'. According to the report non-academic employers of physicists took it as a given that technical or physics skills were associated with postgraduate level qualifications. What they used to distinguish between candidates, however, were the soft skills, of which 'communications skills were mentioned the most often as being important'. However, when the same questions were asked of academic employers, 'some quite striking divergences from the pattern of important skills amongst commercial organisations could be seen.' The report concludes that '[i]n many ways, the skills that are considered important [problem solving, motivation and enthusiasm, proactivity] are a critique of the culture within academic departments ... It is also revealing that the two important areas where employers complain that postgraduates are inadequate ('communication' and 'team working') do not feature on the academics' agenda' (Jagger et al. 2001). Given our best conclusions derived from this admittedly partial evidence, these examples seem to suggest that there is a distinct lack of interest amongst a significant minority of academics in communication skills and teaching.

More detailed research would be required to link this apparent blind spot regarding communication to academic culture. However, it is interesting to speculate whether the inherently parochial collegiate process may reinforce certain communication practices and disapprove of others. In my experience as a student and as a lecturer in four different institutions, the same issue often reoccurred of how students were apparently unable to 'read what it says on the notice/message/handbook'. These complaints – that students do not or cannot read their messages – often elicit the response that students need to study things harder and closely examine the world around them. There is hardly ever any consideration given to the poor instruction, quality or wording of the original message. Thus the student adjusts to academic life – and not vice versa – and those who comprehend and thrive amidst its arcane practices and self-policed authority structures tend to do well. In the worst case, this results in a positive feedback loop where research students become clones of their supervisors, right down to their opposition to skills training and any external demand to respond to social, political and economic pressures.

Objections to generic skills

There are three main issues that make generic skills training a contested area for some academics:

1   Time pressure: The belief that there is already not enough time to educate a research student in the methods, techniques and subject knowledge in order to graduate within the required time frame – to add generic skills training is simply a waste of time.
2   Intellectual engagement and a distrust of the generic skills vocabulary: Research students (and their supervisors) may sometimes see the language of generic skills as 'business-speak' and distrust it believing it to be either intellectually, politically or morally unsound or unprincipled. This is to be expected if colleagues feel excluded from the formal generic skills training process.
3   'It's not our job': Another ground for objection often encountered is that it is the role of industry to train research graduates and not that of the university. This is based on the principle that academia inherently equips its research students in the skills required to be a lecturer or researcher. This objection is therefore political in nature in that it goes to the heart of what it means to provide an education.

Time pressure

The first of these issues is that research students are caught precisely in the crossfire of research versus teaching – a nexus of academic contention in the wake of the research assessment exercise (RAE) and debates around teaching versus research. Within this crucible, the supervisor has a collegial duty to educate, train and develop the researcher whilst ensuring a safe completion of the thesis and the research project itself. The stress of achieving these aims in a limited time frame inevitably causes tensions as supervisors feel the need, rightly or wrongly, to protect their students from the pressures of the research environment. In the current round of the RAE, both the numbers of PhDs and their completions are part of the metrics governing a department's performance and therefore its income. This places further time pressure on issues surrounding training for personal development. Not surprisingly, then generic skills training can be seen as a 'waste of time' by supervisors who either will not or cannot conceive that it will make young researchers any more effective and efficient. The Roberts' requirement of six weeks skills training over three years coupled with other quality of work dispensations such as six weeks holiday a year (stipulated as the recommended time by some research councils) gives rise to the idea that a research degree can no longer be a rigorously thoughtful meander to completion or an exciting if often frustrating or even boring repetition of numerous laboratory experiments and testing. The planned march to a projected conclusion for those supervisors empathizing with the more relaxed approach to completion rates of the 1980s and before may well seem potentially devoid of the more interesting deviations en route. Although research students used to have time to complete at their leisure, that is no longer the case. As such, successful submission – within at least four years – causes some supervisors to look at the training portion of a research degree programme as potential slack that they feel should be cut out of the schedule. Inevitably this view becomes shared by their research students which can create further polarisation in terms of how generic skills training is valued.

Intellectual engagement

The second issue follows on from this perception that dedicated training is superfluous to the research itself. This is the familiar bête noir of the academic, that dealing with the disparate elements peripheral to their own research activity – evaluation processes, attendance at briefings and supervisor 'good practice' workshops, notions of compliance in general, engagement with official university policy, form filling and bureaucracy of all kinds – gets in the way of what they believe to be the true vocation of research, something which, perhaps at its most idealistic, is considered as a sacred duty to their subject area and knowledge in general. The imposition of all this extraneous activity is likened to a 'dead hand' or a 'handbrake' on the speed and efficiency with which papers are published and grant proposals are submitted before deadlines. Grants, research and papers are, after all, their area of expertise, their 'creativity' and within the pressurized environment created by the RAE, this produces incentives to resist and denigrate anything that is not research productive. As the handling of this stress is intimately related to the academic's own skills of time and project management, the line of least resistance can be to instruct the PhD student to ignore the training and to get on with the 'real' work. This link between the 'real' work and the individual's own sense of personal autonomy is very real – their work is connected to them intellectually and emotionally, it is their raison d'être and to threaten this autonomy can be perceived and felt as an attack on the self. Such deep personal involvement in research can produce a hostile reaction to requests from outside an academic's office to service the needs of a larger group such as the university or the government – unless, of course, it happens to be connected to the individual's research goals. Many research skills practitioners now focus on making the connections here in order to embed their practice within the less insular perspectives of supervisors, but it is not easy and the explanation required to justify taking away the research student for a skills workshop can be a challenging and, on occasions, very stressful experience for all concerned if not carefully handled.

Also, the 'real' work is invariably related to money, and research intensive institutions inevitably feel insecure in dealing with colleagues who do not give research top priority. The modern university is in a market for resources and this pressure bears down upon the academic as a 'knowledge worker' whose own productivity then becomes a very real value both in terms of their RAE 'score' and in terms of the money they bring in to the institution. This can be a large amount of money, and some colleagues talk of it as if it is their own. They have control over how it is spent and with the power that such money confers on the individual, it is possible that this affects the rigour with which heads of departments assert the need for accountability. The most powerful academics carry with them the monetary influence of their research agenda and this makes control and delegation a tricky area of responsibility for heads of departments and deans. As a result, some do not bother at all. As William Archer's report for the Higher Education Policy Institute has noted, 'It is hard to think of another sector where managers would need to be reminded that people management is a part of their responsibility. But the feedback from interviews is that this is a major issue in higher education today: many staff either fail to see HR issues as their responsibility, or are inadequately trained to handle them' (Archer 2005: 6–7). In this sort of environment, it is not surprising that the development needs of both research student and supervisor may quietly slip from the agenda lest either of them or both become offended by the thought that they need 'training'. As William Archer discovered, 'the rich heritage of our universities of all ages sometimes translated into a robust resistance to change' (Archer 2005: 5).

Such attitudes towards career management and personal development tend to be found amongst paternalistic organizations and employers where the emphasis is on the strength of the personal relationship a sharing of certain common goals, but coupled with a distrust of external influences unless they can be handled at arms length. The line manager or employer may fear that a broad ranging apprenticeship that developed adaptability and key skills could result in them developing their staff so that others could poach them. When supervisors are trying to build teams of researchers for their laboratory and for the continuation of their research, it would be strange for these fears not to manifest themselves in some as a distrust of the resources that might make their research students more employable and therefore more likely to leave.

'It's not our job': the politics of research training in generic skills

Published opposition to generic research skills training is hard to find but Fellow of Lady Margaret Hall, Oxford, Fiona Spensley published a paper on the Internet (now removed) describing her deep reservations about the JSS of the Research Councils and questions whether generic skills should be part of a research degree programme at all. 'As far as the skills provision is outward looking toward employment' she says that this 'is best provided outside the universities (perhaps funded by the employers) and targeted to individual careers ambitions' (Spensley 2002). Is this symptomatic of a politics attached to opposing generic research skills training? If so what form does it take? As a type of politics it does not have an official constituency to represent nor does it have a generic name that we can readily identify or necessarily identify with. There are no organizations campaigning against the combined weight of the Treasury, the Office of Science and Technology and the Research Councils or asking for the Roberts' initiative to be rolled back. But there is a contest taking place within HE. It is variously described as between an old guard set on preserving what it holds sacred to the spirit of the doctorate and a new generation of academics who are used to quality assessment exercises as well as students and funding bodies that demand extra value from degrees. It is across disciplines, both humanities and sciences, and it could be contested from the holistic outlook of lifelong learning or the focussed scrutiny of the subject specific scholar. Wherever the struggle takes place, a sort of politics will be practised. This political dimension and the contest itself is a good and healthy thing for the HE establishment to both recognize and undertake; indeed, it should be a part of a postgraduate's training and development programme itself. It concentrates the mind of the individual on what education is for and how it relates to the world outside the university. When this political debate is not taking place, the role of the university is being either bypassed or usurped and such debates should be an important part of every student's education.

Even so, if we consider how much the culture of academia steeps the mind of the student after perhaps three years of a BSc, perhaps an MRes and then a further three years of concentrated research for the PhD, it would not be surprising if they felt that HE had a claim on them. The student is so inculcated in academia after such a long time within the institution that it often appears to them that the only thing they are trained for is to become a lecturer, and it is possible to say that sometimes the institution attempts quite blatantly to create doctors in its own image.

Another political aspect to the debate over postgraduate training is that universities perhaps try too hard to avoid the political. There appears to be a reluctance to try and influence the wider world; thus, heads stay down as the university both retreats from being a service for industry and fails as a guide or a repository of wisdom. Such 'academic citizenship', as McFarlane comments, has 'been "hollowed out" by a range of forces affecting university faculty in parallel with the civic disengagement of wider society' (McFarlane 2005: 300). Yet by inculcating in postgraduates the need for a critical mind, awareness of transferable skills, a good sense of general knowledge, and the means to develop their career and be aware of their own potential, universities can and do make a considerable difference to the world of work. Because this is in the interest of the student, it is also in the interest of the university, as the student has the potential to repay the institution with international contacts, future research projects and possibly, for the wealthier alumni, some kind of donation.

The challenge

The idea that it is 'not our job' to train the research student in generic skills is to arrogantly assume, like the academic employers of physics postgraduates, that such skills have no place within HE. I suspect, though I could never prove, that there is, deep within the cultural psyche of the academic institution, a kind of hegemonic possessiveness that helps to inculcate the worst excesses of academic culture. The culprit, as Archer reports, is 'the rich heritage of our universities of all ages' and is born, perhaps, out of academia's religious origins and the progressive reasons for the establishment of the red brick universities in the latter half of the nineteenth century. Inevitably, academia wants to make its best scholars in its own image and personal development in generic research skills is clearly an outside influence. However, Lyotard noted that:

> The transmission of knowledge is no longer designed to train an elite capable of guiding a nation toward its emancipation, but to supply the system with players capable of acceptably fulfilling their roles in the pragmatic posts required of institutions.
>
> (Lyotard 1984: 48)

Any element that allows universities to reprise their pivotal role in the superstructure of society would improve morale, but it would also need vision alongside compromise. Generic skills provision for the academic 'elite' adds an 'edge' to Lyotard's 'pragmatic posts' and should add real value to a research degree. The qualified research graduate should have potential beyond the skills laid out in the JSS. Raffealla Ockinger, President of Eurodoc, the Europe-wide research student association, declared at the 2006 UK GRAD conference that she 'wanted to have her own business *and* have a university post too'. If there is a wide syllabus of skills in things as diverse as critical thinking, epistemology, project management, communication skills and an even broader range of personal development, universities will be endeavouring to take the needs of business into account whilst also playing a role in influencing the wider world of work. Too many academics dismiss the role of generic skills as providing industry (in its broadest terms) with 'oven ready' graduates. Because of the divide between academia and industry, they either ignore or misunderstand that industry requires critical thinkers, sharp minds and effective managers who understand the needs of people, not just the needs of shareholders in order to make a profit.

If universities wish to maintain their credibility in the increasingly pluralist world market for knowledge, they have to consider what they are training research students for. This is not just a question of asking industry what they want, because universities have the responsibility to consider the needs of all stakeholders in (world) society. The problem is what are these agendas? What are the correct things to offer as generic skills to postgraduate researchers? What is politically correct, philosophically correct, ethically correct and epistemologically correct? Many will duck the further questions that arise from this introspection: what kind of industry do we need? What kind of citizens do we want? What kind of business leaders do we want? And, inevitably and most importantly, what sort of scientists and what sort of science do we require? Surely, there is potential here for our training sessions covering ethics, teamwork and business awareness to explosively combine and create those intense 'learning moments' that can remain with the graduate for the rest of their lives. Alternatively, it can be a moment of anxiety for the deliverer of the training – 'Is this what I'm supposed to be doing?'.

In most cases the answer has to be yes, and to keep on doing it, but the anxiety for the institution is whether the political should be allowed or encouraged to surface. If schoolchildren are being taught citizenship, can the same principle be applied to postgraduate researchers by asking them what that citizenship should be and how it should be constructed? The doctorate is potentially the most powerful of all academic qualifications, creating men and women who become gatekeepers in their organizations and society in general, influential in both word and deed; should they be encouraged or even educated mandatorily to have an interest in how their relative power can affect the world?

Conclusion

Research is vitally important to the supervisor, their department, their subject area and their university. Often, particularly in the sciences, the research student is the worker who gets the experiment done, creates the research environment and discovers the next pathway to yet more research and so on. In order to justify the resources that such research consumes, public money is expended. Each stage is a ripple of accountability, and it ultimately becomes important to government, nation and even, in the wake of the Bologna accord, to the future of Europe as an information economy that the research and the researcher fulfil their outcomes in terms of results, thesis and career. All these stakeholders in research want universities to pay increased attention to the personal development of the graduates themselves as the outcome of the research process.

The increased attention of stakeholders and universities is welcomed by skills trainers who practise in this emerging area and who contribute so vitally to this new curriculum. There is an opportunity to realize a new syllabus and establish a new partnership with supervisors who can and should make a real difference to the working environment into which the new PhD will venture. Resources, commitment and a workable theoretical underpinning that gives training pedagogic authority is required to make this partnership work. Skills trainers are the 'new kids on the block' but they must reassure supervisors that they are partners who are there to support them and, most importantly, convince them that what they offer is not just best for research students but also good for the world – and academia – as a whole.

2

What Do Employers Want?

Clair Souter, Sara Shinton and Charlie Ball

With the publication of the report *SET for Success* by Sir Gareth Roberts (Roberts 2002), the training of postgraduates moved away from being a minority interest to a national issue. From the report a range of initiatives have been developed that are designed to help postgraduates and postdoctoral researchers cope with changes in the structure of the labour market for those with doctoral qualifications. Although Roberts dealt with science, engineering and technology graduates, many of the basic principles apply equally to students in the social sciences, arts and humanities, and new schemes have been introduced on that basis.

Roberts made a number of disquieting observations about the attractiveness of PhD study, and how it was contributing to a decline in the supply of doctorates from key subjects into the economy. Many of these observations came as no surprise to keen observers of the sector, but the cumulative effect was to show how important it is now that doctoral study no longer be thought of merely as training for academia.

Roberts expressed concerns about pay and conditions (starkly exposed by bitter industrial action by lecturers in 2006), and about poor prospects for would-be academics. But in stating that 'inadequate training – particularly in the more transferable skills – available during the PhD program' was acting as a deterrent for prospective PhD students, Roberts brought the needs of non-academic PhD employers and those who would work for them onto the agenda.

The 1997 Research Councils survey of 1523 postgraduates from 1987–88 and 1988–89 (OST 1997) showed that postgraduates entered a range of employment sectors, but despite this, the perception of the PhD, amongst both academics and employers, as essentially a qualification for academics, remains strong.

Other surveys of sectors of postgraduate employment, most recently the 2006 ESRC report on social science PhDs (Elias et al. 2006), have reinforced these points – that PhD graduates are valuable employees outside, as well as inside, academia, and that their skills training is sometimes not sufficient to meet the needs of their employers.

The basic conclusions from these reports appear to be that employers prize the problem-solving, project management, research and reasoning skills that are acquired through PhD study, but that these skills are rarely formally developed through training programmes. Furthermore, lack of training means that many students and graduates are unable to articulate these skills in terms that employers understand, and consequently miss out on opportunities. PhDs are aware that they sometimes fail to understand the rules and language of business, and as a result can be nervous or reluctant to engage with employers outside academia, to the detriment of both themselves and the wider economy.

Roberts identified other issues. The changing nature of academic employment means skills training, particularly in soft, interpersonal and communication skills, is becoming increasingly important for the effective academic in managing research, students, administration and staff.

As a result, the government provided £150 million in funding for the period 2003–06 to over 180 organizations. Key developments included the development of the Joint Skills Statement (RCUK 2001b) as part of the QAA Code of Practice (QAA 2004), which covered the framework of research degree programmes. The UK GRAD programme developed their regional networks, or Hubs, to improve the ability to deliver training throughout the country, and it also produced a database of practices related to Roberts for organizations to share. Many organizations undertook training needs analysis, and all of this activity demonstrated that there was an appetite within the sector to improve training and provision for postgraduates.

For all employers to benefit from postgraduate education, training needed to adapt. But to establish how, and to what extent, a number of key questions needed to be addressed. Amongst them are the two dealt with in this chapter: what do postgraduates actually do with their qualifications, and how do they and their employers perceive one another?

For the first time, in 2004, we were able to comment on *What Do PhDs Do?* (Shinton and Ball 2004) when UK GRAD and *Graduate Prospects* published an analysis of the first destination statistics for doctoral graduates. Although the employment of first-degree graduates immediately after graduation has been systematically studied since the 1960s, our PhDs have remained largely invisible. This has fuelled the myth that there are only one or two occupations available to PhD graduates – either remaining in academia or (for the scientific and technical disciplines) moving into research in relevant industrial areas. The truth is far more varied and shows that doctoral graduates also work in the public sector, a range of manufacturing industries and for business and IT companies, as shown in Figure 2.1.

With this basic information on the nature of doctoral graduate employers emerging, new questions have become important. What do these employers need in terms of skills and knowledge? Are they happy with the products of UK research training? Are our doctoral graduates developing relevant skills for the labour market they enter? Whose responsibility is it to ensure that doctoral graduates can perform effectively – the universities that train them or the employers of postgraduates?

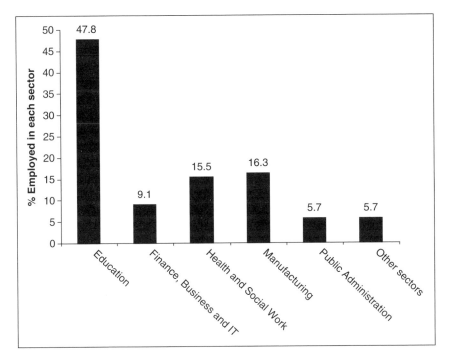

Source: Destination of Leavers from Higher Education (DLHE) survey (HESA 2004)

Figure 2.1 Employment sectors entered by UK domiciled doctoral graduates based on Standard Industrial Classifications returned in 2004

What Do PhDs Do? reports only the destination statistics and gives no information on the challenges of finding work or the perceptions of employers or individuals as they make the transition from student to employee. The questionnaire from the statistics in *What Do PhDs Do?* does not ask graduates if their PhD was 'fit for purpose' in academia or beyond. For information of that depth and quality, we will draw upon the Employers' Perceptions of Recruiting Research Staff and Students (EMPRESS) project supported by Roberts' funding and undertaken by the University of Leeds Careers Service (Souter 2005). From this study, we will present actual responses from employers and former researchers (both recent PhD graduates and more experienced contract research staff). In this chapter, we will present our opinions on what universities and individual researchers need to do to prepare for employment whilst acknowledging the challenges of implementing this in the current academic culture.

Our first look at 'what employers want' is focused at the most significant employer of PhDs – higher education (HE) (which accounts for virtually all of the education sector in Figure 2.1). The persistent unwillingness of some areas of academia to provide a more generic skills base to research students is perplexing, since academia would appear to have the most to gain from better developed and more effective researchers. The basis of most university training provisions is the Joint Skills Statement (RCUK 2001b), which was written by the Research Councils with UK GRAD and the HE sector and 'identifies the competencies that a postgraduate researcher should have or develop during the course of their PhD degree programme'. Much of the list focuses on skills that will enable students to do better research and to accept the personal challenge of doctoral studies. Despite these origins, a significant number of supervisors fail to support (and even discourage or prevent) students attendance at skills training programmes.

So, what *do* academic employers want? In asking that question we begin to identify the root of the problem – the lack of recognition in areas of academia that it *is* an employer and has responsibilities for the development of its staff! Academic success is built upon individual achievement. Those in positions of power and influence have spent their formative years in an environment in which feedback and attention to the 'person' were largely absent. Success depends on publications, securing funding and esteem factors (including examining doctoral candidates, plenary addresses at conferences and editorial positions). This success requires an individual to shine and drives an ambitious academic to focus their attention on grant winning and the *outputs* of their research students and staff (as these improve their chances of success with funding bodies). In working closely with research staff we commonly hear from them that their effectiveness would be boosted if their supervisors recognized their individual needs, acknowledge their need for career development and provide feedback on their performance.

When academics and researchers are asked to describe the personal characteristics of successful academics, a list of skills emerges that is consistent with a research skills training programme. Alongside core competencies such as intellectual ability, come a raft of more generic skills – time management and the ability to prioritize; effective written and oral communication; ability to network with influential people and build a good reputation; ability to attract, inspire and manage good researchers. When recruiting academic staff, universities largely base their decision on evidence of income, esteem and publications. Yet few universities adequately support their own research staff or academic staff by offering opportunities to develop the generic skills that underpin these achievements.

Academia employed more of our PhD graduates in the UK than any other type of employer, but 52 per cent of doctoral graduates in the 2004 survey (HESA 2004) started their careers in other sectors. At a national level there have not been any major studies to look more closely at the experiences of research graduates as they enter new areas – the scope of such a project makes it unlikely. However, some individual research areas (through professional bodies) and universities have investigated employer and employee attitudes.

The EMPRESS project provides more detailed information on the attitudes of employers and employees in the doctoral labour market. Leeds employs or trains over 3500 researchers ranging from very junior (new PhD students) to very senior (postdoctoral research staff with more than a decade of experience on one or a sequence of research contracts). The cohort at Leeds is typical of a leading research institution and the report reveals a complex picture of skills, motivations and aspirations. The individual relationships and expectations of the researchers, senior academics and external partners are diverse.

Whilst interest in postgraduate study grows, in many disciplines there are insufficient academic posts for those who desire them. Equally, as *What Do PhDs Do?* demonstrates, a significant number of researchers believe that their skills and knowledge are not merely valid within the HE sector and consequently they need to market themselves in the wider job market. Since the Concordat (Council of the European Union 1999) was signed in the mid-1990s, it has been accepted that universities have a responsibility to support the career management of their research staff with the dual hope of maximizing their chances of securing academic positions whilst building preparedness for alternative employment.

The Leeds University team that conducted this study had previously investigated the transitions made by researchers into a range of careers and identified a number of the issues facing researchers as they moved from academia to different workplaces. From this, and from numerous career related conversations with individual researchers and external (to HE) employers, it became clear that a wide range of perceptions – few of which were based on personal experience of or contact with the other group – are affecting the transfer of skilled people from academia. In presenting these perceptions, the EMPRESS report gives universities and other employers an opportunity to discuss and eradicate them.

The 47 employer respondents to EMPRESS were almost universally amenable to the idea of possibly recruiting a researcher – even though many of them had no personal experience of interviewing someone from this type of background. Table 2.1 summarizes one element of EMPRESS and illustrates to what degree employers agreed with a set of statements about researchers and their employability outside academia.

The main concerns, unsurprisingly, were about researchers' ability to adjust to a different working environment and the potential cost (in terms of training, time and low productivity) whilst these adjustments were made. Employers were concerned that an academic approach might clash with their own working culture and be hard to cast off, particularly by those who had worked in HE for many years. This, of course, raises an immediate question as to the perceived nature of HE in these competitive times, when it operates with a far more commercial approach. There appears to be a reluctance in some sectors to abandon the notion of ivory towers, a feeling that universities are somehow distanced from the pressures of commercial life.

Table 2.1   Employer responses to sample statements on researchers' employability in non-academic environments (sample size 47)

Statement	Number of positive responses
1 University researchers who have experience of collaboration projects with industry are potentially very valuable to my organization	28
2 I am confident university researchers, at whatever stage, could potentially offer the skills package I am seeking	20
3 I would like to see more people with a university background applying for some of the jobs I advertise	17
4 I would be very concerned that anyone who has been in university research for over 3 years may have lost touch with the reality of the commercial world	16
5 The longer someone stays in university research the less likely they are to be able to make the transition out of it	16
6 I suspect that university researchers have a lot to offer but I'm worried they won't make an effective transition out of HE into my organization	15
7 I believe that experienced researchers are likely to have highly developed project skills	14
8 Retraining is likely to be a serious issue for someone who has spent over 3 years in university research – even if their specialist area of research is directly related to my organization's focus	13
9 I would be/am surprised when researchers apply for positions I advertise	12
10 I would feel differently about taking on someone whose research was in a business related subject	12
11 University researchers would do best to stick to what they do best, i.e. university research	5

Some employers were willing to look beyond the stereotypes, as this comment from an employer in the retailing sector illustrates:

> My concerns (about researchers being able to make a successful transition from the university environment to the industrial/commercial sector) would be mainly related to assumptions which I would actively manage i.e. too academic, too theoretical, may not be able to deal with the pace and interruptions of the business world, may be too narrow and focused. I would consciously put these concerns to one side. There would be no difference for me between a relatively junior or more experienced researcher in terms of concerns – it would depend entirely on the individual.

(Souter 2005: 33)

The benefits of collaborative research and the opportunities this presents for communicating and cooperating with others are recognized by both researchers and employers. Equality of opportunity does not exist and most researchers' experiences are profoundly influenced by the attitudes of their supervisors to collaboration and interactions with a wider community. Two responses from a focus group of researchers illustrate the dichotomy that exists. The question 'what role can your supervisor play in helping to find a suitable role outside H.E.?' evoked the following responses from two research students from different departments:

> The supervisors have different priorities and will not encourage any kind of activity outside academia. In fact I sometimes think they see us as an extension of their ego.

> My supervisor is a great help and has encouraged me to get involved both in conferences and networking with individuals who may help my progression.

> (Souter 2005: 26)

If we compare the responses in Boxes 2.1 and 2.2, we see that researchers make a number of negative assumptions about the way they are perceived by employers outside academia. When pressed (particularly on the subject of teamwork), the researchers were able to illustrate how they could show they possessed most if not all of the skills identified in Boxes 2.1 and 2.2. However, the apparent mismatch seemed to illustrate one of the major issues for employers when it came to recruiting researchers – commonality in language. Researchers do not share the vocabulary of employers as they rarely talk about their own or others' skills development.

In the words of an employer from the manufacturing sector,

> I really want people to lift out the transferable skills i.e. 'I worked on my own initiative ... I worked within x timescales'. I would like people to say things like 'I want to build on my technical and other skills, to be able to develop them within a business context.' For me this sort of focus is far more important than the exact detail of their specific research.

> (Souter 2005: 38)

Similar opinions were given by a health sector respondent:

> Researchers have to manage tight and often conflicting deadlines. They have to manage complex relationships (supervisors/senior staff) and often need teaching/tutoring skills. There's a lot in here but sometimes they don't realise that this is what recruiters look for ... Researchers need to be able to learn and use a different language when presenting themselves outside academia. Researchers at any stage can often be lacking in these necessary 'translation' skills.

> (Souter 2005: 45)

Unsurprisingly, communication emerges as a key factor to connecting employers beyond academia with academic researchers. This goes beyond each individual researcher's ability to identify and communicate skills (although these remain vital for their own career progression). The triangle

---

Box 2.1 Responses from researchers

What skills and benefits do you possess that undergraduates may not?

Maturity
International exposure
Cultural flexibility
HR and day-to-day management skills
Negotiating
Mentoring
Self-motivation
Tutoring
Organizational skills
Presentation skills
Work experience

Which skills are employers outside academia looking for?

Fast learner
Communication and interpersonal skills
Time management
IT
Leadership
Project/people management
Teamwork
Self-management
Innovation
Technical know-how
Ambition
Task orientation
Strategic and creative approaches to business development

---

of communication comprising senior academics/supervisors, researchers and external employers – supported by professional 'enablers' (including career centres and staff development units) – is critical. This goes beyond individual transitions from universities to different sectors. It is critical to the development of academia and its ability to address challenges set by the government (echoed in each region's economic development strategy) to exploit the intellectual strengths within universities and use these to fuel a knowledge-based economy.

In the words of a senior academic at Leeds,

> We must make sure that the post graduate researchers are holistically developed – for example it is really important for them not to become so focused on their work that they cannot communicate it. They need to be able to talk about their work to non-specialists and the general public. Other skills they need are to be good colleagues – team workers.

Box 2.2 Employer responses

What skills do you look for?

Planning and organizing
Analytical
Presentation
Interpersonal
Proactivity
Ambition
Motivation
Adaptability
Creativity
Enthusiasm
Technical
Tenacity
Responsibility
Goal orientation
Commitment

The top three skills, however, were:
Communication
Intellectual ability
Teamwork

> They particularly need to have creative thinking to apply their specific research interests to broader issues such as knowledge transfer.
>
> (Souter 2005: 31)

The broad potential impact of a wide skills base was also seen by a respondent from the oil and gas sector (when asked what could/should universities be doing to support researchers).

> This is not all down to universities. There is considerable onus on the individual themselves to take responsibility for assessing and broadening their skills base. But they do need to have the opportunities to broaden whether through activities or specific training. I feel it is very important that supervisors and professors support the holistic development of researchers. In the end this is likely to be beneficial to universities, researchers and industry.
>
> (Souter 2005: 42)

The question is not about failing as an academic researcher and so looking for work elsewhere. It is all about seeing skills as a currency that can be taken from one work environment to another. It is about how research is positioned as a career, how dynamic it can be and what support is needed to enable the most to be gained from the massive potential contribution of a very bright group of workers. Many researchers either possess or have the capability to develop a raft of highly desirable skills beyond those specific to their research, skills which are relevant to employers in all sectors and have particular value within the hugely competitive academic environment. The most important message emerging from EMPRESS is that experience and training in research can lead to a number of equally valuable but possibly very different options for the individual.

With these insights, we can now return to the question of research training. It is interesting that employers were most likely to see value in collaborative research experience, given that this is also one of the most important developments in academic research. The UK Research Councils and major international funding bodies such as the EU (through the Marie Curie programme) are actively supporting and developing a collaborative research culture. Here, as in so many cases, we see that the needs of employers are strikingly similar, regardless of whether they are in the academic, commercial or public sectors.

What can those in the HE sector, who have responsibility for providing training to research students and staff, do to find a way to operate more effectively? What has to be done to convince the primary beneficiaries of more skilled doctoral graduates (the departments that employ them as research associates or lecturing staff) of the need for training? And what form should that training take?

The first step must be to engage with academic staff and identify the skills they wish to see in their students and staff members. Most institutions do this already and many involve academics in skills delivery where they illustrate generic ideas or principles with examples from their own careers (and in the process see first hand that generic skills are relevant and add value to research training). In addition to consultation with academic staff, training programmes must also map the timing of skills delivery against milestones in the doctoral process so that academics can see the impact of training in the performance of their students. Examples of such milestones are first year progression reports or presentations, conferences for second year students, and thesis writing and viva for third year students.

Those who are unconvinced must be educated on the benefits of developing the skills discussed here. Their attitudes can largely be ascribed to their ignorance of the reality of research training. Research training programme directors and staff regularly face misconceptions about their role that are far more profound than those expressed by other employers about academia. We need to find ways to convince them that it is not about providing our best researchers with the tools to leave academia. It is not about wasting time that could be spent more productively in the lab or library. It is not all presented as management speak that has no relevance. The majority of training offered has a direct positive impact on the performance of researchers. The best training inspires students and researchers to take control of their career development and to become more self-reliant, thus reducing the burden on the supervisor. More importantly, they feel valued by their employer or institution, which rebuilds the motivation eroded by lack of feedback and lack of interest in their personal development.

There is increasing support from those in positions of power and influence to underpin this agenda with tangible signs of the value they place upon it. The research councils now require doctoral research training grant proposals to include reference to the generic skills training that students will have access to. Individual institutions need to follow suit. If students do not attend the courses recommended by their departments or schools and if no alternative training or development has been provided (picking it up as you go along is not a credible alternative), then their supervisors should be expected to explain how this has happened and what remedial actions they will take. If supervisors or departments are discouraging students from engaging in training and development, then institutions must take action.

Individual researchers need to play their parts as well. They should seek out those who develop training programmes and lobby them for relevant support and development. They should explain to academics what benefits they feel have resulted from engaging in development opportunities, as their perceptions will carry far more weight than the opinions of training programme directors. They need to tell their peers about these benefits and encourage them to commit to their own development. More importantly, they need to value the time and resources that are already committed to training and to fulfil commitments made to attend training courses. Their own failure to attend courses without notice is undermining the arguments made by those who are striving to improve the personal and professional development amongst research students and staff.

What we aspire to here is more than a programme of workshops and seminars. Once we have provided the basic building blocks and given our researchers awareness of project management, time management, understanding of how to work collaboratively and how to communicate, we then need to provide the opportunities for these skills to be developed. There are many excellent examples of this, such as the *eSharp* conference and e-journal devised and run by arts research students at the University of Glasgow (http://www.sharp.arts.gla.ac.uk/). A proportion of the Roberts' funding in each institution should be available to students and researchers to support similar initiatives.

As a community, we all need to celebrate the excellence of our research training and make it part of the offer that tempts students and researchers to join our institutions. All universities want to attract motivated, ambitious researchers, so why not learn from the marketing approaches of their main competitors for this wealth of talent. These approaches consistently refer to training and development programmes and promise that working in these environments (particularly the chemical and pharmaceutical industries) will enable you to fulfil your potential. Our research training should be at the forefront of potential students' minds as they consider their offers.

Our message should be 'come here and develop your career, not just in terms of published papers, relevant knowledge or improved methodological approach, but in terms of your own effectiveness'.

When universities and academics engage fully with the responsibilities that are entailed as part of their role as employers of PhD graduates, then the economy at large can benefit. The requirements of academic employers, in terms of soft, transferable skills, are not at odds with those of employers outside the universities. By making a serious commitment to proper skills training of researchers, universities will not only improve the quality of their own staff but also improve the skills level for that majority of their own research employees who will ultimately leave academia, to the benefit of the wider economy.

The employers of our doctoral graduates have consistent requirements. It is not acceptable to hide behind the old chestnuts of 'universities shouldn't subsidise the training budgets of rich industrial employers' or 'these things just develop themselves in the lab'. The universities themselves have the most to gain from excellent, exciting, engaging training and if the by-products of that are highly skilled alumni in a wide range of sectors and roles, then surely we can recoup our investments in them by involving them in future training programmes or research collaborations.

3

PhD, Quo Vadis? Skills Training and the Changing Doctorate Programme

Chris Park

Introduction

This chapter takes a broader-brush approach than many of the other chapters in this book, in seeking to explore the dynamics of the wider context of the changing UK doctorate within which skills training is embedded. The chapter begins by considering where we are now with the doctorate and explains the current 'themes' impacting doctoral change. It then discusses how the doctorate arrived at its current position. With the reviews of the past and present as a basis, likely scenarios for the future are then explored. This approach sets the context within which the skills training and development issues addressed throughout this book will have to adapt and develop in the coming years. Indeed, this year the UK Higher Education Academy has sponsored a national debate 'Redefining the Doctorate' (Park 2007). In looking forward, the chapter adopts a time frame of around a decade; as Barnett and Temple (2006) note in a different context, 'shorter than this, and the context is already set: much beyond this, and the unknowables can begin to outweigh intelligent guesswork'.

This is not totally uncharted territory, because there have been several reviews of the state of postgraduate education and training in the UK (Becher et al. 1994; Burgess et al. 1998). The theme of change in the research student experience is not entirely novel either, because that experience has been changing for some time, to the extent that Pole (2000) describes 'what some would see as confusion around the role and purpose of the UK doctorate'. We can draw some comfort from the fact that other countries – particularly Australia (Pearson 2005) – have also reviewed their doctoral education systems and found the task a challenging one.

Context – where are we now?

It is useful to sketch out what the UK doctorate looks like today, to have a baseline against which to judge possible future scenarios. This section outlines the more important themes.

Firstly, the shape of the UK doctorate. The traditional PhD by thesis remains the norm, although the growth of 'new variants' (Park 2005a) – including PhD by Publication, Professional Doctorates and the New Route PhD (which combines taught and research elements) – continues apace. The full-time research student, working for three years, often with partial if not full financial support, also remains the norm, although the most rapid growth in recent years has been in part-time study, typically self-funded.

Secondly, transparency of process. In the past, the 'secret garden' model of research supervision prevailed; it was a private activity engaged in by consenting adults (student and supervisor) behind closed doors, with few checks and balances imposed on participants. All that has changed over the last decade with the advent of the QAA (Quality Assurance Agency) academic infrastructure, although the engagement of established supervisors with this new reality has been patchy and often sluggish. This academic infrastructure has defined the appropriate academic level for doctoral work (through the Framework for Higher Education Qualifications and subject benchmarks), and established a framework for the research student experience (through the Code of Practice). Both of these have been instrumental in levelling the playing field for research student activities across the sector. Such drivers have promoted a growing emphasis on research culture, infrastructure and the research student experience.

Thirdly, this greatly increased transparency has partly been driven by, and has partly driven, increased accountability, both internal and external to institutions. Internal accountability includes more robust progress monitoring, closer attention being paid to submission and completion rates, as well as to student satisfaction, complaints and appeals. External accountability includes the need to demonstrate alignment with the precepts of the 2004 QAA Code of Practice (which define appropriate policies, processes and infrastructure, including within the skills area), and the need to be held accountable to the Research Councils and HEFCE (and its equivalents) for the use of additional skills development funding (particularly the so-called Roberts money). Universities now have multiple stakeholders to satisfy and many external agendas to serve. Light has been let into the 'secret garden'!

A fourth hallmark of the UK doctorate today is an emphasis on skills training and development. This is even newer than the arrival of the academic infrastructure, and it has been as challenging for institutions to fully engage with and deliver. The two key drivers of skills training have been the RCUK (2001a) *Joint Statement of Skills Training Requirements of Research Postgraduates,* which defines a range of competencies that research students should have the opportunity to acquire or develop during their period of study, and the Roberts' (2002) review *SET for Success,* which (amongst other things) defined ten days of training per year for full-time research students as the norm, and led to the release by the government of additional funding to support the development of research training programmes and skills development opportunities (Roberts money). Roberts money also covers research staff, and there is a move towards creating a clearer continuum of research and training and development opportunities that would develop researcher career paths from postgraduate through postdoc to academic members of staff.

A fifth salient feature is that, today, most higher education institutions (HEIs) across the UK are licensed to deliver research degrees in their own name and under their own authority. Most HEIs now have Research Degree Awarding Powers and award their own research degrees, so there has been some convergence of mission and ambition between the many different types of HEIs in the UK. The net effect of this has been to diversify the range of institutions that are able and keen to engage in research student activities, but at the same time to increase competition for available students. Most of the government funding for research (from HEFCE and the Research Councils) remains concentrated in the pre-1992 universities, but many post-1992 institutions have sizeable populations of research students, typically working part-time and self-funded.

Another hallmark of the current UK research student landscape is a much greater focus on the costs and benefits of research student activities. Universities have long been accustomed to having to seek external funding to support their research student activities, in addition to the HEFCE (R) funding they receive for research students; however, in recent years the fundamental question has been asked whether it makes financial sense to have research students in the first place. This discussion was thrown into sharp relief by the publication of a report by J M Consulting (2005), which concluded that 'current funding for each student varies considerably, but is well below the level of cost, leading to significant levels of under-recovery of costs, almost without exception'.

Finally, there is now much stronger competition between HEIs than ever before to recruit suitable graduates to become research students, and to secure appropriate funding to help attract, support and retain them. Most if not all HEIs have ambitions to increase their population of research students, usually supported by strategic plans. Amongst potential UK recruits these ambitions are challenged by recent graduate indebtedness, the buoyancy of the job market and changing perceptions of the value of higher degrees. Such domestic constraints, coupled with the increased fee income derived from recruiting overseas students (most of whom are self-funding, or bring funding from their home country or sponsors), plus a desire to help build academic capacity in some overseas countries, go some way towards explaining the major expansion in recent years in the recruitment of international research students.

What does become abundantly clear, even from this brief review, is that the research student system in the UK is a system in transition, having to adapt to changing external drivers, changing institutional expectations and ambitions, changing market conditions and changing opportunities (particularly for funding and recruitment). Standing still is not an option, nor has it been over the past two decades. In this sense, future change is inevitable; it is more a question of how, how much and in what form than a question of whether or if.

Retrospect – how did we get here?

Before we look forwards to reflect on what the future may hold in store, it is important to look backwards and appreciate how the present came into being.

Elsewhere (Park 2005a) I have traced the evolution of the British PhD via Germany and the US. The origins of the degree stretch back to the birth of universities in medieval Europe, where the award of a doctorate was a licence to teach, not a recognition of ability or achievement in research. Simpson (1983) stresses that 'Masters and Doctors were . . . the only qualification conferred and cannot in any sense be regarded as higher degrees . . . The twentieth century research degree had no equivalent in the medieval university.'

The doctorate came to acquire special status as a research degree in Germany, when Humboldt founded the University of Berlin in 1810 (Wyatt 1998). The award of a doctorate required successful attendance at seminars, submission of an acceptable thesis and the passing of a comprehensive oral examination; the emphasis was on original and creative research (Goodchild and Miller 1997). Academic staff were required to hold a PhD degree, engage in research and publish scholarly material. From 1815 onwards, German universities attracted smart ambitious graduate students from Britain and America, who had no comparable opportunities at home. Many of the US students subsequently returned home with German PhDs and were employed in colleges and universities.

The US adopted the German approach to research universities and doctoral degrees from the 1860s onwards. The first American university to adopt the PhD was Yale (in 1861); other universities including Harvard, Michigan and Pennsylvania quickly followed. Between 1870 and 1900 graduate education spread throughout North America, and 'by the end of the nineteenth century, the PhD had become the *sine qua non* of American [university] teachers' (Simpson 1983).

The research degree spread from Germany and the US to Britain from 1917, and it then diffused to other English-speaking countries including Canada and Australia (Noble 1994). In Britain, higher doctorates (the DSc and DLitt) had been introduced during the 1870s by the Universities of London, Edinburgh, Oxford and Cambridge, but the lower doctorate (the PhD) was not introduced until 1917, initially by Oxford. Simpson (1983) comments on how 'within three years the PhD had been established in almost all departments of all British universities and with practically identical regulations'.

The shape and format of research degrees in the UK changed relatively little during much of the twentieth century, although there were phases of expansion of provision after the establishment of the then 'new universities' and the polytechnics during the 1960s, and the metamorphosis of polytechnics into universities since 1992 (Pratt 1997).

Inevitably, UK universities have had to adapt over the past two decades to major changes in government policy (Institutional Management in Higher

Education 2003), and particularly to changes in funding (Stiles 2000). A key dimension of this adaptation has been the growth of research student numbers and increased diversity of sources of funding, types of research degree and countries of origin (Taylor 2002).

Two landmark reviews have had enduring impacts on the research student experience and on how institutions shape their provision for research degrees. The Harris Review of Postgraduate Education (Harris 1996) called for a clearly defined national definition and framework for postgraduate awards in the UK, and for better consistency of level and expectations. It inspired and informed the development of the QAA's academic infrastructure, including the definition of academic level. The Roberts' review *SET for Success* (Roberts 2002) established and promoted the new skills agenda for research students and postdocs, including the proposal that the government should provide additional new funding for research training and the expectation that full-time research students funded by research councils should have access to a minimum of ten days of training opportunities each year.

In the UK, skills training, with its emphasis on personal development and the acquisition of professional attributes for both outside and inside academia, appears to be the first change in what I would call the generic content of the PhD since its inception. This has not yet been reflected in the assessment criteria but it is an issue that many will eventually want to address.

Prospect – where are we heading?

The main objective of this chapter is to look ahead and try to identify how the UK doctorate is likely to change over the next decade or so. This task inevitably involves both projecting forward current trends and trying to anticipate new trends and changes. As you might imagine there are always many possibilities and indeed three of the issues highlighted in this section of the chapter are developed and explored in greater detail later in this book. For a fascinating and radical view of the role of the supervisor see Chapter 12. Chapter 13 explores a framework for the doctoral award that would bring consistency to the many different formats of award currently emerging. Chapter 14 adds the further important ingredient to the doctoral mix of the impact of developments in Europe.

What is significant is that the present chapter and others in this book represent an important step forward in that few attempts have been made to forecast likely changes in the research student landscape. Taylor (2002), who only looked ahead five years, envisaged such changes as the continued expansion of student numbers, changes in research training, changing funding arrangements, increased use of information technologies and increased emphasis on quality assurance. Otherwise, the literature is silent on the matter of likely future changes to the research student experience.

In compiling this chapter I have drawn repeatedly upon two very useful recent surveys of expert opinion. One was the report of a think tank of

UK GRAD Regional Hub Coordinators (2006) entitled 'What will the environment be like to researchers in 2012?' The other survey was one I conducted myself, by e-mail, among a sample of people from a range of HEIs who have different roles and responsibilities relating to skills development. They were asked to suggest what they think the three to five most important changes in the research student experience are likely to be, looking ahead ten years from early 2006. I would ideally have wanted to use a more iterative approach to canvass the opinion of experts, such as the Delphi method (Rowe and Wright 1999), but that was not possible because of time constraints. Naturally, the typology used here is only one way of structuring the different themes; the order in which themes appear is not intended to imply relative importance or relevance.

Funding

Anticipating likely changes in funding for research student activities ten years ahead is certainly a case of looking 'through a glass, darkly' because so many decisions are at the mercy of central government.

Continued rise in government funding for research student activity (through the HEFCE Q income and through Research Council funding) over the next ten years seems highly unlikely for two main reasons – budget constraints and workforce needs (the output of doctoral candidates in many subject areas is not seriously out of line with national needs). There may well be some redistribution of government funding towards areas (such as some areas within science and technology) that are deemed strategically important for the country, but this is likely to occur within a constrained total. Thus any sustained expansion in postgraduate research funding and student numbers is likely to come about through a combination of more self-funding by students (particularly on a part-time basis), greater institutional funding by HEIs (though this will inevitably be constrained by tight budgets and competition from other institutional agendas) and external funding from a wider diversity of sources than is available at present (including industry and the charitable sector). This raises questions over the likelihood of continued growth in the number of full-time research students.

A second trend could well be the move by many HEIs to cover the full economic cost (FEC) of their research students, particularly in terms of research training and skills development, in light of the J M Consulting (2005) report on costs and benefits. Without a significant increase in the per capita funding that HEFCE provides to universities to cover the costs of their UK research students, FEC could probably only be achieved by significant increases in fee levels. This could well push doctoral research beyond the financial reach of many prospective UK students and make the recruitment of high fee paying overseas students an even more attractive proposition than at present, tipping the balance of doctoral demographics away from home-grown students and in favour of international students.

Recruitment and admission

One area in which trends that are already under way will almost inevitably continue to intensify is the recruitment and admission of research students; moreover, over the next decade, the demographic profile of the research student population in the UK is likely to change significantly.

Little if any sustained growth in the recruitment of UK graduates is to be expected because of rising undergraduate debt and uncertain career benefits of having a higher degree. Indeed, many HEIs will consider themselves successful if they manage to retain their research student populations at present levels. As the UK GRAD Regional Hub Coordinators (2006) note, by 2012 'we may see a shortage of graduates in some disciplines coinciding with the anticipated difficulties due to the retirement of a significant number of researchers . . . [and] more researchers are likely to undertake PhD study or post-doctoral research overseas'.

Whilst UK recruitment may at best remain static, we can expect continued growth in recruitment of research students from beyond these shores, both in Europe and further afield (particularly in China and India). Competition from individual HEIs to recruit overseas students will inevitably continue to rise because they bring numerous benefits. They are a valuable source of additional income because they pay higher fees, and they also often represent new or emerging markets with future potential. They are often very highly qualified and have great motivation to succeed; overseas students also often complete quicker and are less likely to drop out than UK students (Park 2005b). Overseas recruitment on a large scale and a sustainable basis will become more challenging than it currently is, with existing markets (such as China) declining and new markets (perhaps in South America) opening up, and with competition intensifying from other English-speaking countries (particularly North America and Australia). Competition will also grow as many universities in the donor countries develop their own research capacity using alumni from the UK.

The profile of UK recruitment is also likely to change quite significantly over the coming decade in a number of ways. Continued growth in part-time registrations could drive a progressive switch from full-time to part-time as the core group in most HEIs other than the favoured few 'big players', which would have major implications for support and supervision. The age distribution may change, too, with a growth in mid-career research students (probably part-time) working on doctorates as part of lifelong learning and/or for career enhancement reasons, as well as possibly some growth in post-career students undertaking doctoral study simply out of personal interest, as a challenge or hobby.

Concentration

The net effect of the likely changes in funding will be a greater concentration of research funding (and thus activity) into fewer HEIs than at present. Darwinian 'survival of the fittest' strategies will inevitably become more apparent and amplify underlying change; the big players will get bigger, and research student activity in the rest will decline.

Just how many of the research-intensive 'big player' universities there are likely to be in ten years' time is a matter of conjecture. It may be that as few as 10 or 15 universities across the UK will be large enough, strong enough and sufficiently well funded to compete successfully in research on the world stage. Much will depend on the outcome of the 2008 Research Assessment Exercise (RAE), which will inevitably speed the creation of a two-tier system, with research funding, reputation and momentum concentrated into one group of HEIs, and the other group becoming increasingly teaching-oriented.

As this evolutionary process continues, the gap between the strong and the weak will grow bigger. HEIs that find themselves on the wrong side of the line when this happens will find it increasingly difficult to remedy the situation. The research-intensive institutions will grow stronger, attract more research students, with staff and students working in larger groups and units, with better infrastructure and support, better facilities, stronger teams of supervisors, better institutional frameworks and (probably) better submission and completion rates. Research student activity – along with much staff research – may well disappear from many HEIs, particularly amongst the less research-intensive post-1992 universities and the colleges that aspire to become universities, over the next decade.

There is a second dimension to the critical mass argument, and this is the likely concentration of research student activity in relatively large groups within HEIs, probably based on disciplinary groupings. Again, the process will be driven by constraints on the availability of funding to support students and infrastructure. This dynamic is already very apparent in research in relatively costly subject areas such as science and technology, and it is likely to spread more widely over the coming decade. The lone scholar (in the humanities, for example) is likely to become something of an endangered species in a future research culture, which privileges research concentrated in relatively large groups and teams.

Collaboration

A logical corollary of greater concentration of funding and research is the continued growth of collaborative activities through which HEIs can share expertise, facilities and provision. Collaboration in both research and training is likely to increase, both within and between institutions.

Intra-institutional collaborations, between departments and faculties within an HEI, are already common, particularly in the area of research training and skills development. By grouping small cohorts from individual departments together, economies of scale and increased breadth of opportunity can often be enjoyed by sharing courses, facilities, staff expertise and delivery. Provision will be made more cost-effective through such sharing, probably driven by financial constraints and the desire to create a sustainable critical mass.

Inter-institutional collaborations of various kinds already exist, but they are likely to increase in number, range and reach, again in the pursuit of economies of scale and breadth of provision. But students will derive additional benefits from spending part of their time in another institution within or beyond the UK; these benefits include developing a broader outlook, gaining a wider range of experiences, developing networks and stepping outside their comfort zone by encountering new challenges and viewing the world through a different lens.

Regional collaborations are already becoming more common within the realm of research training and skills development, evidenced for example by the success and growth of the UK GRAD regional hubs and regional graduate schools, both generic and discipline-specific. At the national scale, there are already successful initiatives such as the consortial programme in Scotland for postgraduate research training in human geography (Lorimer and Philip 2005), which demonstrate the benefits for specialized programmes and activities of synergy and collaboration. Such discipline-based collaboration is likely to become more common and widespread in the future.

International collaboration in the development of research student activities is as yet in its infancy, but here again growth is likely as leading research-intensive UK universities seek to build global strategic alliances, some of which may include staff and research student exchanges as well as shared programmes and activities. As possibilities in this area open up, turning them into reality will get easier; information and communication technologies will continue to develop and make place and location less relevant than ease and cost of access (real or virtual).

Internationalization

Internationalization is not just a matter of recruitment. The UK GRAD Regional Hub Coordinators (2006) envisage that it would challenge traditional notions of the UK doctorate in a number of important ways. By 2012, they believe, 'UK researchers will be working in an increasingly competitive international market. There will be a need for them to stand out and add value . . . More researchers will undertake part of their training abroad and more overseas researchers may be employed in the UK . . . researchers will be working in multicultural teams collaborating with other institutions in the UK and overseas. Distance collaborations and the use of remote communication tools will be standard practice. As a result, skills relevant to working in multi-disciplinary and international research teams will be of increased importance, such as cultural awareness, language and communication skills.'

A second trend relating to internationalization that will become more prominent in the future is the so-called Bologna agenda, which will drive the harmonization of research degree programmes across Europe to take account of the mobility of labour (students and staff) and the creation of trans-European research networks and projects (Musselin 2004). As plans progress to develop a European Higher Education Area and a European Research Area, the differences between postgraduate research students and postdoctoral researchers will diminish and both groups will be treated as a seamless group of 'early career researchers'. If the UK follows the rest of Europe, research students are likely to have the rights and status of employees on proper contracts rather than students supported by tax-free stipends.

New managerialism

What ties many of the recent changes together is the professionalization of this area of activity within universities. It has become one of the last areas of academic freedom to become more open and transparent, as well as more accountable in terms of both use of public funding and performance measurement (such as completion rates and attrition rates). This increased professionalism is reflected in a number of ways, including much more cohesive institutional structures and practices for dealing with postgraduate research students (particularly relating to the realm of skills development) and much greater formalization of roles and responsibilities (particularly for supervisors).

This professionalization reflects the emergence of a culture of new managerialism within UK higher education, one which Deem (1998, 2004) attributes to radical policy changes from the 1980s onwards and sees expressed through the changing role of the academic as a knowledge worker. Within the world of research student activities, hallmarks of this new managerialism include the new prominence being given to such factors as improved institutional management and control, evidence-based decision-making, accountability and performance measurement.

Institutional organization and management of research student activities are becoming much more formal than they were previously, as witnessed for example by the growth of graduate schools (as both physical and organizational entities) and of clearly defined research degree programmes. Formalization is driven particularly by what the QAA calls the 'academic infrastructure,' which includes the Code of Practice, the Framework for Higher Education Qualifications, subject benchmark statements and programme specifications. This trend towards greater formalization will inevitably continue in the future, driven particularly by the need for external accountability.

Institutional management is becoming increasingly strategic and informed by evidence-based decision-making based on more comprehensive monitoring of performance and more widespread strategic use of key performance indicators. This type of management by fact will become more prominent and sophisticated in the future, as HEIs seek to fine-tune performance management, make better informed strategic decisions and compete more openly and proactively in the world of league tables (national and international). Inevitably, there will also be much greater emphasis in the future on accountability to external stakeholders, both financial (to research funders, for example) and academic (to funders and the QAA).

Mode and length of study

We should expect to see some major changes over the next decade in the way in which research students study as the system adapts to changing circumstances, particularly in terms of funding, recruitment, competition for students and changing institutional strategic objectives and priorities.

A key trend is likely to be the continued growth (both relative and absolute) of part-time study at the doctoral level. This will be driven partly by increasing undergraduate debt and more competitive graduate starting salaries, but wider socio-economic changes will also make it both easier and more cost-effective for research students to combine study and employment. New developments in information and communication technologies (particularly digital technologies that make the sharing of information and access to information much easier, quicker and cheaper than previously) will open up new opportunities for working from home and studying at a distance, so that location becomes less of a constraint on regular access to facilities, support and people. This will fuel the shift towards part-time study, and towards study away from the host institution, which would be popular amongst overseas students who would be based in their home country but still be supported and supervised at a distance by UK HEIs.

New patterns of delivery will be developed to meet the needs of distant and part-time research students, including increased use of block-mode study (in which the student mainly studies away from the HEI but has periodic visits there for supervision, support and access to particular facilities), perhaps supported by local cohort-based learning sets or support groups. Mixed-mode or blended learning, based on a combination of face-to-face and e-learning situations, is already becoming more common amongst undergraduate students; over the next decade it is likely to be quite widely adopted at the postgraduate level. Whilst distance delivery at the doctoral level can, if carefully devised and managed, be better suited to the needs and constraints of part-time and distant (study away) students (Combe 2005), it is not without problems, including the challenge of developing an effective community of practice in an academic context (Wikeley and Muschamp 2004).

Length of study is also likely to change over the coming decade, with four years (1+3 or 4 years for PhD) becoming the norm for full-time doctoral study in most disciplines, to allow appropriate time for research training and skills development.

Research

As well as changes in the environment in which research students carry out their research, we should also expect to see changes in the types of research they engage in. This will be driven by a combination of factors, including the changing funding regime and opportunities, changing career opportunities (real and perceived), and changing strategic missions, niches and priorities of research-intensive universities.

The coming decade is likely to bring a swing in emphasis away from research in purely academic subjects towards more applied research, particularly in disciplines such as engineering and applied sciences (Leonard and Barber 1998). As interest declines in purely academic research in areas without obvious vocational relevance in both relative and absolute terms, it will be replaced by a growing emphasis on more applied research, which has greater knowledge transfer potential and more obvious commercial applications. But this will further intensify a tension that already exists, which is the pressure on research students to produce high quality academic outputs (particularly peer-reviewed articles in high rating journals) to contribute to the academic reputation and prestige of their host department.

The UK GRAD Regional Hub Coordinators (2006) forecast that 'new academic disciplines will emerge' by 2012, but more likely is the emergence of new approaches, methodologies and focal points within existing disciplines. Equally likely is the continued growth of interdisciplinary research or what Metz (2001) refers to as 'intellectual border crossing', which could well turn out to be a particularly fruitful area of growth for the foreseeable future. Such a change in focus and emphasis could pose serious challenges to the ability of traditional departments and disciplines to adapt.

As research becomes more applied, research students will be expected to make the fruits of their research more accessible beyond the academy by engaging more proactively in knowledge transfer, both as a means of attracting research funding and also to benefit the economy and society. By 2012, the UK GRAD Regional Hub Coordinators (2006) believe that 'there is likely to be a greater emphasis [in research student training] on business awareness, particularly in science and technology. Researchers will need to be more flexible, more effective at communicating their research to

non-specialists and better at establishing good working relationships ...
there will be more emphasis on the researcher as a vehicle for Knowledge
Transfer and a greater awareness of IP and ethical issues.'

Diversity of awards

The range of degree programmes and academic awards offered by UK HEIs
is likely to continue to increase over the next decade, in response to changing market opportunities (both within and beyond the UK) and changing
employer needs.

Diversification of qualifications and types of doctoral award is already
apparent in the emergence and growth of a range of novel forms of doctorate, particularly the Professional Doctorate (such as those in Engineering,
Management, Education and Clinical Psychology) or, as Harman (2004)
calls them, 'industry-ready doctorates'. The Professional Doctorate is already
becoming more common in Australia (Neumann 2005) as well as across
the UK, particularly in the more vocationally oriented post-1992 universities
(Bourner et al. 2001; Thorne and Francis 2001). Other relatively recent
innovations in the UK include the Practice-based Doctorate (Collinson
2005), for example, in Creative Writing, Art and Design, Dance and Drama,
as well as the PhD by Publication and the New Route PhD (which combines
taught and research elements).

There is also likely to be continued growth of MRes and similar Masters
awards, which serve as launch pads from which graduate students can proceed to doctoral study, and of 'early exit' awards (such as a Postgraduate
Diploma or Certificate in Research Training) for those who successfully
complete approved sections of a doctoral programme but leave before completing the research element.

Supervision

Whilst the main focus of this chapter is on the research student and their
experience, the relationship that students have with their supervisor(s) lies
at the heart of that experience, and it can have a significant and enduring
impact on it. The traditional 'secret garden' relationship between student
and supervisor is already changing, as HEIs exercise greater control of the
process and as supervisors take more seriously their institutional responsibilities. Institutional control of the supervisory process will inevitably be a
matter of growing importance in the years ahead.

One significant change has been to replace the traditional model, in
which a research student is supervised by one particular supervisor, with a
more open approach involving supervisory teams. Team supervision provides cover for absences, allows mentoring of new supervisors and gives the
student access to a range of academics who might have different strengths,
outlooks and experiences.

Traditionally, supervisors were expected to supervise as part of their normal workloads, without explicit reference to workload norms or the balance of activities that are taken into account. Although this is already changing, as more HEIs start to include time spent supervising research students within workload allocation models, in the future making this process more transparent and equitable in this way will inevitably become standard practice.

An even bigger change has been the new emphasis on supervisor training and development, designed to share good practice, improve personal development and enhance the quality of the student experience. New supervisors are often required to undergo some form of formal training before they are allowed to serve as main supervisor, but experience from across the sector shows that many experienced supervisors are very reluctant to engage in such training on a voluntary basis. It is quite possible that many HEIs will make 'refresher' training and personal development of all supervisors compulsory within the next decade.

The nature of the working relationship between student and supervisor will also change, with roles and responsibilities more clearly articulated and codified, and expectations made more explicit and better grounded in reality. As Dinham and Scott (1999: 2) put it, 'the student–supervisor relationship has the potential to be wonderfully enriching and productive, but it can also be extremely difficult and even personally devastating'. In the future it will be in the interest of HEIs to be more sensitive to these tensions, which will encourage them to take more seriously their responsibility to provide appropriate training and support for supervisors.

Research training and skills development

Research training and skills development for postgraduate research students is already a hallmark of the UK doctoral experience, and one that is admired by many other countries. Nonetheless it is clear that it will grow in importance over the next decade, with the overarching objective of producing research students who are more employable and who have skills and competencies that are relevant to national needs.

We should expect skills development to become even more formalized within HEIs, with the further development of formal Research Training Programmes at faculty and institutional levels. Skills development for research students should also become much better embedded in the fabric of the research student experience in all HEIs in the years ahead. National expectations and requirements are already fairly well established across the sector in the UK, thanks to the 2004 QAA Code of Practice, the Roberts funding and the RCUK (2001a) *Joint Statement of Skills Training Requirements of Research Postgraduates*, and these instruments are likely to remain operative for the foreseeable future. There is no need for a 'national curriculum' of skills development for research students in the UK – as Gilbert (2004) has hinted at for Australia, for example – because the skills framework in the UK is already quite tightly defined, and the alignment with it of individual HEIs has recently been audited by the QAA through their Special Review of Research Degree Programmes (2005–06). The UK GRAD Regional Hub Coordinators (2006) expect that 'personal and professional development will be an intrinsic part of researcher training and careers' by 2012.

We are also likely to see more collaborative provision of training and skills development opportunities, within and between HEIs, and more outsourcing of some training activities that individual HEIs are unable to deliver on a cost-effective and sustainable basis in-house to specialist providers (such as UK GRAD).

Many stakeholders hope that the next decade will see the establishment of a much-needed evidence base through the collection and publication of empirical research on the impact of skills development on the employability and early career progression of recent research student alumni.

Assessment

As skills development becomes a more integral part of the research student experience, questions will increasingly be asked about whether and how the examination of doctorates should be revised to include the formal assessment of students' skills and competencies (process) alongside the more traditional assessment of the thesis (product). Whilst producing the thesis is undoubtedly an important stage in the development of deep learning skills (James 1998), as far back as the early 1990s Salmon (1992) argued that 'doctoral research is a process, rather than an outcome or product'.

There is a need for a national debate about examining the doctorate (Park 2007), which could lead to calls for a wholesale review and possible revision of expectations of what a doctorate is, and what it is for. Broadening the viva voce to embrace competencies as well as expert knowledge will be a challenge, but there is already momentum to adopt more transparent and consistent criteria and procedures within and between HEIs (Morley et al. 2002; Denicolo 2003; Park 2003).

Quality of the student experience

To date few HEIs have devoted much attention to evaluating the quality of the research student experience on a systematic basis. This will doubtless change over the coming decade, as research students are seen increasingly as consumers with associated rights and expectations. A focus on the student experience will pay dividends to HEIs; after all, the best adverts and ambassadors for an HEI's offerings are satisfied alumni, and there is thus a direct link with recruitment and therefore also with critical mass and financial health. The reverse side of the coin is also true; as the 'student voice' becomes more vocal both within HEIs (through elected and trained student representatives) and across the sector (for example, through, the National Postgraduate Committee), demand from students for better access to facilities such as work space, study space and social space is bound to increase, as will the number and range of student complaints and appeals.

Understanding of what makes for a high quality experience for research students is currently limited, and there is great scope for the development of survey instruments – such as the Postgraduate Research Experience Questionnaire approach developed in Australia (Marsh et al. 2002) – which focus on the student experience rather than on student satisfaction per se. Such instruments are likely to be widely used in the future, allowing benchmarking between universities and disciplines, and oriented towards enhancement of the student experience.

There is also likely to be greater interest in how experiences vary between different groups of research students, such as females (Leonard 2001), international students (Deem and Brehony 2000) and part-time and distance students (Lindner et al. 2001). The status of research students in the institution or department is also likely to come under closer scrutiny as their research and supervision become better embedded in departmental procedures and practice.

An important dimension to the student experience is the multiple roles they play, sometimes out of choice but often out of necessity. Today many research students work part time, including acting as graduate teaching assistants (Park 2004) to support their studies, and this will doubtless increase in the future. Such multitasking broadens experience and increases employability, but it comes at a cost – time lost to the research. Many research students also have to juggle multiple responsibilities (for example, as carers and parents), and this constraint is likely to increase in importance if the research student population in the future is older than it is today. Such a shift will require greater support and more flexible approaches by supervisors and HEIs.

Conclusions

This chapter has touched on many themes as it tries to envisage what the UK doctorate might look like in ten years' time. All forecasting must have health warnings attached to it, and this is particularly the case in this area. Inevitably, much that is envisaged here is largely based on projecting forward trends that are already apparent; predicting radical changes in government policy and in higher education strategy is a step too far, given the many uncertainties that surround these realms.

The scenario suggested here is that within a decade funding to support research student activities will be concentrated into larger teams operating in fewer institutions, with full economic costing of these activities, greater collaboration within and between institutions, and more international emphases and practices. It envisages a more managerial approach, a research student population that is more heavily balanced towards overseas and part-time study, as well as a greater emphasis on applied and interdisciplinary research and knowledge transfer. It anticipates that institutions will have a wider range of more specialized awards on offer, that supervisors will be required to engage more routinely in personal development and the sharing of good practices and that supervision will be formally included in workload models. It expects that research training and skills development will be more formalized and better embedded within institutions, that more delivery will be on a collaborative basis and that evidence will be available to demonstrate cause–effect links (impact) between skills and employability. It predicts that traditional approaches to the assessment of doctorates will have been broadened to encompass competencies as well as the thesis, and that institutions will pay much closer attention to the quality of the research student experience.

4

Normalizing the Part-Time Student Experience: Making the Rhetoric of Diversity Real

Alistair McCulloch and Peter Stokes

The UK skills agenda

Over the years, the UK skills training agenda has been driven by a number of key stakeholders in the research training arena. Early enthusiasts included the Research Councils (lead by the ESRC) and the (then) Department of Education and Science (now DfES). These were joined later by the higher education funding councils (HEFCE, SHEFC, HEFCW) and the Office of Science and Technology (OST). Interestingly enough, there was little evidence of student or university demand for these developments, which have frequently been resisted by individual students and their supervisors. These developments were associated with a change in the focus of doctoral study from the production of a thesis to the production of a trained researcher.[1]

Following this initial, rather piecemeal, approach to skills training, the agenda was pushed forward in a significant way by the award by the Higher Education Funding Councils of England, Scotland and Wales of a contract for a project designed to 'determine the role of threshold standards and conditional funding in improving standards in research degree programmes (RDPs)' (HEFCE 2002: 4). The resulting report, 'Improving standards in postgraduate research degree programmes', was intended to 'review good practice and identify indicators that could form the basis of threshold standards' and that could institute the first of three phases. The report stated that: 'Phases two and three of the project will develop these threshold standards, systems for assessment and monitoring, and the funding models needed to support such a system – and so deliver an improvement in the standards of RDPs throughout the UK.'

The report was publicized at relevant conferences and workshops and was subject to significant criticism for the proposed threshold standards it mooted. In particular, its intended use of departmental research assessment exercise (RAE) scores as a surrogate indicator of the quality of individual supervisors, and the quality of individuals' ability to monitor progress and act as examiner attracted particular criticism. When added to the suggested use of metrics regarding completion rates, the potential implications of the report generated significant opposition from across the sector. The strength of the feelings aroused by the report can be judged from the fact that, for the only time to date, the funding councils felt obliged to conduct an 'informal consultation' on the proposed standards (HEFCE 2003a). This 'informal' phase invited 'higher education institutions to contribute to the development of threshold standards for research degree programmes (RDPs), prior to formal consultation on this issue in spring 2003'. The formal consultation began in May 2003 (HEFCE 2003b) and this contained none of the RAE-related thresholds, but it did retain a threshold standard relating to completion rates.

Over the next few months, the HEFCE considered how best to take its agenda forward.[2] The resolution surfaced in late summer 2003 with QAA being approached and asked to revise Section 1 of its Code of Practice relating to postgraduate research degrees to take account of the concerns of the funding and the research councils. The working group contained representatives drawn from all sections of the higher education community, including the HEFCE and its Scottish equivalent SHEFCE. The revised Code of Practice was published in September 2004 (QAA 2004); it represented a significant shift away from the use of metrics and recognized explicitly that the UK's diverse collection of higher education institution (HEIs) contained a diversity of research students with different backgrounds, motivations and needs. While early drafts of the code had included a requirement that all research students should undergo a programme of skills training irrespective of their individual circumstances or needs, discussion within the working party resulted in the requirement in the final code that institutions should provide access to appropriate training, paying 'particular attention to the differing needs of individual postgraduates, arising from their diversity'. This training was to be based upon the document 'Skills training requirements for research students: joint statement by the research councils/AHRB' (RUCK 2004).

Diversity of student, mode of study and institution

This recognition of the diversity of research students is refreshing in an area where 'policy is based largely on the stereotype of the young, full-time, funded student who is geographically mobile, without dependents, studying in a metropolitan area and intending to pursue a career as a full-time researcher or academic' (McCulloch 2004). Diversity is not, however, only a feature of the research student body, it is also a feature of the types of doctorate for which they are studying, and also of the institutions in which they are studying.

Even as recently as 25 years ago, it could be safely assumed that UK doctoral students were almost all studying for what can be termed loosely as a 'big-book PhD'. In the early years of the twenty-first century, that assumption can no longer be made. Students can achieve the title 'Doctor'[3] through a variety of means. These include:[4]

- The taught doctorate (and its close relative, the 'New' PhD)
- The practice-based doctorate
- The PhD by published work (there are two variations here, the PhD by work published by the candidate previous to their registration as a student and the PhD by publications produced as part of doctoral study)
- The doctorate purely by research thesis[5]

There have also been large changes over the last 25 years in terms of the mode of doctoral study. Whereas once part-time students were relatively rare, they now comprise approximately half of the total research student population. Green and Powell (2005: 13) present HESA data to show that of 108,610 research students registered in 2002–03, 53,340 were studying on a part-time basis. As they say, 'if discussion relates to full-time mode only, there is a failure to take account of over 50,000 students' (Green and Powell 2005: 14).

Finally, the UK contains a significant diversity in types of HEIs. In addition to the Russell Group of large, research-intensive universities, there is also the 1994 Group (smaller, research-intensive), and the group Campaigning for Mainstream Universities (consisting primarily of the universities created post-1992 from the former polytechnics). Many universities remain non-aligned and there are, in addition, the Colleges of Higher Education and specialist colleges. The balance of subjects offered and the types of research students attracted to these institutions varies. By and large, the more research-intensive institutions have higher absolute numbers of research students and a higher proportion of full-time postgraduate research (PGR) student activity, while the less research-intensive tend to have a more equal balance between full- and part-time activity. (It may be worth noting here, as an extreme example, that the University of Cambridge only admitted its first part-time research student as recently as 2004.)

Who are these part-time research students? They do not constitute a single group. Green and Powell's (2005: 14) comment that 'it becomes ever more apparent that the concept of "the doctoral student" is one typified by heterogeneity (rather) than by homogeneity', applies just as much if not more to part-time research students as it does to the entire PGR student body. Some of them are in full-time employment and are pursuing a doctoral award as part of their own continuing professional development or to address an issue or project of particular interest to their employer. Some part-time research students are drawn from the ranks of those who are not in formal work either through redundancy or retirement, or because they have dependents to care for. Others may work part-time across a wide range of occupations. Some may move in and out of employment during their time as a research student.

Generally, part-time research students tend to be more mature and, as a result, possess significant life experience. In post-1992 universities and colleges of higher education, and in the professional disciplines such as business, education and nursing where there is a strong tradition of recruiting practitioners without doctoral qualifications, some are fellow academics. Most of those pursuing the alternatives to the traditional 'big book' thesis are part-time students.

While there is no significant body of research on the issue, anecdotal evidence suggests that the motivations of part-time students overlap with, but are not the same as, those of full-timers. Some want to become academics or, in the case of those already employed by HEIs, remain academics. Many more do not. Some, as has already been noted, are doing projects related to their employment and professional development. Others, in the spirit of one of education's former mobilizing slogans, 'lifelong learning', want to learn for its own sake. Some simply want to pursue a particular, often long-held interest in a more structured and directed way once they have both the time and the opportunity.[6]

Funding

The general rationale for skills training was a concern that students who had engaged in research leading to the production of a thesis did not have the skills and knowledge required by industry or the entrepreneurial skills necessary to support the development of a wealth-creating and enterprising society.[7] The skills training agenda was finally formally recognized in a resource sense by the provision of 'Roberts money', which was allocated to institutions on the basis of the number of research council funded students they had in post. These students have been distributed very unevenly across the sector. The result is that, in 2005, 80 per cent of the career development and skills training payments (by value) went to 17 per cent of the recipient institutions, and in the financial year 2005–06 just under £18m of the £19.3m to be issued went to 50 institutions.[8] The remaining £1.4m was shared between those of the remaining 118 institutions fortunate enough to host research council supported research students. The problem with this approach to funding is that the distribution of resources reflects the unequal distribution of research council funded students across institutions.[9] Institutions in receipt of Roberts money are free to use it to provide skills training for all of their students, as long as the students funded by the research councils (the ultimate source of the Roberts money) are not disadvantaged by this strategy. The mode of allocation does, however, leave a significant number of institutions in a position where they receive little or no resources but are nonetheless expected to deliver the same skills agenda as those institutions which are well resourced.[10]

A similar concentration has been occurring with regard to quality research (QR) funding. QR funding is the resource accruing to HEIs as a result of their performance in the previous RAE. Since 1992, when English HEIs received funding for departments rated at 3b (meaning that at least

50 per cent of their research activity had been assessed as being of national levels of excellence), the threshold for funding has moved, initially to 3a and subsequently to grade 4.[11] Where this has had its biggest impact is in the decision to tie the funding given to HEIs, for the provision of facilities and supervision of research students, to the RAE grade at which QR funding kicks in. What this means is that research students in England studying in departments graded at less than 4 in the 2001 RAE, almost all of which lie outside the pre-1992 universities, are effectively unfunded by the government money.[12] This falls particularly hard on part-time research students who tend to study in the very departments which now find themselves unfunded (Shepherd and Davis 2005; *The Independent* 2005).

The problem at hand and a potential solution

This background of diversity in individual, institution and mode of study, the concentration of QR funding in an increasingly small number of institutions and the allocation of Roberts money by reference to numbers of full-time research council funded research students (almost all of whom it should be noted are full-timers) combines with two other factors to produce a significant problem. These two other issues are the near monopoly held by the research councils and the funding councils on the development of the skills agenda, and the disparity between the nature of the student body supported by the research councils and the total body of research students.

At the risk of oversimplification, institutions are now increasingly being required to make available to all students a relatively fixed menu of skills training, irrespective of their topic of study or the personal situations in which they find themselves. This raises issues that institutions have, to date, largely only dealt with in relation to their full-time students but are now, as a result of the QAA Code of Practice, having to address for all students, including part-timers. Institutions can respond to the skills needs of part-time PGR students either in the same way as they have tended to respond to undergraduate part-timers, which is to treat them as a strange variant on the 'normal' full-time students and hope that they do not take much notice,[13] by taking what is offered to full-time students and trying to repackage it for part-timers, or by pursuing a third, more radical option. That more radical option would be for universities to treat the part-time student as the norm and create a skills training package suitable for that mode of study. In effect, the aim should be to provide a facility such that, if a research student were (for whatever reason) to be unable to move beyond their home environment, they would still be able to access resources such that they would be able, should they so wish, to fulfil the requirements of the Research Councils' Joint Statement on Skills Training. This extreme-case approach would have the advantage of ensuring that, provided it was actually accessible to part-timers, whatever was offered would, by definition, be accessible to full-timers.

The question to be asked initially is, 'in addition to literature and data relevant to their topic of study, and communication with and guidance from their supervisory team, what do students, whether full- or part-time, need access to in order to successfully pursue a doctoral qualification?' Answering this gives us a number of elements to be considered.

1   They need to have their individual requirements in both research and generic skills identified.
2   If a research deficiency is identified, they need access to appropriate research skills development.
3   If a more general deficiency is identified, they need access to appropriate generic skills development.

These first three elements are identified and discussed in the QAA Code of Practice (2004) and are very recent arrivals on the PGR stage.

4   They require encouragement to address their needs. This requirement is traditionally met to varying degrees by supervisors, departments/faculties, and institutions.
5   They require access to learning and development opportunities through which they can address any identified needs. In the traditional model, these are delivered on campus through the media of courses, mentoring, conferences and workshops. In more adventurous institutions, these face-to-face sessions may be delivered in the evening or in blocks at weekends, but they are largely extensions of the conventional 'university-based' model of learning.
6   They require pastoral support[14] for their learning and development. This has traditionally been delivered through campus-based learning and student support departments or through Graduate School Offices, or else through faculties and departments where graduate functions are devolved. They may also be provided through less formal arrangements such as student networks and individual peer counselling.

What the authors of this chapter are arguing for is a solution to the problem of delivering access to the full range of skills training for the student who, for whatever reason (financial, social or personal), cannot attend campus to access provision. Provision of this sort would not only benefit part-time students, nor should access to it be limited to part-time students. It would benefit full-time humanities and social science students who differ from laboratory-based science students in that they tend to spend less time on campus due to their need for data collection and visits to libraries and archives. It would benefit full-time students whose research involved them in extended periods of study away from the campus, whether in a collaborator's premises or undertaking long-term fieldwork in another country. Indeed, there are many science research students who undertake significant amounts of fieldwork and who could, therefore, benefit from such a solution. It would also enable universities to offer places to study to appropriate overseas students without the necessity for them to have to commit to the expense of extended residency in the UK. It might also offer universities a way of offering doctoral opportunities to research students unable to overcome visa difficulties.

One approach that seeks to do this is currently being explored in the North West of England through a collaboration developed from discussion at the regional UK GRAD Hub.[15] The initiative uses the possibilities made available by communications and information technology (CIT), but takes as a fundamental starting point the principle that any solution must be 'learning' rather than 'technology' driven. This means that the solution must be based on pedagogical not IT imperatives. Accordingly, the following discussion takes the six elements discussed above and seeks to utilize the expertise of SOLSTICE, the Edge Hill University CETL (Centre for Excellence in Teaching and Learning), to offer a design for a regional PGR distance skills and support facility.[16] It is suggested that the region (rather than the nation or the locality) offers the appropriate geographical organizing principle for such an initiative, given that it allows for economies of scale and can build on existing relationships between universities while also allowing for the development of appropriate face-to-face events for doctoral students to attend should they be able.[17] The basic model for this initiative has been presented to and discussed extensively in two separate workshops at the 2005 North West Hub Good Practice Conference; in addition, it has been discussed at the North West University Association Research Group and has been the subject of a consultative workshop at the 2006 UK GRAD national conference.

Strands of e-activity

As noted above, research students may need a number of 'diagnostic' elements and a number of 'access' and 'support' elements in order for them to be able to navigate their way through the doctoral maze. These can be organized into four strands of e-activity:

- knowledge and doctoral process,
- peer support,
- advice and
- reflection.

Students may require access to these either on an ongoing or a sporadic basis, and, depending on the situation, that access may be either open to anyone who chooses to take advantage of it or closed, meaning that sensitivities about the nature of the discussion or the support being provided is such that a closed environment is necessary. The model is shown in Figure 4.1 and is elaborated below.

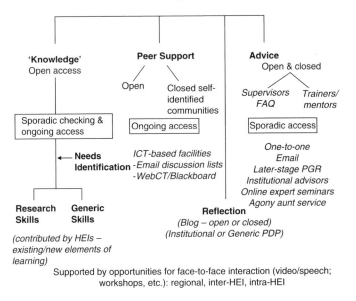

Figure 4.1   A model for student access to strands of e-learning activity

Knowledge

This strand contains nothing that might be considered sensitive (although it will address issues concerned with sensitive research) and thus will be 'open access'. It will comprise modules and learning objects concerned with two aspects of the PGR experience, research skills and generic skills. These will be drawn largely from the (rapidly expanding) publicly available stock of learning resources currently available on the World Wide Web and those currently used by partner institutions. Some resources, particularly those concerned with the development of generic skills, will need to be developed from scratch. The resources should address the various elements included in the Research Councils' Joint Skills Statement. With recent and continuing developments in CIT, these resources need not (and should not) be of the type that has earned e-learning a bad reputation in some quarters. Dynamic, well-designed e-learning opportunities should be the norm, not the exception.

It is this aspect of a student's development needs that will need to be analysed and determined early on in her/his research degree programme. This can be done through a variety of mechanisms and may involve the use of Personal Development Portfolios that are commended in the QAA Code of Practice, or it may involve some other institutionally determined mechanism. However it is organized, its implementation must be carried out. Some institutions may wish to test a student's skills development, while others may simply require a student to demonstrate that the issue has been considered. In either case, the system would have to include provision for an institution to link to it its own bespoke skills offering. It would, of course, be necessary for a 'generic' Learning Needs Analysis tool to be developed as part of the facility for those institutions or those students who may wish to use it rather than develop their own. Additionally, for those institutions that might wish to introduce some form of assessment, that could be done through local arrangements and would only require the acceptance of the principle that learning can be undertaken separately (geographically, institutionally and temporally) from assessment.

Peer and other support

Support is a crucial part of any research student's journey to success (Phillips and Pugh 2000; Tight 2003: 96–8; Rugg and Petre 2004). Typically, this support can come from a variety of sources, amongst which peers, friends, family and the institution itself are the most common. Some of these sources, family for example, cannot be entirely substituted no matter what the quality of the CIT. Virtual communities can, however, provide settings in and through which support of various kinds can be delivered. This delivery can be through one of the existing virtual learning environments such as Blackboard or WebCT. It can also be through e-mail discussion lists, bulletin boards and associated resources. The important thing to remain aware of is that while some peer support can be best delivered through open forums, on occasion it will be required to be made available in closed, 'safe', spaces. This requirement, which also applies to the facility's 'advice' section, may arise from a number of sources including the fact that, from time to time, support is required because of what someone else close to the person who is seeking support (for example, a fellow student or supervisor) is doing with regard to that person (Leonard 2001; Delamont et al. 2004: 30–2).

If all those using the facility (both staff and students) are regarded as the population, then that population will contain a significant number of 'communities'. These communities can be defined a priori by the facility's designers (examples of this could be students and/or supervisors in a cognate area, students in a subregional geographical area, those interested in a specific methodology, and so on) or by the members themselves according to specific needs, interests or desires.

Advice

Most students need advice as they proceed through a doctoral programme (Cryer 2000; Phillips and Pugh 2000; Rugg and Petre 2004). Sometimes the act of seeking advice is reassuring simply because it shows the seeker that others have faced the same issue or problem. Sometimes offering the solution to the problem brings about its own resolution. In any event, a research student requires ongoing access to appropriate advice. This can be provided online in a number of ways including:

- one-to-one,
- by e-mail responses to specific enquiries,
- online expert-led seminars,
- an 'agony aunt' service and
- frequently asked questions.

It can also be provided by

- later-stage research students,
- institutional advisers,
- PGR mentors,
- supervisors and
- subject experts.

For some of these, there are resource implications (although, in many cases, there are already people in place who are employed within institutions to offer advice), but increasingly the content that makes up the 'virtual' world is being developed by users themselves. Of particular note here is 'Wiki' technology, which allows participants to contribute to the development of virtual content and which lends itself very well to this type of initiative.

As noted above, an important element of the 'advice' section of the facility is to recognize that there need to be both 'open' and 'closed' areas of support and that the participants should be able to define the latter as their need determines.

Reflection

Research informs us that reflection is an integral part of learning (Kolb 1984; Daudelin 1996). While there are some who prefer to reflect in a very informal way, for others the discipline provided by a formal structure is helpful. This is what is provided by a personal development plan (PDP). An effective reflection program should include both a generic PDP designed for research students and also the facility for institutions to 'plug' their own PDP into the system. This generic PDP should be associated with the other sections of the facility so that all dimensions of the research students' experience can be reflected upon and linked back to the elements to which the reflection refers.

Another relatively recent aspect of the Internet that many people have embraced is the 'blog'.[18] Blogs are used in a way analogous to either private or public diaries and include an individual's thoughts on whatever is exercising them at a given time. Blogs made public by research students could feed into the peer support and advice function provided by the facility.

Conclusion

This chapter has sought to identify a major tension in doctoral education in the UK. This tension arises at the nexus of the increased degree of concentration of funding for both research and research students, the increased requirement for institutions to provide all research students with access to skills training, and the fact that the policy regarding these two elements is made to a significant extent on the basis of an ideal type of student who is not typical. In particular, this tension is played out most severely with respect to part-time students. The tension also has a number of potential implications for UK doctoral training, and this chapter has focused on one currently exercising the sector, the provision of skills training for part-time students, for which it has also offered a potential solution. There are, however, other potential implications that emerge from the skills agenda; one of these concerns the fundamental nature of the PhD.

The defining characteristic of a doctoral graduate in England, Wales or Northern Ireland is someone who has demonstrated the following:

(i)   the creation and interpretation of new knowledge, through original research or other advanced scholarship, of a quality to satisfy peer review, extend the forefront of the discipline, and merit publication;

(ii) a systematic acquisition and understanding of a substantial body of knowledge which is at the forefront of an academic discipline or area of professional practice;

(iii) the general ability to conceptualise, design and implement a project for the generation of new knowledge, applications or understanding at the forefront of the discipline, and to adjust the project design in the light of unforeseen problems;

(iv) a detailed understanding of applicable techniques for research and advanced academic enquiry.

(QAA 2001a)

These characteristics are all of a higher level than is normally associated with skills development and relate to the development of cutting-edge knowledge and high-level conceptual activity. They are also 'output'-related threshold statements and all of them are assessed through the thesis and the viva undertaken on the basis of the thesis. It is very difficult to sustain the argument that the 'outcomes' identified above in the Qualification Framework cannot be achieved unless an individual has attended or participated in 'skills-related' activities of the sort being provided through the Roberts money. What appears to be happening is that, through a process of policy development and the associated regulation, a new type of PhD is emerging by the back door. This new PhD, involving both the research project and also a significant element of associated and career development, is welcome for those who wish to pursue it. It is less welcome, and arguably not necessary, for those who are already in careers (for example, those pursuing professional doctorates) or for those who are pursing life-long learning for its own sake.

It may be time to consider the possibility that the 'PhD' as a single uncontested concept has had its day. There may well have to be different types of doctoral degrees, each of which has a different character, to meet the needs of different audiences or consumers.[19] These types might be as follows.

1   A 'research career training' doctorate with a full portfolio of associated generic skills training attached.
2   An 'academic practice' doctorate combining a full portfolio of associated generic skills and higher education teaching training attached.
3   A continuous professional development (CPD) doctorate similar in nature to the current professional doctorate.
4   A doctorate by practice, a category which could include not only the existing 'practice-based doctorate' but also the doctorate by publication.
5   A doctorate by thesis only, essentially, the traditional PhD.

The danger of pursuing the current agenda is that, by concentrating on one of the types, there is a risk of alienating significant, other audiences. Currently, it is the first and second categories (and the associated primarily full-time audience) that are being privileged. These are also the types of doctoral study where the balance is largely in favour of the full-time student. The other categories are much more likely to be the preserve of part-time students. They are also much more likely to be the preserve of the post-1992 universities, those institutions which receive a very small proportion of the available PGR and QR funding. These are also the institutions that historically have been best at widening participation. Higher education has because more effective at widening participation and lifelong learning with respect to undergraduate studies, where it is now accepted that most students are effectively part-time. If the government, higher education sector and individual institutions believe that lifelong learning is a good thing and believe further that doctoral study is a part of lifelong learning, it is time that policy and practice reflected the reality of today's diverse research student body.

If too much is asked of research students in terms of compulsory skills training, institutions risk losing a potentially large market and, more seriously, individuals will lose the opportunity of studying in a supported setting at the highest level. The contribution to intellectual and socio-economic development, which can be made both by people within careers and also by people who have moved beyond paid work, would be lost to academe and society more generally. If the diversity in types of research students and their needs and motivations as well as the diversity in the institutions and the types of doctoral study already being effectively offered to these students is not recognized and provided for, then notions of widening participation and lifelong learning will effectively stop at the level of the taught programme. As the UK increasingly becomes a society in which intellectual capital is the key to economic development and in which over one-third of the population has left the paid workforce, it would be socially and economically ill-advised to allow a system to develop that ignored this segment of the population's potential contribution through doctoral study. This chapter has argued for a recognition and embracing of diversity, and it has outlined a proposal which would go a long way towards assisting all universities to make doctoral study truly a part of lifelong learning.

Acknowledgements

The authors would like to acknowledge the considerable part played by Dr Simone Kruger and Mark Schofield (both of Edge Hill University) in the development of the proposal that forms the final part of this chapter. We would also like to thank the participants in the workshops referred to later for their contribution.

Notes

1   These demands for an increasing 'skills-dimension' to the research degree should be seen as part of a general move towards the concentration of funding council resources for research in a smaller number of 'elite', research-intensive institutions.
2   This agenda was driven largely by HEFCE, the English funding council.
3   This does not include the rather different uses of the term 'Doctor' for medical practitioners.
4   See Green and Powell (2005) for a wider discussion of these issues. The current discussion draws on this very timely study.
5   For one attempt to identify the range of titles of doctoral (and masters) awards, see Bourner et al. (1999).
6   For an early discussion of some aspects of these, see Duke (1997).
7   As with many developments in the area of postgraduate education, these concerns were never subjected to systematic interrogation and developments were based largely on anecdotal evidence.
8   Information supplied by RCUK in a personal communication.
9   This policy was given formal voice in the 2003 White Paper (DfES 2003). Policy on QR and PGR funding is largely responsible for the significant wedge that has been driven between the various parts of the higher education sector and is directly responsible for the development of the different institutional interest groups. These are The Russell Group, The 1994 Group and The Coalition of Modern Universities.
10   By 2006–07, some individual institutions were receiving an amount approaching £500,000 per annum for resource skills training.
11   Other arrangements involving lower thresholds for funding have been adopted by the Scottish and Welsh funding councils.
12   The exception to this is seven 'emerging subject areas where the research base is currently not as strong as in more established subjects', where research students are supported in those departments whose research was graded at 3b. For details of these subjects, see HEFCE (2003c).

13   One research-intensive university refuses to allow full-time research students to graduate unless they have followed the institution's skills training programme, but is content to allow part-time students to graduate irrespective of whether they have engaged with the programme. This is despite both sets of students being assessed against the same set of regulations. In an increasingly litigious culture, this practice appears to hold significant risk for the institution.

14   By this we mean practical and emotional support for life and the social dimensions of studying for a doctoral degree.

15   The membership of this Hub includes all the universities and higher education colleges in Cumbria, Lancashire, Greater Manchester and Merseyside. It thus represents the full range of institutions.

16   SOLSTICE is focused on the development of innovative approaches to, and the use of, e-learning.

17   This may seem contradictory to the purpose of the proposal, but the authors accept that a model involving face-to-face interaction is preferable to one that does not have this dimension. Where practical, these can be provided within the region and participants can travel to them. Current examples are Hub events and those developed by individual institutions, which are then made available more widely to other HEIs. They might also be delivered through virtual networking using appropriate CIT hardware, for example, increasingly inexpensive web cam technology. The purpose of the proposal is to enable provision where the traditional model does not fit well.

18   The term stems from a shortening of 'WebLog'. In addition to the sites established purely to provide 'blog space', MySpace (www.myspace.com), which at the time of writing has 130 million members, provides a blog facility and almost half a million blogs are posted every day. There are also other social networking sites offering the same facility.

19   It would be ironic if the recognition that there are different types of consumers of doctoral education enabled a more traditional style of doctoral study to make a comeback.

Part 2

Practice

5

The Challenges of Research Training Practice

Steve Hutchinson and Tony Bromley

Introduction

Part 1 of this book discussed the political issues of relevance to skills training and raised a host of challenges for the sector. This second part examines the practicalities of implementing a successful research training programme that reflects these many challenges. The chapters in this section examine the key challenges in some detail. Part 2 culminates with three universities describing their practice and illustrating how they have responded to the challenges.

This chapter attempts to focus the broad picture set out in the book so far into a summary of the practical issues which need to be addressed when creating skills training provision for researchers. This chapter unashamedly poses far more questions than it answers, with a view to allowing the reader to make up their own minds based on the rest of the section and the specific needs of their own institutions.

A summary of the key issues is provided in Table 5.1a and b.

Stakeholder needs analysis

As many project management courses illustrate, a good starting point for managing a project is a stakeholder needs analysis. If institutions are to put together training programmes and courses that fulfil a purpose and meet needs, then they need to know what these needs are and where they originate. So who *are* the stakeholders here and what needs do they have?

Postgraduate researchers – a diverse group of professionals?

A sensible place to start this discussion must surely be the researchers themselves. For a long time the sector retained the notion (and catered accordingly) that its researchers were 23 years old, British, middle-class students who had finished a Masters or Bachelors degree and were staying

Table 5.1   Summary of the main issues for consideration in programme design

(a) Stakeholder needs analysis and programme structure

Stakeholder needs analysis		*Programme structure*	
PG researchers	Home/overseas Previous experience Part/full time On/off campus	Who leads the programme?	Staff development? Graduate school? Faculty/school Other?
Government	Meet QAA Code of Practice Roberts agenda Knowledge economy	Programme style	Compulsory? Embedded/bolt-on Credit rated?
Other research funders	Enterprise Commerce Industrial R&D	Training style	Group size 'Module' length Lecture/workshop
Academic employers	Research funding skills Learning and teaching Publications	Training progression	1st/2nd/3rd year programme Different registration dates
Non-academic employers	Commercial awareness Project management Communication	Quality assurance	Evaluation Reporting Monitoring
Your institution	Publications Research standing Completion rates	Coherence amongst all providers	IT service Careers Library

(b) Programme components and resources

Programme components		*Resources*	
Aims and objectives	What are they? e.g. improve research, employability	Training and development staff	How many? Required capacity? Professional trainers
Personal development planning	Personal/discussed Compulsory/optional Paper/online	Support staff	Workshop co-ordinators Web designer Web developer
Development/ training needs analysis	Basis? Joint Skills Statement Online?	Training rooms	Plenary room(s) Breakout room(s) Common room
Progression monitoring	System? Online? Paper?	Training materials	Budget? IT? Stationary
Workshop programme	Generic/subject specific? Induction Subject content		
Broad opportunities	GRAD school Researchers in residence		

in the sector. However, even if this were once true, we know that this is no longer the case. The Roberts report (while a great lever for change within the sector) has done little to disabuse policy makers of this notion.

The cultural shift in postgraduate student populations has had huge impacts on the sector as a whole – not least via the difference in fees levied and the resultant development of universities' interests abroad. It has also made waves in research training, and providers have a duty to ask themselves the following questions while putting their programmes together, as all of them will have major ramifications for the content and make-up of training interventions.

- Who are the researchers themselves?
- Are they home, EU or overseas?
- Are they studying on a part-time or full-time basis?
- Do they spend substantial amounts of their research time on campus or off campus (either a few miles away or further a field)?
- Are they straight from a first degree or are they returning to study after years working outside education?
- What previous training and experience have they had – either in the form of another higher degree or in the form of industrial or business training?
- What are their expectations of training and development within a research degree context?
- What is their cultural background – and what ramifications might this have for their perceptions of training and development?
- What is their exit strategy or preferred career trajectory after their research degree?
- What would motivate them to attend training? (And what would block their attendance?)
- What training do they want and need? What do they think they need? (The QAA Code of Practice for research degree programmes (RDPs) has raised the bar considerably in terms of placing training needs analysis (TNA) and personal development planning (PDP) at the heart of the research degree.)
- Would accreditation of training be a motivating carrot or a restrictive stick for the researchers? (And who would do the accrediting, and what credibility would it have?)
- Would embedding training serve the needs of the researchers or would it simply detract from the core objectives of the research itself? Are bolt-on courses what works for busy researchers?
- What is the 'vertical progression' (that is, continuity before and after) with any training that the researchers may have received as a taught student and any future training they may receive in the research sector? The current vogue is to refer to 'early stage' or 'early career' researchers, and this seems to set a tone that there should be continuity of provision. Do researchers actually benefit from any joined up thinking?

The government – what really is their agenda?

A question which often taxes training providers (amongst others no doubt) in this post-Roberts climate is 'What does the government really want here and how does that impact us?'

In the interest of brevity, the earliest points of involvement worth mentioning here are the Harris (1996) and Dearing (1997) reports, which raised the Key Skills agendas in universities and laid much of the ground for the thinking of students as consumers. The involvement of the Research Councils in the formulation and endorsement of the Joint Skills Statement (RCUK 2001b) also sent clear messages to the sector from the government about what the PhD should be. In addition the report by Prof. Sir Gareth Roberts (Roberts 2002) reinforced these movements stating that 'minimum standards [for PhD] should include the provision of at least two weeks of dedicated training a year, principally in transferable skills . . .' and that this should be linked to the ability of institutions to drawdown money for research. Roberts also states that 'skills acquired by PhD graduates do not serve their long-term needs. Currently, PhDs do not prepare people adequately for careers in business or academia'. It is clear to see, therefore, that the direction of UK government thinking is drifting away from the 'traditional' PhD.

In general, the rationale for the government's support of this agenda lies within the 'knowledge based economy' concept and the belief that in the future knowledge creation and commercialization will be key wealth generators (DfES 2003). It is this notion, and the associated need for skills development, that is driving the research councils, the 'Roberts monies' and much of the policy making and substantial increase in training activity from the sector as a whole. Practically, the government's 'needs' as a stakeholder, with respect to designing a training and development programme are embodied in the new Code of Practice for research degrees developed by the Quality Assurance Agency (QAA 2004).

The other funders – a majority shareholder?

However, in addition to the UK government there are a multitude of other funders of research students, ranging from charities, overseas governments, business and industry (either in partnership with the host university or not) to a variety of others (notwithstanding those researchers who are self-funded), each with their own demands, agendas, requirements and views. As already stated, the training and developmental agenda is currently being led by the UK government, yet research council funded students do not make up the majority in most (if any) HEIs, and in many there are next to none. Some within the sector are starting to question this discrepancy in which the 'demands' of the few are affecting the lives of the many. Later chapters of this book speculate upon the possible futures of training policy and funding.

Employers and the employability agenda

If the Roberts' review is the catalyst that helped to shape the current landscape, the skills agenda (especially in this context) has been shaped by one concept – employability. This is again confirmed by Roberts (2002).

There are of course a number of deep-seated problems with 'employability' as the foundation stone upon which all this activity is based. Primarily, a researcher's role model within the sector (the supervisor) often received little or no training in this area and 'ended up' in a career much sought after by the junior researchers. Employability is thus not a word that many training practitioners use if they are trying to convince supervisors to engage with this agenda.

Secondly, it overlooks the fact that previous PhD graduates were not 'unemployed'. (Such a notion is clearly an oversimplification, but is certainly not untrue.) Thirdly, such a driver of 'employability' is heavily weighted to the 'traditional' PhD student (whom we have already highlighted as an endangered species) at the start of their career.

The national findings of surveys such as Careers in Research Online Survey (CROS 2005) have shown that the majority of research staff with a PhD aspire to research careers within the academic sector – even if in reality this is a numerical impossibility. The perceived trajectory of many students and their supervisors is one of an academic career. The sector overall has been slow to make the realization that academia (including the academic-related professional) is the biggest employer of PhDs (as evidenced in reports such as the UK GRAD-commissioned *What Do PhDs Do?* (Shinton 2004)), and we have been even slower to realize that academics are actually 'employed'.

The real problem with employability as a reason for 'up-skilling' our PhDs is that it is very difficult to convince an institution to engage with an agenda whose benefits may only be visible five years after the student has left.

Universities are therefore presented with a dilemma – how to meet the needs of a variety of stakeholder groups when the shots are being called by a minority (but significant) group and also how to meet their own needs as research institutions.

In short, it could be argued that in order to meet these conflicting stakeholder demands, institutions are in danger of forgetting what they are actually here for – to do research!

The universities and research institutions – so what do we want?

The heading 'universities' is an enormously broad one, and despite the fact that this book deals with doctoral researchers as a catchall term, the institutions in which they sit are enormously diverse. This diversity of institution stems from history (in terms of old or new university) and is also dependent on current and future priorities (that is, whether an institution aspires to be research or teaching led). Any government research assessment exercise (RAE) and emergent government policy over the next few years will obviously shape this agenda further.

In addition, with the increasing pressure on academics and universities, there is often a real scepticism that the training agenda is, at best, merely another drain on time and, at worst, 'just another initiative'. To their credit, it should be remembered that HEIs have nearly all embraced the notion that any Roberts' funding can be used altruistically to support all of their researchers (staff and student). The desire to not have a two-tier system is a laudable one, yet it is a desire that has not been followed by matched financial input from the other major research funding bodies.

So, when establishing and reviewing a training programme, it is necessary to take into account the strategic priorities of all of the stakeholders (from institution, down to schools, faculties, departments and research groups). Such consideration will often have a dramatic effect on the commitment to the training from all parties (Box 5.1).

Box 5.1 Strategic buy-in – an example from the Faculty of Medicine at Leeds[1]

While considering how to spend the faculty allocation of Roberts funds within the Faculty of Medicine and Health at the University of Leeds there was some debate as to how best to use the resource. The faculty had recently undergone a strategic review and one of the priority areas for development was within the field of Knowledge Transfer (KT). The Roberts agenda and the KT agenda are closely aligned, and so a strategic decision was made to use the Roberts allocation to train researchers in communication and KT. A number of initiatives were established – presentation skills training, poster creation, communicating with non-specialists courses and a host of others. The faculty ran cross-discipline conferences with KT themes, which they used to build communities of researchers. As a result of these initiatives, several researchers went on to win regionally and nationally prestigious communication and KT awards. In addition, the faculty used the results of such training and efforts to promote *its* work to the general public – as was laid out in its strategy. The ramifications of such activities were that the strategic needs of the faculty were met, as well as the needs of schools, researchers and supervisors. *Because the faculty, combined with advice from the University's centre, had the vision to treat the training agenda as part of a bigger whole, the buy-in from the academic community was a powerful force for cultural change.*

Training provision design – the big issues

With training requirements explicitly detailed within the QAA Code of Practice and the RCUK's Roberts reporting mechanisms leading to a direct policy link between the skills training provision in RDPs and potential future research income, universities are for the first time being compelled to address this issue at the highest level. Institutions must surely then consider some of the major issues that surround training practice.

Should training be compulsory?

A programme of training that a student is compelled to attend may well be an attractive option (to the host institution) for several reasons:

- such a programme will ensure high student attendance at skills training and development activities;
- such attendance is far easier to police, monitor and report externally;
- high attendance will provide financial security for a programme;
- programmes such as this have potential to drive through cultural change at a faster rate than non-compulsory programmes.

However, there are a number of other issues with such compulsory programmes.

Perhaps the most significant of issues for the compulsory approach is whether to allow 'failure' if a student does not attend a compulsory part of the RDP and the subsequent ramifications of such an action. To illustrate the issue, take the question to the extreme. You may have an exceptionally gifted researcher who has produced high quality research but not attended the requisite skills training and development 'credits'. In this scenario you may have to fail the student or send them back to complete the required credit. However, such issues can be tackled. For example, see Chapter 9, which refers to practice at the University of Sheffield.

There are a number of other issues that need to be confronted. What aspects of the programme are compulsory? All parts of all three years of a programme or just an initial TNA or development needs analysis (DNA) and ongoing PDP? If any elements are compulsory how are they to be assessed? For the larger universities in the UK with research student numbers running into thousands any 'exam' type of assessment would be a significant undertaking. Therefore, is the option to put assessment of skills development down to supervisory judgement? Or should there be a simple 'time-served' approach? Does 'time-served' provide a satisfactory indicator of progression in skills development?

If research students have completed some compulsory training and development, should they be awarded something in recognition of this beyond the award of the PhD itself? Options could range from 'credit' to a certificate or diploma. How do you handle mature students with significant prior skills development? Is a PhD with a significant compulsory training and development component an attractive option for students from overseas when there are other institutions internationally that appear to allow a researcher to simply 'get on with research'? What about the ramifications of attempting to train rooms full of unwilling and resentful participants? What about the sheer numbers of participants that result from compulsory attendance in a programme? Finally, is 'compulsory' training applicable for the diversity of research students? Should it be a tailored programme for each individual?

Non-compulsory programmes also have their issues. Primarily, will a programme with no compulsory element foster any form of the cultural change identified by Roberts (2002) and previously discussed as necessary? If cultural change does not occur, will this leave a university open to losing the ability to drawdown funding for research from government? In terms of provision, how do you schedule and fund a programme without a good idea of likely attendance rates? How do you manage a programme where students know attendance is not compulsory even if they have signed up to attend a training course or workshop?

Finally, and perhaps ideally, a cultural shift may move towards a state where skills training is truly embedded within the PhD research. Is this best achieved through a compulsory or non-compulsory programme? If you have a compulsory skills training programme set apart from the research, is this truly embedded?

Accreditation – what does this count towards?

If our modules, programmes and courses are to be accredited, then we need to address the positive and negative incentives inherent in such an arrangement, as well as the practicalities of actually running such a scheme.

If a programme is to be accredited, for many practitioners this sends out the message that the skill development is a bolt-on extra that can be assessed separately. Vocational qualifications (*and is that not really what a PhD is?*) do not as a rule have various isolated components. And if such accreditation is made mandatory, will we not surely end up with researchers taking courses just to complete the doctoral process? A trainer shared with us recently a tale of a participant on a 'Thesis Writing' course who had already completed his/her thesis, but was attending just to get the credits needed to pass the accreditation. Surely this type of scenario is to be avoided.

A final question, left open here, might be who will actually recognize the accreditation (that is, will the accreditation – as opposed to the training – be of any use to candidates in addition to their thesis when they move on with their career)?

Some institutions have implemented a policy of full accreditation for their skills training components, and examples of this are reported later in the section.

Of course there are options currently being used, such as a professional doctorate with a Management Diploma.[2] However, does this disconnect 'training and development' from a research degree rather than embed it?

The student demographic – back to the stakeholders

A criticism of the Roberts' review and subsequent agenda is that it leans towards catering for the 'standard' student progression route from high school through a degree programme to PhD. However, as Chapter 4 illustrated, there is a huge variety in the backgrounds and motivations of PhD candidates. For example, what about the training needs of the mature 'hobby' PhD student or the mature student re-entering higher education for career progression? How do you assess and accredit prior learning and experience of an individual who has been running a multimillion pound business or department? Do you send them to the project planning workshop or do you let them deliver it? Are short courses really the answer for a body of students, many of whom may increasingly have to hold down part-time employment even if they are 'full-time' researchers[3] and who have a multitude of other agendas? *Until our thinking breaks away from an image of standard students attending short courses and truly embraces the diversity of student population and the possibilities of a myriad of delivery vectors, we will never achieve the cultural change to which we aspire.*

Generic or subject-specific training?

A common debate in skills training and development provision concerns what material can be provided generically to a cross-campus student group and what material really has to be covered subject specifically. Strong opinions are commonly found across this debate. Superficially, as an example, it would appear that many aspects of communication skills training and development would benefit from cross-university groups whereas research methods would appear to be most effectively delivered at the faculty or subject-specific level. However there are pros and cons to both these models, and years of experience delivering short courses to research staff and students from many disciplines has taught us that often the subject specificity of the title on a handout is as important as the content inside.

Is it 'training' or 'development'?

Is the skills training agenda about simply trying to get researchers to a prescribed set of learning outcomes or levels (in which case, if they arrive with these levels attained already, can we leave them in peace?) or should it be about helping to move people forward from their level of entry? Do we aspire to a research skills 'driving test', or something focusing on the needs and individual skills, behaviours, knowledge and attitudes of each individual? If it is the former, then we are destined to fall into the trap of creating a homogenized cohort of cloned researchers, and if the latter is the case, we are building a system which is near impossible to properly evaluate and accredit.

Another way of looking at this issue is to consider an analogy for a training and development programme. Should we have a development programme associated with a career path (which could be argued to meet the current life-long learning agenda) or should we have a set of unified, rigid, prescribed learning levels? How do we cater for the increase in skills training and development throughout all educational levels, from primary, secondary and tertiary through to postdoctoral programmes? Should universities have a co-ordinated structure of training and development learning outcomes for each level in higher education from a Bachelor's degree through a Masters to a PhD and beyond?

Programme components

Skills training and development programmes are not just about 'workshops'. There are a myriad of other elements that need consideration and implementation, including PDP, TNA/DNA and progression monitoring. Each needs a robust system, be it online or paper based.

The issue of evaluation

The twin agents of full economic costing and the RAE mean that increasingly researchers are being asked to justify the money that is invested in them. The training agenda is no different, and yet (with the light-touch RCUK reporting mechanism for the Roberts monies) there is little evidence (whether in existence already or even in the planning-to-collect stage) that any of the provision of training *actually makes a long-term difference*. Moreover, there is no research base in the sector to provide meaningful baseline data. Many providers of training will tell you that they know 'in their heart' that training has an impact, and many collect post-course feedback. However, as we will see later in the section, such feedback really only scratches the surface and rarely gets at either long-term behavioural change from the researchers or the training's cultural impact within their institution. *To put this in more familiar language – there is a real need for research to back up the thesis!*

If institutions are to properly engage with the culture of training, we need as a sector to be able to demonstrate that this activity has a payoff for the institution and current academics, as well as to the employability of the researchers themselves. If we as providers are to truly convince the cynics, then we must provide evidence of impact – and moreover we must do it properly. If an institution can show that its investment in training in, for example,

Writing for Publication has led to an increased RAE submission rate from its postgraduate researchers, then suddenly the impacts and benefits to all parties may become clearer.

This duty to ourselves, our students and our funders must look beyond simple 'bean counting'; as such, the challenge that the sector faces is that measuring the behavioural and cultural impact of such diverse interventions is fiendishly difficult and could legitimately employ whole social science research faculties for many years.

Evaluation is recognized as a highly significant issue in the sector and a topic richly debated as part of the 'Rugby Team' (2006), a sector initiative backed by HEIs nationally in response to RCUK. It is sincerely hoped that the result of this debate is meaningful, funded research into the effects and long-term benefits of much effort and financial investment.

To quote something of a truism about training and development from Professor Norman Staines[4] 'Better researchers do better research'. *As a sector we must prove this truism to actually be true.* Evaluation is the subject of Chapter 8.

Styles and methods – what should training and development be?

There is much written on training and development in the workplace, and this book is not meant to supersede any of the years of practice within the private sector. However, to many within the academic establishment, the notion of teaching sessions that move beyond straight chalk/PowerPoint and talk lectures is a move into alien territory. Much of the sector has never experienced training that comprises facilitated experiential learning, review sessions, group discussions, learning 'journeys', role-play, storytelling, icebreakers, play as training, so-called buckets and ropes exercises, emotional learning, coaching, participants training each other, designated and recorded reflection, vicarious learning, spacious sessions to allow embedding of learning and a host of other staples of a quality trainer's toolkit. Even the language of training, with 'participants' instead of 'students', is more inclusive and less segregating than the normal language of academia. Decades of training practice developed outside academia is trying to gain a toehold in a world where 'we teach and they learn', 'they are the students and we are the masters', and students are weighed and measured in a largely summative fashion.

Chapter 6 examines the different rationales for how and why we do what we do, alongside a review of the Research Councils' GRAD schools that have for nearly 40 years been delivering experiential (industry/management) training to researchers.

Location, structure, deliverers and credibility

The skills training agenda has some impact across every university campus. With any such cross-university activity, an important question is 'who is best placed to lead the provision?' In some universities, activity is led from a central unit, in others it is faculty or school-led. Activity can be based in staff development units or graduate schools. Commonly, the rationale for this placement lies somewhere in the history and culture of the university and the respective university ethos regarding the intrinsic value (both financial and moral) of skills training and development activity.

Additionally, there are questions of credibility. Can research methodology be 'taught' at the university level generically or is it better done at the faculty, school or supervisor level? Can you cover communication skills in a school or is such activity better placed at a central level? Do all 'trainers' require a PhD to be credible and stand in front of research students on any topic? Some universities clearly think so and thus source most or all of their training provision from within the academic body.

Another option might be to bring in external trainers from training companies. Buying-in trainers who do not have a research background is fraught with pitfalls, and feedback from participants on 'nice people with no idea of what it means to be a researcher' is common in these circumstances. We should not forget that our 'customers' are highly demanding and highly intellectual and do not suffer fools gladly.

A solution here (especially if your institution or department has only a few researchers) may be collaboration with other universities both regionally and nationally (many examples of this stem from the UK GRAD regional hubs[5]).

There are of course pros and cons inherent with any of these decisions (not least of which being the time pressure on busy academics), yet it is essential that an institution has truly considered all the angles before investing in a strategic model.

What about the developers?

A final stakeholder not previously mentioned are the training and development staff themselves. The explosion in provision nationally has led to an explosion of people involved in the sector. What is the career path for these people? What are their training requirements!? Do we look to industry and accredited training such as that provided by the Chartered Institute of Personnel and Development?[6] Is training any different from the skills base established in higher education through a history of learning and teaching experience? Do they all need a PhD?

Resources

Finally, a note on resources. A training programme has both human and consumable resource needs that require significant consideration. The human resource must reflect the required capacity of the programme. As an example, a research-led university such as Leeds has around 2500 research students. For a workshop group size of 20 and taking Roberts' view of two weeks 'training' per year for each research student, this would amount to a requirement of 1250 workshop days per year (taken literally!). In addition, there is a requirement for administrative support staff and training rooms.

Concluding remarks

This chapter has illustrated that the challenges in creating a successful skills training and development programme are many and varied (summarized in Table 5.1). The following chapters illustrate how a range of institutions have begun to find answers within their own specific contexts for many of these issues.

Notes

1   Reported in discussion with Susan Haymer, Heather Sears and Trevor Batten of the University of Leeds.
2   Manchester EngD programme. http://www.eps.manchester.ac.uk/graduate school/engd2.html (accessed 15 October 2006).
3   With the significant increase in student undergraduate fees in the UK, PhD researchers may well be starting a research degree with significant personal debt.
4   Quote reported in conversation with Professor Norman Staines, Kings College London.
5   The UK GRAD programme is a research council funded programme for post-graduate research students. It has a national Centre of Excellence in Cambridge and a number of regional 'hubs' (www.grad.ac.uk, accessed 15 October 2006).
6   CIPD provides accredited qualifications for the Personnel industry, guaranteeing to employers that individuals have achieved a required standard of personal development facilitation skills. Further details are available from the CIPD website: http://www.cipd.co.uk/default.cipd.

6
Training Practice and UK GRAD: Why They Do What They Do?

Al Richardson

Introduction

The postgraduate research degree is changing. 'It is no longer just about producing an original piece of research', says Mary Ritter, Pro-Rector for Postgraduate Affairs at Imperial College, London, and Chair of the UK GRAD Programme Steering Group that supports training for postgraduate researchers (PGRs) in universities, 'Now, producing a trained researcher is an equally important output.'

These sentiments are echoed by Sir Gareth Roberts in his foreword to this book: 'The product that the PhD student creates is not the thesis – vital though it is to their subject area through the creation of original knowledge; rather, the product of their study is the development of themselves.' Sir Gareth emphasizes that the rate of change needs to accelerate to keep pace with the needs of the major stakeholders who stand to benefit from a PGR who is not only capable of original thought but also capable of more mature deeds. In this context, it is perhaps the researchers themselves, as the most important stakeholders, who may find that unless they engage with training opportunities and acknowledge the need for wider learning they may look back on the research itself as a 'waste of time'[1] if they cannot find a suitable outlet for their talents.

This is now not only an important issue but also a matter of urgency to the UK economy and other important stakeholders. A biting illustration, provided by Sir Gareth, is that of a major City of London recruiter of individuals with computational and mathematical skills no longer looking to the UK for these skills but instead preferring the US. The reason given was that, 'similarly talented American research graduates had greater maturity and were less likely to come with a negative attitude towards business needs'.

Within the 'Practice' section of this book, three institutions describe their way of dealing with the challenges raised by the Roberts report (HM Treasury 2003) and the Joint Skills Statement of the Research Councils. The purpose of this chapter, however, is to add some context to both why we do what we do in relation to training practice styles appropriate to PGRs as well as to the role of the UK GRAD Programme, the longest established provider of experienced-based training to the sector.

The Research Councils set up the UK GRAD Programme in its present form in 2003 to support the academic sector in providing personal and professional ('transferable') skills within research degree programmes. Run by the Careers Research and Advisory Centre (CRAC) in Cambridge, it aims to: raise the profile of the importance of these skills, encourage opportunities for researchers to acquire them, deliver provision of exemplars in developing transferable skills and share good practice within higher education institutions.

When Sir Gareth Roberts' report *SET for Success* (2002) noted that PGRs were not prepared adequately for careers either in or outside academia, the government provided funding through the research councils for HEIs to implement Roberts' recommendation to provide PGRs with 'two weeks of transferable skills training per year'. UK GRAD has played a pivotal role, not just in raising the awareness of the logistical implications of the Roberts report for the PhD, but it has also championed the value of research skills to the economy and their impact on the productivity of researchers.

In a series of interviews held during 2006 Janet Metcalfe, Head of the Centre of Excellence for UK GRAD claims they have done this in a number of ways. Firstly, UK GRAD has been successful in bringing together all stakeholders interested in developing PGRs both nationally and through eight regional Hubs based in universities. By building networks, holding good practice events and enabling institutions within the locality to create their own resources while accessing the materials and courses of others, the organization has effectively built up expertise and capacity across the country. 'Universities are usually competitive with each other but UK GRAD has created an environment where they work together to promote and develop skills training', says Metcalfe. This cannot be easy and it would be naïve to pretend that institutions enjoy sharing resources such as courses freely, especially if delivery costs are high. It must be tempting for the larger HEIs within these hubs to let the smaller ones struggle on with the expectation that eventually they will inherit the local research student market. Tensions could arise if the Hubs attempted to share subject-specific training – such an initiative may well be seen to create a conflict of interest with a university's market for a particular research area. However, regional identity, and the recognition that there is much to gain from the Hubs facility keeps the generic skills agenda running.[2] It says much for the skill of the UK GRAD Hub Coordinators that these potential conflicts have not arisen and that a spirit of cooperation prevails.

The generic skills initiatives within research degree programmes, both those that are facilitated within and by Hubs and those that are funded by Roberts' money inside HEIs, are evolving and UK GRAD plans to evaluate whether the Roberts money has indeed made an impact. This will be done by surveying researchers, supervisors and employers about how they see the benefits of additional skills training. UK GRAD will endeavour to identify ways to measure the economic impact of research training by investigating whether employees with PhDs make a difference to a company's bottom line, and will also work out methods to measure the factors that enhance the employability of researchers in the early stages of their careers.

Another aim of UK GRAD policy is to close the gap between the expectations of PhD researchers held by the general public, employers and reality. 'People often think that PhD researchers are too "academic" or not worldly', says Metcalfe, 'where as, in fact, they bring a bundle of competencies that are attractive to any employer. They can work independently, handle complex issues, solve problems, motivate others, and manage projects. But this is still not necessarily recognised enough.' In 2004 UK GRAD published *What Do PhDs Do?*, the first ever analysis of the initial employment destination of UK PhD graduates (Shinton 2004). This demonstrated that half of all PhD graduates leave academia upon graduation and enter all sectors of the employment market.

To support the skills agenda UK GRAD runs national, regional and local courses for PGRs, including week-long GRAD schools that have been going on for almost 40 years. As part of encouraging and embedding provision within HEIs, it also supports the delivery of HEI-led local GRAD schools and organizes 'train the trainer' courses for supervisors and training providers. It holds national and regional conferences, good practice workshops and provides downloadable resources and advice, such as databases of training resources and examples of institutional practice. It also publishes reviews of issues in postgraduate research training.

The situation

There are no plans as yet for research degrees to be evaluated on the basis of an individual's generic or transferable skills as well as their subject knowledge. However, it is clear from the movement towards skills take-up, as facilitated through UK GRAD and Roberts' money, that the environment is changing. Individuals within that environment, be they researchers, supervisors or institutions themselves, feel the need to change. This continued evolution of the doctorate is summarized by Chris Park in the 'History' section of 'New Variant PhD' (Park 2005a). It charts the progress of the research degree from monastic trial by ordeal to the current wide choice of research degree programmes for PGRs offered within HEIs across the world and delivered in the English language. The defining factor of the twentieth century PhD being that individuals select a subject area which plays to their intellectual strengths and that their suitability is initially confirmed through qualifications that have tested their knowledge rather than performance or a wider range of skills.

Park talks of a lack of harmony within HEI culture, 'It is useful', he says, 'to distinguish between the PhD as a product and the PhD as a process'. The essential differences between the Process PhD and the Product PhD appear to divide supervisors. The PhD supervisor who emphasizes Product will have a greater emphasis on demonstrable outputs such as the content of the thesis and whether the candidate has adequately demonstrated their subject knowledge through the strength of their argument. Alternatively, the Process PhD supervisor is likely to highlight the journey towards being a fully fledged researcher capable of delivery at a sustained high level. The Process supervisor is perhaps more teacher/tutor/facilitator orientated, whereas the Product supervisor is more interested in results and takes the mentoring role for granted, as something that goes with the territory. Gaining the Process PhD assures the examiners of their fitness for purpose in the community of researchers; accordingly, it is not just what they know that matters but also whether they have acquired and developed the mental acuity to use their knowledge to the best advantage. For the Product PhD holder the step-up to employment can be problematic. For the Process PhD such a step-up should be something they have at least anticipated experientially through a UK GRAD school or an equivalent form of enlightened training.

Is more (training) better?

In the case of the Product PhD, focus on content leaves little room for the personality of the PGR to be admitted into the examining equation (in theory at least). Training in wider matters that may be thought to detract from the clinical elegance of the thesis and viva is therefore discouraged. The Process PhD, however, requires the PGR to express a sufficiently rounded self (augmented by suitable training) to convince prospective peers of professional worthiness. Arising from this balanced mix, individuals perhaps encounter a much higher level of experiential training and emotional roundedness. Ironically, PGRs often only realize the source of their emotional roundedness much later – often years after graduation. The idea of the Product PhD thus prompts the question of whether it is appropriate to the person and that the benefit to the individual and society may take time to emerge. The Process PhD on the other hand, makes it clear to the PGR and the subsequent graduate that their training has a purpose beyond the submission of the thesis and this teleology should help to motivate them during their studies. Consequently, the fact that Roberts money has been made available may go some way towards softening the blow of institutional expenditure in that it could procure strategic outcomes such as more engaged research students who are prepared to contribute to their department's research environment, produce faster completion rates and, to paraphrase the Roberts report, help to make research graduates 'adequately prepared for an academic career' (Roberts 2002).

What factors are affecting current training practice styles?

Roberts money has been beneficial in creating an environment where the Process PhD is not just encouraged but frequently consciously realized and implemented. Evidence for this is available at institutions such as University of Liverpool and University of Sheffield that have implemented compulsory training in transferable skills for PGRs. These HEIs have made a policy decision to send a message to stakeholders, including their own supervisors, the research councils as well as the potential and current research students themselves. Institutions such as these claim to deliver a full six weeks of training in generic skills over the three years of the PhD. Nationally, resources have been greatly improved through the appointment of over 300 staff recruited through Roberts money for research student skills development and for careers advisors, so there has been a meaningful impact in the delivery of best training practice. However, this is mainly confined to those institutions – Russell Group and the larger campus universities – that have enough research council funded PGRs to drawdown the funding which goes with such a research 'critical mass'. The progressively savvier PGR may eventually gravitate towards those universities that adequately cater for their career opportunities – a trend which potential students are generating worldwide.

This brings us back to both the advantages and also the potential political problems inherent in the UK GRAD Hubs because, to compensate for lack of resources, smaller HEIs may find they have to (rather than elect to) either collaborate with neighbouring HEIs or deploy further afield contacts, networks and co-ventures to offer the best possible training at an economic price. Independent or semi-detached suppliers will often become favoured suppliers of training, 'leaving faculty to do what it does best'. This may reduce the need to dedicate staff to a function, which remains difficult to resource and manage for a variety of reasons. What this does not do, unfortunately, is enable the learning achieved through training in an institution to be developed and nurtured internally.

For the less research orientated institutions, in order to compete, there are other options, but they are not as secure as dedicated research council funding. Without larger amounts of Roberts' monies, these HEIs have to formally embed generic skills provision within the working relationship of supervisor and PGR – this is probably part of a lexicon of best practice but it is by no means easy. QAA standards require training opportunities to be available, and the Code of Practice states that:

> In providing research students with opportunities for developing personal and research skills, institutions will wish to pay particular attention to the differing needs of individual postgraduates, arising from their diversity. It is expected that a range of mechanisms will be used to support learning and that they will be sufficiently flexible to

address those individual needs. For example, the development needs of research students already employed to undertake research may be different from those of other students. The emphasis in formal training should be on quality, relevance and timeliness.[3]

Such a 'range of mechanisms' that are 'flexible' and the implication that at least some of this training is 'formal' and 'quality' inevitably infers a degree of cost and many HEIs with small numbers of PGRs could question whether the kudos of having research students is worthwhile in the long run. More alarmingly, perhaps for those with research student numbers in the low hundreds, HEIs will have to innovate and offer work placements or attract funding from industry and other sponsors. Such activities, specifically for dedicated training in generic skills, could be welcomed, or they could be contentious with staff. Either way, such projects would require commitment of resources and impetus.

Embeddedness is clearly the key to a successful transition to the Process PhD. 'Rather than just tacking training courses on to a PhD degree programme, we believe skills development should be embedded within the day-to-day experiences of researchers', explains Janet Metcalfe. 'This involves bringing about a cultural change in both researchers and their supervisors. We want researchers to reflect on the development of their skills as a researcher in much the same way that they reflect on the progress of their research. Part of the supervisory process is for supervisors to be able to support researchers to identify how they can improve their skills, for example, through developing their project management skills, or having an opportunity to practise their presentation skills. It is about making explicit what is implicit in good supervision.'

The role of the UK GRAD programme in training

UK GRAD provides courses and creates course materials to the highest standard available such that the mainstream requirements of a succession of cohorts of PGRs have amply and demonstrably been fulfilled since 1968. Their programme of GRAD schools was recognized by a National Training Award in 2000 for exceptionally effective training. More importantly though, the learning is imbued in a different, more caring and collaborative fashion than would be possible from the resources of many institutions. The GRADschools website section www.grad.ac.uk/GRADschools and the UK GRAD Programme 'Guide to Gradschools' provide an illustrative timetable and statistics on learning outcomes (UK GRAD 2006: 2, 5). Participant feedback indicates that 93 per cent of participants were motivated to complete their PhD and that 97 per cent could identify ways to develop themselves. Furthermore, 81 per cent were confident about working in teams and 93 per cent were confident about their employability. Finally, 94 per cent could see the relevance of their skills in different environments.

These high ratings do not happen by accident. The fact that something different happens at a GRAD school, the three to five day residential training course spent away from the home HEI, is readily verifiable from a long list of GRAD school alumni. This high level of caring arises from the focus on the participant PGRs themselves in addition to what they need to know. This is sensitive and places a particularly high duty of care upon course directors, tutors and mentors who themselves must satisfy stringent quality standards.

The extended period of immersion in the training and developmental objectives of the GRAD school enable participants to reflect on topics relevant to them as people; in addition, it is possible to apply a new awareness of personal skills and competencies to research issues. This approach may be the first time that some PGRs find themselves being treated not just as adults but genuinely as equal participants in the learning process.

GRAD school creates a safe environment within which questions may be asked of self and other consenting participants prompted by well tried and tested models, profiles and theories including the use of the Kolb Learning Cycle (Kolb 1984). For some PGRs this starts the whole process of context creation and appropriateness awareness in relation to themselves and the possibility of working better in teams. At the PGR stage, being able to articulate personal needs in a variety of ways reduces the danger of key matters remaining undiscussed with respect to fundamental life and career decisions.

There is a collegiate rather than pedagogic approach taken by both tutors and participants to the point where the terms teacher and pupil are somewhat blurred since those drawn to providing such programmes do seem to understand the need for mutuality of learning in education. Part of the PGRs' growth in learning is derived from the tutors' expectation of mutuality such as the sharing of learning outcomes. Based on recurring researcher feedback, this obviously works best in the tutorial groups (usually of up to ten people) where tutors are skilled in encouraging a high quality of debate within a stimulating but safe environment. The plenary sessions seem to benefit from the participants' progressively greater expectation of a civilized share of 'airtime' and the more open, questioning approach of all proceedings.

An additional benefit of courses away from one's institution is to participate in a different form of engagement with tutors, mentors, course directors and course designers. For many students this is liberating in terms of more mature ways and means of engaging with others in positions of responsibility. The learning dynamic is enhanced when the arbitrary, hierarchical barriers to learning are reduced or eliminated.

This non-hierarchical environment for participants extends to the 'local' UK GRAD courses that are enabled, validated and monitored by UK GRAD and CRAC and supported within the regional hubs. This roll-out to local HEI delivered GRAD schools is a much needed counterpoint to that which is originated by UK GRAD and, as an example of knowledge transfer, can go deep into the next generation of academics if those participants are positively influenced enough to imitate UK GRAD school practice.

The long-standing gulf between the needs of PGRs and the needs of their stakeholders had been addressed patchily until the post-Roberts era. There is still a fair distance to travel; indeed, the ethos of lifelong learning to which UK GRAD no doubt aspires requires that the journey never stops. This means that UK GRAD has to facilitate the future development of generic skills provision and anticipate the continued evolution of the PhD. They provide a forum which enables national stakeholders to air views and share ideas on practice, evaluation, ideas, provision and many other related topics.[4] UK GRAD acts as a filter, catalyst and broker providing leverage when needed across the relevant communities. Creating awareness, context and back-up regarding the bigger picture and where an idea may be best incubated is another perspective they provide. Bearing in mind that researcher education is a global marketplace, UK GRAD coordinates and provides a source of feedback to both educators and funders. This is an invaluable source of intelligence to ensure that the British doctorate remains competitive and of enduring value to world-class researchers.

The training practice styles

Training is an everyday thing. On-the-job training dispensed, often informally, is thought by many organizations to be quite sufficient for the needs of the workers and apprentices, not least in universities. By providing the Roberts money, the government has acknowledged that supporting the development of life and job skills is helpful not only to PGRs but also contributes to the economy in the form of more rounded, open-minded and understanding citizens. However, despite the availability of 'free places' for researchers funded by the research councils, only 30 per cent on average attend a GRAD school. This is a conundrum, as significant funds have been made available for places which will at the very least enrich a PGR's learning experience and 'add value' to the PhD. This does not mean that HEIs believe they are able to deliver a better service, but rather that many remain unconvinced of the need to put such training higher up their agenda. For many HEIs this would mean challenging the control of the supervisor and the personal autonomy of the research student who may choose to be 'unaware' of either the opportunity or the virtue of a GRAD school.

Part of the deeper answer to this question may lie in learning styles. The proposition of spending several days sequestered with other unknown researchers, exploring your motivations, competencies and career goals may only appeal to the 'activist' or the 'pragmatist' within the models of learning. Strategic thinking in training aimed at producing a consistent and yet flexible programme for PGRs may fail to match the learning styles of those PGRs – for instance, those who are from the more pragmatic reflective or theoretical segment in their approach.[5] Intuitively, perhaps, one feels that there should be some pedagogical benefit to be derived from knowing more about the student, and if HEIs and trainers were prepared to invest more in facilitating such self-knowledge, then many of the problems concerning 'resistance' to UK GRAD style learning experiences could be greatly disarmed. The Learning and Skills Research Centre (LSRC) publication – *Should We Be Using Learning Styles?* (Coffield et al. 2004: 8) – however, is less convinced of such a proven benefit. The publication provides an evaluation of 13 of the profiles most used in post-16 age-group assessments of learning styles to draw out the implications for pedagogy and rejects most as unproven or incomplete to achieve the pedagogic objective.

For example, performance improvement derived from Kolb and then Honey and Mumford's (1992) widely used profiles on learning styles were found to be inconclusive when set against the main frameworks used to define pedagogy. All the definitions, whether devised by psychologists, sociologists, on-the-job trainers or adult educators, mention the 'facilitation of learning' as the common purposes of education. More resources are needed to produce authoritative answers on profiling given that the LSRC publication's assessment of the Myers–Briggs Type Indicator (MBTI) and its effectiveness was: 'It is still not clear which elements [of MBTI] are most relevant for education.' This is at odds with the widespread use of MBTI in most sectors. Coffield et al. are scornful of the lack of coherence in the learning styles arena:

> The sheer number of dichotomies betokens a serious failure of accumulated theoretical coherence and an absence of well-grounded findings, tested through replication. Or to put the point differently: there is some overlap among the concepts used, but no direct or easy comparability between approaches; there is no agreed, 'core' technical vocabulary. The outcome – the constant generation of new approaches, each with its own language – is both bewildering and off-putting to practitioners and to other academics who do not specialise in this field.
>
> (Coffield 2004: 54)

Along with most personal development trainers and, increasingly HEIs, UK GRAD uses some of the profiles reviewed in the LSRC publication on its GRAD schools. However, this is more to create self and team awareness and to provide an objective language by which to improve the quality and depth of conversations between people. As Coffield et al. explain in their section on 'Positive Recommendations', it is better to facilitate metacognitive behaviour rather than to not do so; making participants aware that there are such things as learning styles is thus probably fruitful. However, the endorsement gap remains.

One further positive to emerge from the Coffield et al. study is that the ability to have the time and space for reflection is an important part of all learning styles. The Dearing report (Dearing 1997) and the Harris report (Harris 1996) recommended that more skills training related to research support be undertaken and that this should take place where the research-active staff are based. Individual HEIs have responded by providing some level of 'on-the-job' training for PGRs. However some training, particularly that which needs a deeper and extended period of participation and uninterrupted reflection, is best done off-site, ideally incorporating more than two nights away from base for maximum learning. At its very least it prevents those participants who are obsessed with their research and unimpressed with the need to reflect on their 'self' from sneaking back to their desk or laboratory.

The PhD can be a seminal moment in a researcher's life. For some, it is a transition from being a student to an early career researcher or for others it is a demonstration of a capacity to produce an original piece of research and as such is a rite of passage. Perhaps the greatest value of GRAD school opportunities is that they give research students the space to reflect on the momentous nature of the enterprise that they are undertaking. This should be a reflection not just on their research outcomes of course but on themselves as character material that they have the ability to shape and transform.

The bigger picture

There are indications that the government at last realizes the need to engage with the research community in a different way and that the Roberts initiative represents the beginning of a better understanding of the value brought by the research community to UK society. Bearing in mind the money spent annually on research through the research councils and institutions (let alone research undertaken in each of the government departments directly and indirectly), it is hardly surprising that the government is looking for a tangible, demonstrable return from some proportion of this research. The current government-set targets and incentives for researchers to turn some of their research into cash has produced a level of success below the level even of tokenism.

Performance statistics against which UK governments are evaluated by the media have seldom included higher education or the precious intelligentsia of the future. As a nation which now has to survive on its wits, the UK has at last recognized that some of its best brains are not yet committed to making a greater contribution to society. This is not because they do not want to, but rather because it has not yet occurred to them how they can do so. However, as the saying goes, it is not rocket science. The Lambert report is one of the latest to shine light on the divide between the needs of industry and those of academia. Lambert is yet another calling for this divide to be narrowed, at least to jumping distance. Lambert wants to see more entrepreneurial training, more work placements and more on-the-job training as '[e]vidence suggests that a large proportion of the initial skill-deficiencies reported by employers relate to skills and knowledge that are best acquired on the job' (HM Treasury 2003: 111). When the on-the-job training of the research student is so ostensibly dedicated to the reproduction of their supervisors' academic qualities – whatever their virtues may be – the resulting learning tends to favour academic culture rather than that of the industrial entrepreneur.

Conclusions

The Product PhD could be accused of losing touch with society and its stakeholders and to have outlived its usefulness. Losing touch with prospective PGRs, only some of whom will have the ability to discover and describe something original without help in their personal development, could prove suicidal. The world has moved on from the monastic origins of academe. To have a PhD heavily dependant on originality of insight at the expense of practicality of outcome may be unnecessarily off-putting by being too abstract even for extremely academically capable people. The intellectual struggle needs to be a combination of the outward bound debate with external forces and the inward bound debate with self to build the competence and confidence which comes with training, development and transformation. A similarly ambitious outcome, but one with a greater recognition of the support needed by PGRs in the achievement of a thesis worthy of their potential, seems more readily achievable by virtue of the Process PhD. To be able to effectively deploy both inward and outward knowledge in a project that embraces both the individual and their subject should be the target of the new PGR and their supervisor. Through the enlistment of the UK GRAD programme and its concomitant partners within institutions, that dual goal is being increasingly realized.

Notes

1   This phrase has entered the lexicon of training officers throughout UK higher education as one of the most common saying of supervisors who are opposed to their research student attending generic skills training sessions or workshops – such as those offered by UK GRAD.

2   It is interesting to think here of the political tensions within hubs where the smaller and medium-sized institutions drive the agenda in order to gain some of the resources from their larger neighbours.

3   Code of Practice for the assurance of academic quality and standards in higher education. Section 1: Postgraduate research programmes. http://www.qaa.ac.uk/academicinfrastructure/codeOfPractice/section1/default.asp#development.

4   See the 'Resources' section on the UK GRAD home page: http://www.grad.ac.uk/cms/ShowPage/Home_page/p!eecddL.

5   See Kolb (1984).

7

Evaluating Student Skills and Development: Current Practice and the Imperial College London Experience

Esat Alpay and Elaine Walsh

Introduction

Although present in many universities for a long time, the quantity, range and importance of skills development work for postgraduate researchers (PGRs) has increased dramatically since the introduction of Roberts funding via the research councils in 2003–04. Attendant upon this increased activity is a need to evaluate its benefits. A wide range of possibilities exists and no sector-wide approach has been agreed upon. When considering the evaluation of student skills and development at a fundamental level, questions arise as to the main purpose and benefits of a given evaluation method. At one extreme, the evaluation may in fact refer to a mechanism for generating student self-awareness and encouraging appropriate personal development planning; at another, the evaluation may involve performance criteria of importance to the overall standing of the institution, such as completion rates and employment destinations. Of course, these two measures of skills development are not mutually exclusive but rather can lead to very different evaluation cultures between institutions. Many tutors and teachers on skills development programmes would argue that the priority should be student growth in personal and professional areas. Indeed, a recent strategy paper from the Rugby Team (a sector-led working group formed following the 2005 UK GRAD Policy Forum) (Rugby Team 2006) recommends that skills evaluation should be focussed on enhancement and not measurement, and that any evaluation 'should not be focussed around submission/qualification rates as a proxy for effective skills development' (Rugby Team 2006: 5). Nevertheless, the summative assessment culture of UK higher education inevitably leads to pressures for objective and quantifiable evaluation. Moreover, the formal evaluation of skills development may become increasingly important in the justification of future funding from the research councils.

Given the complex nature of student motivation and aspiration, which not only rely on personal qualities but also on social, contextual and situational factors, any objective, one-shot and *ex-situ* evaluation of a skill competence is likely to be difficult. Likewise, a clear definition or description of a skills area is often elusive in itself, which may either lead to some superficial categorization, such as 'I am able to work in groups effectively', or to a list of descriptors or attributes of that skills area which are not necessarily exhaustive of the full possibilities in which the competence manifests. A second concern to educators is a reliable measure of the impact that any skills development programme is having on the participants. Difficulties of an objective skills measure are likely to be further augmented by the highly variable student experiences within their immediate research environment. For example, over the course of a research degree, it would be difficult (and perhaps impossible) to decouple fully the supervisor input into skills development from the benefits gained from explicit training/development programmes. For individual short courses and workshops, post-course feedback from the students is common and often does provide some indication as to how effectively learning outcomes have been met as well as any subsequent expected gains in competence. Nevertheless, such gains are often qualitatively inferred from the feedback, with little attention to pre-course standings of competence. Although such difficulties in the evaluation of student skills exist, opportunities for some evaluation do at least give the individual a basis for self-reflection and appraisal; in addition, they raise to the forefront the skills that, one should be concerned with.

In the following text, a brief survey of current practice in skills development evaluation in UK higher education is presented and a discussion of some of the issues surrounding various approaches is given. An overview of experiences at Imperial College London is also given, with particular emphasis on a *skills perception* method developed with the aim of reflecting good practice and addressing both student and institutional needs. The chapter concludes with some general guidelines for skills evaluation and a discussion on the scope for future development in this area.

Current practice in UK higher education

As mentioned earlier, there is a wide range of evaluation methods that can be used to gauge skills development, but to date no systematic or sector-wide approach to the task exists. One outcome of the Rugby Team's strategy paper was the recommendation that HEIs receiving Roberts funding should work to identify the most effective ways of evaluating and enhancing the support and training offered (to both research students and staff). The team also identified four indicators for possible use by the sector, namely, increases in both the opportunity to engage and actual engagement in skills development, how researchers have been encouraged to reflect on their skills development and how researcher feedback is embedded in development of skills programmes. A clear recommendation was that evaluation should not be focussed around submission or qualification rates; it should focus on skills enhancement rather than measurement. In other words, institutions should be encouraged to continue improving their skills development provisions and not simply work to reach a benchmark.

The Rugby Team (2006) also recommended the continued use of the UK GRAD Database of Practice as a means of sharing examples of good practice which have arisen or been developed in response to the Roberts agenda.[1] The current UK GRAD Database contains 32 entries under the 'Skills Assessment/ Training Needs Analysis'[2] practice category. One way to group the various entries is by the main stakeholder/agent the practice is intended for, or indeed owned by. Specifically, the following categories arise:

1   Student-needs led, for example,
    • student-owned training needs analysis/personal development planning (TNA/PDP) system
    • evidence-based/reflective portfolio production
    • student perceptions of skills levels before and after a course
    • student perceptions of relative abilities in different skills
2   Supervisor-needs led, for example,
    • TNA/PDP (with heavy supervisor involvement)
    • monitoring supervisor perceptions of student performance
3   Programme needs, for example,
    • attendance at workshops
    • evaluations of workshops attended
    • focus groups
4   External/institutional needs, for example,
    • PhD submission rates
    • employment destinations
    • take-up of TNA/PDP systems
    • feedback from employers

It should be noted that of the 32 entries, several give no or minimal information about what is actually assessed and/or the methods used. Several use methods from more than one category and indeed there is much overlap between methods. Specific issues arising with each of the above practice categories will now be considered in turn.

Student-needs led

Student-needs led methods are often of great interest to tutors, as these evaluation methods have arguably the greatest potential to be tools for the user's development in their own right. The most widely used method seems to be some type of TNA/PDP system. This is at least partly in response to the QAA

Code of Practice for research degree programmes, which includes a precept relating to PDP. Amongst PGRs, significant support and positive feedback exists (Shaw et al. 2004) which, for example, states that 50 per cent of the sample 'found these useful mechanisms for personal reflection on progress'.

TNA/PDP

These methods can act as a powerful conduit for self-reflection and appraisal – a benefit appreciated by some PGRs in relation to setting targets, identifying needed improvements, writing a CV and so on (Shaw et al. 2004). A challenge with any TNA/PDP system is to make an active connection between the outcome of the TNA/PDP process and the development opportunities available within the institution. It is unfortunate, from the brief evidence available in the database, that few institutions explain whether or how they make this link. It is also clear that the debate about 'true PDP' (Shaw 2005) has not been resolved – that is, there is some confusion about the true purpose of PDP, a tension between using it as a means of producing a record of development and using it as a truly dynamic planning process. Also, the issue of ownership and confidentiality of any (electronic) documents created remains somewhat problematic. Of course, if total confidentiality is assured, then the TNA/PDP is wholly owned by and private to the student and therefore tends to be totally isolated from institutional planning. This was identified as a 'frustration' at the 2005 National Postgraduate Committee (NPC) summer conference (Shaw et al. 2004); that is, if PGRs are not able to access relevant training to meet their identified needs, 'the PDP process is frustrated and undermined'. Nevertheless, clear explanations and guidelines from institutions can minimize these difficulties and maximize the benefits realized.

Portfolio production

Much of the above discussion could also apply to the production of evidence-based/reflective portfolios, mentioned by, for example, the Universities of Durham, East Anglia and Lancaster. This is likely to become a more popular practice, as encouraging researchers to reflect on their skills development is in accordance with the third of the four indicators recommended for consideration by the Rugby Team. Students may need support in being able to produce worthwhile portfolios. For example, the University of East Anglia runs half-day workshops, 'which examine the nature of reflective practice and provide guidance on how to maximise learning from experience'. The same institution also mentions a challenge in convincing supervisors 'that learning the generic skills of a professional researcher can come from engagement in a wide range of activities not always relating to the research itself'. This is potentially one of the most rewarding means of evaluating skills but is highly dependent on the understanding and enthusiasm of the participants. In an acknowledgement of the value attached to the best of these portfolios, at least two universities (Durham and Lancaster) report in the database the possibility of submission of such portfolios for academic credit (in one case for an optional skills award, in the other within a research masters' programme).

Before-and-after skills perceptions
This approach, as employed at Imperial College London, potentially gives a clear indication of the perceived enhancement in various skills levels as a result of course or workshop attendance. Such an approach may help to decouple the effects of specific development events from interactions with supervisors and other informal development activities. Care is needed in such evaluations to ensure that the students can effectively gauge a given competence within themselves. This may involve questions which relate directly to the immediate student environment and concerns and/or to the level of competence in completing a specific task related to a skill. Further discussion on the Imperial College London approach and specific evaluation concerns related to this are given in the next two sections of this chapter.

Student perceptions of relative abilities
This is often part of a TNA system, and the work done at the University of Manchester is particularly interesting (Bromley et al. 2007). New PGRs self-assess their skills on a four-point scale with the view that as the exercise is repeated over time, there will be a means of monitoring their progress. The results have been used to help decide the priority training areas for graduate development programmes. The method has also highlighted some differences in skills sets in specific student subgroups. The authors identify the need for further work to verify the accuracy of the self-assessments in comparison with actual ability levels. This could involve interviewing students and supervisors and observing students exhibiting or using certain skills. A similar process is described by the University of East Anglia in which students complete a self-assessment form on an annual basis, which may then be used as a possible means of assessing distance *travelled* over an entire study programme.

In summary, each of the above models needs strong backing from institutions to become established, as they may be perceived as being time-consuming or superfluous to the technical PhD programme. Further, there exists a potential conflict between the student's own responsibility for considering their competencies and the desire of HEIs to use the results of such assessments for their own purposes. Successful resolution of the confidentiality issue and a clear statement of purpose of any evaluation are prerequisites to success. With these in place, however, the goal of 'developing reflective, independent, self-directed learners' (R. Bingham (in Shaw 2005)) must surely be within reach.

Supervisor-needs led methods

The supervisor-needs led category is certainly the smallest and it is arguable how much it is, in fact, a separate category rather than one end of a continuum of TNA/PDP type practices. Along this continuum, institutions, and in some cases individual supervisors and students position themselves. As the quasi-employer of the research student, the supervisor is normally well placed to comment on the skill level and development of their own research students. This facility has been consciously employed as part of the assessment by some institutions to a greater or lesser extent, for example, the Universities of East Anglia, Wales (Aberystwyth) and Ulster. The latter describes a system encouraging 'negotiated frameworks' for development between 'supervisors and supervisees'. The responsibility of supervisors in identifying training needs and developing action plans is mentioned. However, interestingly, the level of access that supervisors have to the system is controlled by the research student.

Committed supervisor involvement is an important feature, identified as a future need by several HEIs (for example, University of Wales, Aberystwyth). However, there is an issue around how heavy the commitment of supervisor time might be and how it might sit within other competing demands. Confidentiality is also an important issue and was a major concern to the respondents of the 2005 NPC survey (Shaw et al. 2004).

It should also be noted that some supervisor and student-needs led skills development is achieved through formal institution-instigated report processes, often every 6–9 months. This typically involves both student and supervisor contributions, and is an ideal opportunity for project review. However, much variability is anticipated as to the amount of attention given to skills development and planning outside the immediate remit of the technical work. Ultimately, a cultural shift may be required for many supervisors to become skilled and willing to engage with such systems; clearly, the quality of the key relationship between supervisor and student will be a crucial factor in any success. Nevertheless, these systems can offer a powerful means by which student–supervisor communication and relationships may be improved and thus potentially lead to better research outcomes.

Programme needs

Programme needs are probably the most simple measures to obtain and can produce large amounts of quantitative data. Inspection of the UK GRAD Database of Practice reveals that this is by far the most commonly used measure. These methods respond directly to the first two of the four indicators suggested by the Rugby Team. Whilst it is clearly an advantage to be able to see by how much both the opportunity to engage and actual engagement in skills development programmes have increased, these are not the most robust of measures, often yielding fairly superficial information. As was made clear by the Rugby Team, there is a risk of overplaying the importance of the more readily accessible measures, with linked risks of the creation of league tables, which may in fact mislead on the quality of the student learning experience. It appears to be accepted by the sector that numerical data cannot be the only method of assessing how well the Roberts agenda is progressing. Nevertheless, the monitoring of programmes also yields qualitative data, from feedback forms and perhaps more informatively from focus groups, and useful information can be distilled to improve the programme on offer.

External/institutional needs

External/institutional measures are important for all institutions since they relate to external drivers such as, for example, adherence to sector-wide policy, positions in league tables and potentially to the continuation of Roberts funding. They also commonly make use of large amounts of quantitative data that are collected for other purposes and so do not necessarily represent a major increase in the administrative burden on staff. At least two entries in the UK GRAD Database of Practice mention the use of four-year submission rates as a means of assessing their skills development programmes, which as stated earlier, goes against the recommendations of the Rugby Team and perhaps fosters a rather narrow interpretation of the benefits of skills development.

Employment destinations are also mentioned as part of current evaluation practice by some institutions (for example, Babraham and Sanger Institutes). Data on first destinations are normally collected by institutions at six monthly intervals for return to the Higher Education Statistics Agency. However information is required only for UK-domiciled students and even for this population, the return rate is highly variable. It should also be noted that it is the first job/destination that is reported for this survey and it would almost certainly be preferable to look at longer-term career paths with a longitudinal survey. Career destinations are also subject to many complex factors, such as economic downturns.

PDP systems have been a requirement for PGRs since the 2005–06 academic year.[3] Several institutions report monitoring the take-up of TNA/ PDP systems (for example, Lancaster). Of course, this in itself gives little information on the specific benefits gained by the students in undertaking the TNA/ PDP and is a good example of a relatively easy-to-produce measure, which is vulnerable to a rather superficial approach.

Finally, the anticipated value of feedback from employers on the skills of their new recruits is often mentioned by HEIs (for example, University of East Anglia, Babraham Institute). Since many universities have yet to see a cohort of PGRs graduate since the full effects of the Roberts agenda have been felt, such feedback could be misleading and even discouraging at this stage. However, it could be reasonably expected that 'post-Roberts' PGRs are now better prepared as they begin to face employment selection processes. To complicate things further, a pre-Roberts datum of feedback has not been established, and thus it is difficult to measure direct benefits accruing. Externally or institutionally driven measures clearly have a role to play, but they must be treated with caution and superficial treatment must be avoided.

The Imperial College London experience

Given the variety of evaluation approaches described earlier, it would be appropriate at this point to consider the ideal skills evaluation scenario. At the onset, the development programme needs to be mapped onto the prior skills of the student, as well as their personal prioritization of the areas needed for development. The latter requires a process which raises student awareness of appropriate and valued skills, and importantly generates motivation for development. To this extent, the design of the skills evaluation method and the design and delivery of the skills workshop/course/ programme should not be carried out independently. Likewise, just as for attending a workshop, students should see the benefits of undertaking any skills evaluation. Furthermore, the evaluation itself should give specific feedback to the tutors and course/programme leaders, with sensitivity and insight to any academic, cultural or gender issues. Ultimately, the motivation to actively assess and develop one's own skills may in itself be viewed as a higher level (meta-)skill, and therefore a critical (but rarely mentioned) measure of the success of a transferable skills programme may be the attitudinal shifts gained towards the perceived benefits and value of skills development.

A skills evaluation method developed at Imperial College London has been designed specifically for a skills development course which most first-year postgraduate researchers undertake. Although such an evaluation method only partly addresses the above-mentioned needs, several of its features support and exemplify such good practice. Nevertheless, like many other HEIs the college implements a multifaceted approach in evaluating skills development, which includes general post-course questionnaires, informal feedback from academic staff (supervisors and directors of postgraduate studies), as well as basic measures of, for example, course attendance and access (that is, *number of hits*) to Web-based sites pertaining to the skills development programme. To help students further raise their awareness of skills development prospects, a Web-based TNA-type questionnaire is also being adopted, which has the added feature of being directly linked to course and resource information to encourage and support PDP.

Skills Perception Inventory (SKIPI): basis and design

The Skills Perception Inventory (SKIPI; see Figure 7.1) was developed to gauge the influence of a three-day residential course on the skills development of early PGRs. Although there is much anecdotal evidence of the benefits of focussed, residential training programmes (cf. the national UK GRAD courses), much of this is based on post-course student feedback. The assessment of specific skills development is often not addressed in any quantitative rigour. However, the broad yet intense nature of residential courses leads to ideal opportunities to measure any pre- and post-course

Research Skills Development Course – SKIPI (a)
Please take a few minutes to complete the questionnaire.

name:			
department / division:			
gender:	female ☐	male ☐	
residential status	home ☐	EU ☐ overseas ☐ please specify:	
stage in research (months)	<3 ☐ 3–6 ☐ 6–9 ☐ 9–12 ☐ >12 ☐		

Expected level of comfort / confidence with the following situations or issues. **1 = very uncomfortable / very unsure** **2 = uncomfortable / not confident** **3 = slightly uncomfortable / slightly concerned** **4 = comfortable / at ease** **5 = very comfortable / very confident**	**1**	**2**	**3**	**4**	**5**
1 working with others on an interdisciplinary group project					
2 being able to communicate with people of different cultures					
3 effectively prioritising my work to minimise distractions					
4 recognising excessive stress in myself					
5 being able to appraise the strengths of other group members					
6 being able to give constructive feedback to peers and other students					
7 using effective strategies to plan my work over the course of a term					
8 being aware of strategies for dealing with stress					
9 having my ideas listened to by other group members					
10 dealing with conflict with my supervisor or peers					
11 being aware of the level of accomplishment needed to successfully transfer from MPhil to PhD registration					
12 having a realistic awareness of how I am perceived					
13 being aware of the different roles within a good team					
14 having to communicate with people I don't know very well					
15 keeping up-to-date with the research literature throughout my project					
16 being able to enhance my creativity when I need to					
17 coordinating a group project					
18 understanding how my and others' personality-types influence work interactions					
19 making use of feedback opportunities in the planning of my work					
20 understanding and maintaining my motivation for work and study					
21 being able to describe the facets of good team development					
22 networking with academics and senior scientists / engineers					
23 being able to realistically monitor the progress of my research					
24 being aware of my specific areas for further development					
25 being able to develop cooperative relationships					
26 receiving feedback and dealing with criticism of my work					
27 being able to set realistic research goals					
28 having an awareness of my strengths and weaknesses					
29 being able to enthuse a non-expert about my work					
30 being able to apply creative methods in tackling research problems					
31 appreciating a programme of non-technical skills development					
32 writing a good abstract for a research paper					
33 being aware of the different career opportunities open to me after PhD					
34 having a good understanding of research ethics					
35 being able to describe the good attributes of a conference poster					
36 being aware of the ideal PhD thesis structure for my subject area					

Figure 7.1 Skills Perception Inventory (SKIPI)

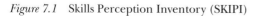

Please indicate your level of agreement with the following statements. SD = strongly disagree D = disagree A = agree SA = strongly agree	SD	D	A	SA
1	workshops for transferable skills development are generally not useful				
2	PhD students should be encouraged to attend more transferable skills development workshops				
3	workshops for skills development are only important for some students				
4	I wish I had more skills training as an undergraduate student				
5	attending GSEPS / GSLSM workshops is distracting to my research				
6	I can understand the benefits of transferable skills training				
7	most skills training is obvious and can be more effectively covered by reading a book				
8	I plan to be proactive in developing my transferable skills throughout my PhD				
9	at the end of the day, my academic performance will be the only thing that's important to my employment and career progression				
10	the GSEPS / GSLSM workshops are likely to help refine my behaviour and change my outlook on life				

Figure 7.1   (Continued)

differences in several skills areas. Likewise, where such courses are run for students early in their research careers, an opportunity exists to gauge any favourable attitudinal shifts on the value and benefits of skills-focussed programmes. Thus, SKIPI was specifically designed to:

1   provide a direct measure to the tutors of the impact of an intense skills development course, with quantitative feedback on specific areas of benefit;

2   enable students to reflect on the development experience and any specific benefits gained from this;

3   raise student awareness as to the kind of skills which are of value in the research environment;

4   gauge any attitudinal shifts on the perceived value and benefits of skills training in general;

5   enable investigation of any cultural, gender or discipline-specific influences on skills development;

6   provide a basis for studying the longitudinal development of transferable skills.

The residential course at Imperial College London has been designed for first-year research students with the primary purpose of enhancing both the personal and the research effectiveness of the participants. The course also acts as a platform for promoting other skills development workshops and opportunities within the college. In the development of SKIPI, attention was given to four skills areas: group work, communication, personal awareness and planning and project management. For each skills area, several question items were chosen to cover the key facets of that area and provide an overall perception-score which did not rely on a single response. Mean scores for all the items pertaining to a specific skills area were then calculated for each individual.[4] The questions were chosen to closely map onto the learning outcomes of the residential course, with the exception of items 34 and 35. These latter items acted as a check on the validity of the questionnaire as a measure of actual improvement in a skill, rather than a general feeling of competence as a consequence of course attendance (for more details on Hawthorne, *halo* and *placebo* effects, see Draper (2005)). For example, in this particular course no formal discussion of the issue of research ethics or the attributes of a good conference poster takes place, and therefore no change in pre- and post-course beliefs are expected to exist. Ten items (1–10 in the second part of the questionnaire; see Figure 7.1) were also included at the end of the inventory to measure any change in the student beliefs towards the value and benefits of skills training in general. Such items included both positively and negatively worded phrases, and were measured on a four-point Likert scale. The items could then be scored to give a single measure of attitude.[5]

The inventory was administered to students at the very start of a course (that is, the evening before the first day of activities) and again at the very end of a course. Students were informed that the collection of background information was for the purposes of investigating trends and that once different questionnaires were collated, no name entries would be recorded. Thus, although scores for any item are subjective, the design of the questionnaire enabled changes in perception to be tracked for any given individual, and overall statistical significance could be evaluated through an appropriate paired-samples test (see below). The inventory was administered for eight courses between June 2005 and May 2006. Each course typically consisted of 32 participants of mixed academic and cultural backgrounds. However, SKIPI is considered an integral part of the Research Skills Development (RSD) course, and its administration will be continued in future courses. Specifically, the inventory is not just an evaluation tool but also a means of raising student awareness of the various skills areas. The continued and post-course administration of the test is likely to lead to insights on the longitudinal influences of skills development throughout the PhD programme.

SKIPI as a tool for assessing skills development

With reference to Figure 7.2, differences in pre- and post-course scores in areas pertaining to (a) group work, (b) communication skills, (c) planning and project management and (d) personal awareness are shown. As a check on the statistical significance of the score differences, paired-samples *t*-tests were carried out; see Table 7.1. The results indicate statistical significance (<0.1 per cent probability level) for all four skills areas. Likewise, statistically significant differences were measured between the pre- and post-scores responses to each individual item, except for the test items 34 and 35. The results suggest that such a questionnaire provides a clear indication of the benefits of course attendance in areas which correspond to the intended

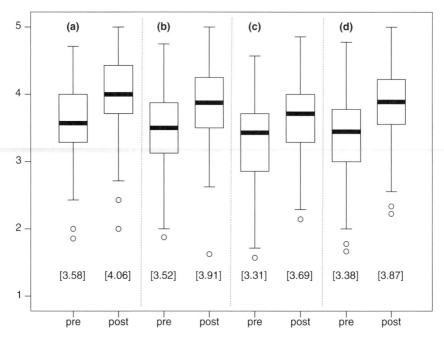

Figure 7.2 Boxplots of the SKIPI data: (a) group work, (b) communication skills, (c) planning and project management and (d) personal awareness. Mean scores for each scale are shown in square brackets (maximum score = 5). Sample size = 215. (Boxplots indicate the median (bar), 25th and 75th percentile range (box), smallest and largest scores which are not outliers (whiskers), and outliers (circles), i.e. scores which are 1.5 box-lengths outside the box.)

Table 7.1 Paired-samples *t*-test for the SKIPI data

	Paired differences					Significance
	Mean	Standard deviation	Standard error mean	*t*	Degrees of freedom	(probability) 2-tailed
(a) Groups	−0.48	0.58	0.04	−12.37	222	0.000
(b) Communication	−0.39	0.54	0.04	−10.79	223	0.000
(c) Planning	−0.37	0.54	0.04	−10.17	220	0.000
(d) Awareness	−0.49	0.56	0.04	−13.22	223	0.000

learning outcomes. Post-course discussions with several students also indicated that carrying out the questionnaire in itself was useful in explicitly identifying attributes of, for example, good teamwork and personal awareness.

With reference to Figure 7.3, differences in pre- and post-course scores pertaining to the value and benefit of skills training in general are shown. A favourable shift in student attitudes towards skills training is indicated. A paired-samples *t*-test for this case again demonstrated statistical significance ($t = -7.5$, probability < 0.001). Such a favourable shift in student attitude

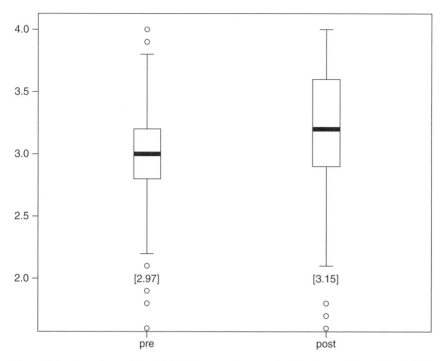

Figure 7.3 Boxplots of the SKIPI data on the perceived value and benefits of skills training. Mean scores for each scale are shown in square brackets (maximum score = 4). Sample size = 215

(even if a short-term effect) is expected to lead to more concerted and considered personal development planning. Marked differences were found to exist between British and other (EU and non-EU) students for certain skills areas; see Table 7.2. In all cases, the self-perceptions of British students were found to fall below those of other students, and although statistically significant improvements in skills perceptions were found for all groups of students, differences remained between British and other students on perceptions relating to PhD planning and project management. Such results generate a number of interesting questions concerning the antecedents of such differences, and have recently led to further qualitative investigations.

Although SKIPI was developed to evaluate changes in skills perception as a consequence of attending a specific course, it is also intended to use the questionnaire to track skills development throughout the research degree programme. As a first step, therefore, some measure of test–retest reliability was required. Such a measure was undertaken by asking a cohort of students to complete SKIPI for a third time, approximately three weeks after the 'post-course' questionnaire. The data indicates no significant differences

Table 7.2 Areas in which statistically significant differences exist in the skills perceptions between British and other students. No differences were found to exist between EU (non-British) and non-EU students

	Pre-course	Post-course
British students (113) and EU students (43)		
Planning and project management	$p < 0.01$	$p < 0.01$
Communication	$p < 0.05$	
Value/benefits of skills training	$p < 0.05$	
British students (113) and non-EU students (80)		
Planning and project management	$p < 0.01$	$p < 0.01$
Personal awareness	$p < 0.01$	
Value/benefits of skills training	$p < 0.01$	

in the four skills areas scores between the post-course and retest questionnaires, but even further improvement in scores relating to the value and benefits of skills development programmes ($p < 0.002$). Of course, ultimately such information should be accessed and retained by the student as a measure of their personal progress in skills development. However, over a large time period, such an inventory would not necessarily help to identify the specific experiences and programmes that had the most impact on a student. Similarly, it would be in the ultimate interest of the student if skills development in an area could be mapped onto their confidence and self-belief in very specific tasks associated with mastery in that area. This would suggest some evaluation which goes further into the specific attributes (and behaviours) associated with a skills area, and subsequently into the realm of domain-specific self-efficacy; see discussions below.

Guidelines for skills evaluation and scope for future development

Experiences at Imperial College London have led us to consider the evaluation issue as one that needs to be multifaceted in order to cover the full spectrum of evaluation needs. Such needs range from checking that the learning outcomes of a course are being achieved to the impact of the whole skills development programme. Successful skills development workshops typically have a strong student centredness and encourage involvement and personal application. In a similar way, evaluation procedures need to focus on specific student gains, and to work effectively they must engage and involve the student clientele. Thus, for example, if the TNA and PDP processes are effectively integrated, then the evaluation is less likely to be viewed by the student as an external imposition, but rather as a tool for their own development. Nevertheless, any monitoring of such a process would require sensitivity to student confidentiality.

Post-course qualitative data is always useful feedback to the front-line tutors, but immediate and specific benefits, and thus development, may be hard to ascertain. Before-and-after skills perception questionnaires such as SKIPI, which directly relate to the learning outcomes of a course, may provide a more quantifiable measure of student perceptions and attitudes and at the same time prime student expectations of their development and promote self-reflection on their skills. Translating such a questionnaire to specific course contexts is relatively straightforward, but the approach itself may be particularly suited for extended and broad-ranging courses where attitudinal shifts towards skills self-efficacy and a personal development ethos are more likely. Alternatively, a more precise, domain-specific approach to the skills perception analysis is the use of self-efficacy measures for gauging the level of confidence and self-belief of an individual to perform particular tasks (see, for example, Bandura 1997; Mau 2003; Lucas and Cooper 2006; Lucas et al. 2006). For example, each learning outcome of a training programme could be evaluated through a range of questions relating to highly specific tasks that may be performed as a consequence of achieving the learning outcome. Such an approach would inevitably increase the size of the questionnaire, but it could further help raise student awareness of desirable skills, as well as focus the design of workshops and programmes on how to better address specific task-based skills. Trials of self-efficacy questionnaires which complement the more general (learning outcomes based) SKIPI are planned at Imperial College London.

As a reflective and ongoing method of skills tracking, the portfolio approach offers many advantages. Such documents may help to promote a sense of student ownership and control, and also offer a tangible basis upon which effective coaching may be offered by the supervisor or even other peers. A student-centred ethos with a direct relevance to the research and work environments is again likely to help to enthuse participants. The portfolio approach is one example in which the overall effectiveness of a skills development programme may be gauged. Other institutions (including Imperial College London) have attempted to measure such effectiveness with general questions, or indeed a single question. Needless to say, such a general-question approach can be criticized on the grounds of construct validity, and lead to little or no insight as to areas of good or poor practice. More radical but far-reaching evaluation options exist, some of which are akin to the quality assurance of degree programmes. Such options include:

- The development of a national task-based skills inventory as a uniform evaluation tool across the different institutions. Such an inventory can be used before and after the PhD programme as a means of impact analysis.
- The requirement of a personal statement on skills development within the PhD thesis, which would be then formally assessed by the examiner against some national guidelines. Unlike the PhD itself, this component could be scored on some quantifiable scale.

- The use of skills coaches for guiding students towards personal development, and collating case studies of student achievements and problems on this front.
- The regular use of structured and representative discussion/focus groups to ascertain the tangible student benefits of a skills development programme as well as any shortcomings.

As mentioned earlier, perhaps any effective skills development programme should in itself be self-promoting. As noted by one academic staff member at Imperial: 'These are smart kids. If they can see the real benefits [of skills development courses], then they'll carry on attending these courses and learning from them. Any evaluation should then give some positive information.' It may be desirable therefore that the evaluation should also consider the attitudinal shift towards transferable skills courses as a consequence of, for example, initial student experiences with workshops. Long-term changes in the attitudes and self-beliefs of adults can, of course, prove difficult. The consistency of attitudes has been widely considered in the research literature, and theories range from high consistency, in which attitudes form an internal logic to create a coherent belief system or ideology, to non-consistency, in which attitudes are not organized around any particular ideology; see the discussions of Hogg and Vaughan (1998). However, in the context of adult learners, some evidence indicates that significant changes in attitude, self-belief and self-efficacy may be achieved through programmes in which individuals are encouraged to challenge any subjective norms as well as perceptions of controllability over their behaviour (see, for example, Dweck 2000; Aronson et al. 2002; Lucas et al. 2006). Student exposure to and critical reflection on the belief systems and approaches of their peers to personal development is likely to help overcome any fundamental self-inhibitions. Likewise, opportunities for 'authentic mastery . . . vicarious experience . . . and the appraisal of an individual's skill' (Lucas et al. 2006: 3) is likely to help enhance and sustain self-efficacy. Thus, although evaluations methods may be concerned with improvements in and the acquisition of skills, the attitudinal shift of individuals towards continued personal and professional development may be the true measure of a successful skills development programme.

Given current institutional and research council commitments to postgraduate skills development, attitudes towards the premise of PhD training will inevitably change. Perhaps this is already happening through both *top–down* and *bottom–up* mechanisms. The former is exemplified by the high-exposure of skills-related workshops, courses and information that students encounter, which is likely to lead to a greater personal awareness of potential growth areas and opportunities and intrinsic needs for continued personal development. With the awakening of such needs, students themselves are likely to provide the critical and perceptive evaluation of skills development programmes. At the same time, new lecturers are being exposed to the importance of postgraduate transferable skills through their induction programmes as well as indeed through their own experiences of skills development as research students. Interestingly then, what if the hoped-for *culture shift* that is often mentioned actually happens? What influences would this then have on skills evaluation? Perhaps in this ideal situation, a truly integrated skills development approach may emerge, in which there is a concerted commitment by the supervisor, student and supporting staff. Evaluation could then focus on development as perceived by the student, with objectivity and guidance given through appraisals and other direct feedback. Students themselves would then become increasingly discerning regarding the quality of workshops and courses, and likewise many supervisors might choose to be proactive in supporting and developing workshops which may have previously been viewed as external impositions or irrelevant to the knowledge–content focus of the PhD. TNA/PDP type methods would then solely act as tools for facilitating development and course evaluations as a means of collating the views of motivated learners and as a check as to whether the intended learning outcomes are being achieved.

Finally, if the fundamental aim of skills development is to create more successful researchers, managers or entrepreneurs who are effective at both interpersonal and intrapersonal levels, then the ultimate evaluation of the Roberts agenda may arise from the feedback from alumni in the years to come. For greater objectivity in this, employer feedback will also be essential. Indeed, past input from employers has been the antecedent for Roberts funding, and it is their future input that is likely to influence continued funding. Other measures such as the health of alumni societies and the strength of continued links with alumni may also be indicative of the improved worth of carrying out a research degree at a university that had a material effect on the broader development of the individual. Moreover, it may even be the strengthening of alumni societies, and specifically the greater involvement of employers and managers as role models within skills development programmes, that leads to highly motivational and effectual training.

Acknowledgements

The authors would like to thank Tony Bromley (University of Leeds) and Melissa Shaw (University of Central Lancashire) for their input in the preparation of this chapter.

Notes

1   See http://www.grad.ac.uk.
2   Many educators, including the present authors, believe that the phrase 'development needs analysis' is more appropriate than 'training needs analysis'. However, as the latter has become a common and widely used phrase, it will be employed within this text.

3   See www.qaa.ac.uk/academicinfrastructure/progressFiles/archive/policystate-
     ment/default.asp.
4   In order to test the reliability of items forming a hypothesized skills-area scale,
     Cronbach alpha (α) coefficients were calculated to determine the average inter-
     item correlation, and thus the overall internal consistency of the scale. For all
     scales, α coefficients were found to exceed 0.78 (based on a pilot study involving
     48 participants), thus indicating a high internal reliability.
5   An α coefficient of 0.84 for this scale again indicated high internal reliability.

8

Evaluation and Review of Skills Training Programmes for Research Students

Peter Lewis and Ged Hall

Introduction

As the early chapters of this book have shown, research skills training is undergoing a major re-appraisal in UK universities. Increased research student numbers have gone alongside debates about what they might expect from their training. The research councils and a government questioning the value for money in the sector (Roberts 2002) have been key drivers for improvement. The requirement for all public services to demonstrate the quality of service delivery led to the explicit expectations defined in the QAA Code of Practice (QAA 2004). The fact that we are preparing researchers for a varied career in an international and changing job market (Moynagh and Worsley 2005) has also led to more specific requirements relating to research students (HM Treasury 2002). In this context UK universities need to be able to demonstrate the impact and effectiveness of their research degree programmes.

This chapter places the University of Nottingham's experience of evaluating research skills training alongside the relevant literature. It highlights challenges facing the sector and concludes with links to the evaluation of initiatives under the Roberts funding of researcher skills development. We have deliberately drawn on both the academic literature and our experience of short course evaluation in the wider world of work and professional development. This provides a useful perspective connecting academic skills training with lifelong personal development, something all skilled adults in both academic and non-academic employment undertake. We begin with a brief survey of this wider literature on short course evaluation and the implications for university research training.

What the key literature on evaluation says

The literature suggests that the practice of training evaluation rarely matches the importance ascribed to it. In industry and commerce the evaluation of staff development is discussed more often than it is done and much actual practice is simplistic (Industrial Society 2000). Building in evaluation from the start and working within a clear cyclical approach to planning training is by far the best approach. As shown in Figure 8.1, Daines et al. (2002) presented one of the best diagrams of this approach. Here, good evaluation depends on a clear planning process, and the judgement of the effectiveness of training must be weighed against stated aims and objectives.

Evaluation is thus a continuing process of feedback. Indeed, there are loops across the middle from assessment/review to content or methods and resources to allow refinement during the delivery of a course by trainers faced with groups of participants with competing needs and different levels of understanding. Therefore, evaluation should be taking place continuously and not just at the end of training. The cycle also points out the link between identifying training needs and evaluation, and it highlights the extent to which evaluation is a shared task and not just the responsibility of those who commission or run the course. There are roles for those who identify training needs, research supervisors and the researchers themselves.

Rogers (2001) summarizes the distinction between 'validation', where one checks whether the training met its objectives, and 'evaluation', which judges the benefits of teaching or training to the participants or those who sponsored their attendance (often two different groups). She reminds us of the separate task of assessing whether the teaching or training meets an agreed standard.

Since most training is a response to a need someone has identified, it makes sense to match the evaluation method to the original diagnosis of need (Rae 1997). We might ask: What evidence was used to make the original

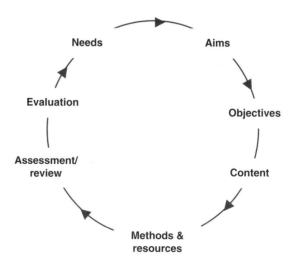

Figure 8.1   A cyclic approach to planning training (Daines et al. 2002)

decision to mount the training? What aims and objectives were set and how could their achievement be measured?

The Occupational Standards for Training (TDLB 2002), in defining good training practice, identify different stages of evaluation. They refer to the *selection of appropriate evaluation methods*, highlighting that a range should be used (within available resources). They distinguish the process of *conducting the evaluation* (in ways that reinforce the learning but do not disrupt the participants' activities) from the *analysis and interpretation of data* to report on and develop training practice. Therefore, trainers need to be able to say *why* they are doing an evaluation in a particular way and *how* the results will be used to give appropriate feedback and develop practice. An evaluation of a research training programme needs to be purposeful and should fit that purpose. For instance, is the current evaluation informing one or more of the following needs: How to run the next part of a modular course? How to run the next full modular programme? Whether the current round of courses have achieved what they set out to do? Or what further future needs for training are there?

This highlights the continuum from varying degrees of formative evaluation to the more summative evaluation of whole programmes or of the research training function within the university. The most frequently cited model of evaluation is Kirkpatrick's Four Levels of Evaluation (summarized here from Forsyth et al. 1995):

1   Reaction: Gathering information about learners' feelings and opinions; helpful in adjusting materials, content, pace, methods or facilities.
2   Learning: Measuring the knowledge, skills and attitudes gained from the event; to check whether the learning objectives have been met.
3   Behaviour changes: Can learners demonstrate that they can apply the skill after the intervention? A follow-up of practice or behaviour may be needed with feedback from supervisors and others about whether the learning has been internalized and can be transferred into new situations.
4   Results or impact evaluation: Does the changed behaviour bring about the required benefits (for example, higher quality research outputs, more smoothly operating research teams, better managed career transitions)? Additionally, it may also measure the overall impact of the research training function in the institution.

Applying this literature to research training

Although the proportion of UK organizations evaluating at levels 3 and 4 has grown, it is still small with many organizations only operating at level 1 (Lowndes 1998). It is unlikely that universities are very different in this respect.

The early experiences of the University of Nottingham's Graduate School of offering a Research Training Programme in 1996 reflect these issues. The programme was a suite of less than ten different courses delivered by an equally small number of tutors. Since the programme used strategic development funds from the university, a detailed evaluation strategy was required to determine whether this investment would continue.

Focus groups were used to ascertain initial needs. The degree to which these needs were met was assessed via end-of-course evaluation forms, followed up by further focus groups. These were collected at two points in time: the first around one month after the course ran (for participants from that course); the second at the end of the academic year used a sample of participants from all the courses to examine the whole suite.

In addition to this focus group approach, the small number of tutors coupled with the relatively small number of participants allowed the development of reasonably close relationships between the two stakeholders. This gave another less formal and richer feedback mechanism. Taken together these measures covered some elements of all four of Kirkpatrick's levels, which we discuss in more detail next.

Despite the tendency to regard end-of-course forms as 'happy sheets', they can usefully check reactions at level 1 if they are designed with more than personal comfort in mind and are focussed, specific and timely. However, it is unclear whether positive reactions to training are either an indicator of learning or necessary for it. Research suggests that in some instances, negative reactions can indicate the discomfort required for real learning, whilst in others they can be a barrier to learning (Alliger and Janak 1989). Rogers (2001) argues that simple level 1 evaluation can be very useful, but that high scores here might not reflect whether anything was learnt and low scores might reflect something else rather than the content or design of the event. This reminds us that it is important to be clear about what we think we are measuring, and therefore we should be cautious about reading too much into reaction evaluations.

Within level 2 (measuring the knowledge, skills and attitudes gained from the event) it is important to distinguish different kinds of learning. Since it is relatively easy to check on the acquisition of knowledge, we may over-rely on that. What we are really looking for may be the acquisition of skills, requiring considerable resources to evaluate and perhaps only testable during the participant's research – not during the course (Bee and Bee 1994). Well-defined learning objectives make this easier to determine if they make clear the behaviour and the standard of performance that is sought after the training.

In workplace learning clear links with competences and occupational standards help this, although they can ignore how the learning process itself worked as well as unanticipated learning (Newby 1992). In the research training context we need to be more clear about the standards we are working towards by either developing relevant competency frameworks (Bromley 2006) or 'filling out' the skills specified in the Joint Skills Statement of the Research Councils (RCUK 2001a). Clear learning objectives for the programmes and meaningful descriptors of what participants will be able to do at the end are helpful to those identifying whether a particular course is appropriate, and they also provide a basis for evaluating whether the skill has then been acquired.

In thinking about what constitutes best practice in short course evaluation, we must remember that since it is expensive (and intrusive) to do a full-scale evaluation, it will be useful to have 'proxy' measures, or indicators of those features which make learning more likely. These might include:

- The training followed sound principles of adult learning; enjoyable, participative and allows participants to identify personal goals and their own learning at different points.
- Support for the implementation of the learning back into their own work through supervisors and research teams.

Brookfield (1986) argues that adult learning principles suggest that evaluative procedures are partly the responsibility of the learners, who need to be engaged in the process early on. Again Knowles (1996) suggests that if one is using a before-and-after test, there is less in it for the learners if it is seen as an evaluation of the training inputs. However, presenting it as a fresh training needs diagnosis helps the learner to think about 'what's next for me?', and then they may invest in it.

Lessons from the Nottingham experience

The initial simple but multilayered evaluation system in the University of Nottingham inevitably came under strain as the programme grew. The growth was in two stages:

- The number of courses tripled within three years.
- The number of repeat sessions required to meet the demand for courses then grew.

As long as the total number of individual evaluations remained relatively stable, the original approach worked. However, in the second stage of growth the total number of participants, and therefore evaluations, grew. This meant that the follow-up focus groups were unsustainable and a larger number of tutors were required. The nature of the tutor group therefore changed from a small group, closely connected to the university and regularly in touch with one another to share feedback and experiences, to a wider group that included external tutors who were less likely to be in touch with each other.

The result was the gradual loss of 'richness' from the evaluation process – a richness derived from the multilayered opportunities for feedback, both structured and informal. This richness had shown the demand for the programme and confirmed that it was satisfying those needs.

Initially, no replacement to the focus group system was considered because:

- A small group of core staff managed the programme and still provided the informal feedback mechanism between the participants and the tutors.

- Additional three-yearly reviews of the whole programme were performed, involving the internal stakeholders (supervisors and researchers) and taking account of the requirements of the research councils.

Overall this produced a more formal process.

In terms of Kirkpatrick's levels the evaluation process was now focussed on level 1, with some at levels 2 and 4. This was primarily due to the extremely different timescales involved. A secondary issue was the paper-based nature of the evaluation forms and the large absolute numbers of individual completed evaluation forms, making full understanding of the data problematic. These two issues coupled with a lack of ownership of the programme, as voiced by the internal stakeholders, led us to conclude that the model was inadequate.

The literature warns against an over-reliance on single methods of evaluation and suggests that, just as a variety of methods are the safest form of training needs analysis, so different methods of evaluation will enable you to 'triangulate' and check any hypotheses (Rae 1997). Observation of skills on the course might need to be cross-checked by supervisors in the context of the research. Score sheets at the end of a course can give spurious exactness to very subjective measures and need other evidence to go alongside them. Whilst tests, quizzes and case study exercises can be used to check how much has been learnt on the course, subsequent learning logs and personal journals can help individuals make structured assessments of their own learning.

Bramley (2003) usefully describes ways of building evaluation into each stage of the training itself so as to make the delivery of the training a learning process for the trainers – an activity which sees them improving their effectiveness whilst ensuring that the training focuses on the changes it aims to bring about. His approach emphasizes the importance of finding congruence between the training objectives and the participants' individual learning objectives. Making these connections explicit heightens the commitment and motivation of all involved.

With respect to the overall evaluation of a piece of training he argues that individual methods of evaluation give very partial pictures of its effectiveness since they are pieces of a complex jigsaw of both organizational and educational processes. He would rather cluster methods according to whether they relate to changes in effectiveness, changes in behaviour, the acquisition of skills and/or knowledge or changes in attitude. Each method has strengths and weaknesses, with some pitfalls of which trainers should be wary. The message for us is that a mix of methods and a very open planning and review process are the best ingredients for evaluating our provision.

The importance of the context in evaluation

In order to rectify the perceived lack of ownership, Nottingham's evaluation strategy and processes were reviewed. This coincided with a broader review of research training across the university to provide both a benchmark prior to the introduction of Roberts funds and an indication of how, where and on what the money should be spent (Murphy et al. 2004).

The review of the evaluation strategy focussed on the different timescales involved and what better use could be made of the post-course evaluation forms. An important constraint on the review was that any recommendations were cost neutral. The key recommendation was the development of an evaluation-recording database. In-house development meant that no cash expenditure was required and allowed close specification of the format of the data reports.

This database had significant advantages. It enabled a yearly assessment of the full year's evaluations for each course, therefore bridging some of the gap between the evaluation of each course and the tri-yearly reviews. Generation of richer and timelier reports was possible, with data sorted by tutor, by course and by specific instance, for example. However, tests of the speed of data input coupled with an estimate of the likely number of forms showed that an additional 0.7 full-time equivalent administrator would be required. Due to the cost neutral constraint on the review, this was not possible.

Therefore, rather than recording all the courses, an acceptable compromise was to record one quarter of the programme each year. Since the programme is mapped onto the Research Councils' Joint Skills Statement (RCUK 2001a), careful selection of the courses recorded ensured that all aspects of the Skills Statement were assessed each year; the full range of provision being assessed over four years.

As well as looking at the processes and systems involved in the evaluation of the programme, the review also looked at links between the training and the wider activities of the university. Not surprisingly, levels 3 and 4 of Kirkpatrick's model show how important it is to get organizational factors right if training is to make a difference. How much people learn during a training event is a very poor predictor of what they will do subsequently (Alliger and Janak 1997; Bramley 2003). In many short research skills courses there is little time to check how well something has been learnt, and we are dependent on setting up the application (and reinforcement) of that learning in the research setting. We know that, in the workplace, changed behaviour and the application of learning will be dependent on a range of organizational and context factors, of which the level of management support is the most obvious. Bramley (2003) picks out supervision as a critical factor in supporting or undermining 'transfer behaviour'. The importance of the first few days and weeks after the training has been highlighted in terms of the support and feedback in applying new learning (Warr et al. 1999).

All these points underline the critical role of research supervisors in supporting the learning after the short course. Our own research suggests supervisors are often not following up such training and sometimes feel that they do not know enough about course content to be able to reinforce it (Murphy et al. 2004). Part of the Roberts money development work at the University of Nottingham has attempted to develop tools for improving the researcher/supervisor dialogue about training and sought to find ways to highlight best practices amongst supervisors to offer models of what is effective.

The wider review also suggested that there was a perceived disconnection between the training provided centrally by the Graduate School and that provided locally in each school. This reinforced the view that schools and research students did not feel that they 'owned' the central programme. Increasing the academic leadership within the Graduate School aimed to address this by connecting the academic staff and research students more directly with the central programme. The Graduate School now has faculty-based associate deans, senior academics from each faculty, to guide its strategic direction and activities.

Additionally, the connection between the central programme and the academic schools is currently being enhanced by increasing the size of the Research Training Team. This increase will allow each faculty to have a direct contact with the Graduate School via a senior academic and a dedicated trainer (known as a Research Training Convenor). This will allow academic staff to have two routes through which they can influence the scope and nature of the training provided. Research students will also be able to build a relationship with their dedicated Research Training Convenor. Taken together these components will build the 'rich' informal feedback mechanism back into the Graduate School's evaluation strategy.

A further development that will provide supervisors and research students with a greater ownership of the research training agenda is the growth of faculty-based programmes to supplement central provision, linking initial training with the day to day activities of the research students.

The literature suggests a number of reasons why the Graduate School should engage at faculty and school levels. The context for applying learning is crucial and a wide range of studies testifies to the importance of self-efficacy in workplace performance – the specific belief that it is possible to carry out a task successfully (Bandura 1986). Whilst this is partly about individual levels of confidence and self-belief, it critically includes learners' views about the context and culture of their environment, the availability of resources and equipment or the support of colleagues and supervisors.

It has been suggested that raising the learner's sense of self-efficacy (through positive feedback, praise and encouragement and the experience of performing new skills) can contribute vitally to learning on a course and the likelihood that the learner will risk trying the new skills (Stajkovic and Luthans 1998; Salas and Cannon-Bowers 2001). These aspects of the context have led many commercial and public sector bodies to invest in ways of measuring how valued different groups in an organization feel (Walters 1996; Huczynski and Buchanan 2001) and this can also provide data for training needs analysis.

What next?

It is worth thinking about what would be the equivalent of this whole organization approach to skills development in the case of researchers at a university. We would suggest there should be more systematic engagement with programme users and with other key stakeholders at school and faculty levels to provide measures of this context for learning. In terms of surveys of whole groups, there is some experience of this with research staff (CROS 2006) and we can see the need for more systematic means of capturing the experience of postgraduate researchers. The recent developments of an audit inventory tool at Oxford (Trigwell and Dunbar-Goddet 2005) and the potential of the PRES approach (PRES 2006) are encouraging, although we would urge that such tools should be broad in their approach, encompassing wider transferable skills and recognizing the importance of the routes that many postgraduate students will take outside academia.

Experience of training evaluation outside universities suggests that medium-term feedback (has the learning from a course impacted on research practice six or nine months down the line?) and longer-term studies of alumni (what aspects of their research training and experience were useful two to three years after their doctorate?) are required. The Arts and Humanities Research Council have recently published research which seeks 'to understand the career progression, employment patterns and skills of AHRC-funded postgraduates, and to examine their likely impacts in academia and beyond' (AHRC 2007). This is to be welcomed and we would encourage further work in this area beyond the AHRC's discipline remit.

Identifying training needs does not necessarily equate with developing yet another set of short courses. The literature suggests that staff development responses should be more varied than that (Rae 1983; Bramley 2003). The emergence of human resource management encourages trainers to look at a wider range of development opportunities, including learning 'on the job', support for self-directed learning programmes and attempts to change organizational cultures (Huczynski and Buchanan 2001). Given the educational base of HEIs, it is perhaps surprising that the learning organization approach has not been adopted in UK universities to encourage a whole systems approach to development (Senge 1990; Pedler et al. 1997).

Equally, in the light of the earlier cited research regarding evidence about the limited value of short courses, a 'research-based approach to skills development' would look beyond simply adding to the range and number of such courses for researchers. For these reasons, at the University of Nottingham the Roberts money has been seen as a chance to promote other developmental strands alongside short course training (see University of Nottingham 2006). These new strands, and indeed the whole Roberts initiative within the university, present another challenge in terms of evaluation, one that has encouraged us to go back to some of the principles identified in the first part of this chapter to seek to develop a multilayered approach to evaluation that shares responsibility across a range of stakeholders.

At the national level the need for RCUK to demonstrate to the Treasury the return on the investment of Roberts money (RCUK 2005) is not dissimilar to the demand for an HR department to be able to demonstrate value for money in terms of a range of development opportunities. Attempts by the 'Rugby Team' to identify ways of evaluating the development of researchers (Rugby Team 2006) already mirrors the way many organizations have sought to extend Kirkpatrick's model 'upwards', and to identify the contribution of development programmes in terms of organizational performance and financial impacts on both the organization and the national economy (Hamblin 1974). There has been a growing emphasis on the 'return on investment' of training (Kearns and Miller 1997), and we can expect the central government increasingly to look for measures of this wider impact. Although difficult to do at the level of an individual university, collaborative steps to demonstrate research training effectiveness will be more and more necessary, and the suggestions above about follow-up and alumni feedback will assume greater importance.

A remaining major challenge, posed earlier in this chapter, concerns the need for clarity of purpose and aims for training. The pressures on academic staff and researchers to ensure timely completion of PhD research and to meet other centrally imposed targets on university research mean that research trainers are often constrained by what individual supervisors or the strategic managers of the university think the PhD is a preparation for, and the skills supervisors have to address this. The Roberts report (HM Treasury 2002) has opened up a debate about the value and role of the PhD and the contribution of universities to the research and development base of the nation's economy. There is a danger that too many of the responses to this challenge are simply in terms of trying to do more research training, or 'better' research training, without the fundamental purposes being addressed at all. More and better short courses are only part of the answer, and those working in this field will need all their creative skills to develop the innovative approaches required.

Our own exploration of evaluation is a continuing journey in which new phases constantly present themselves and lessons from recent experience need to be identified and applied. We continue to value a multilayered approach in which findings can be tested and observations triangulated. Whilst resources require us to be selective in seeking more detailed and less structured feedback, we aim for a process that keeps trainers both in touch with a range of stakeholders in an open dialogue and communicating well with one another. Yet HM Treasury will require the sector to take seriously the longer-term economic imperatives which drive this agenda, and universities must accordingly do more to promote a process of lifelong learning and continuing professional development beyond the postdoctoral phase, whether in academia or not. We therefore see the need to widen the dialogue with stakeholders to include government, research councils and employers, whose agendas will inevitably challenge internal providers of training and require more evidence of longer-term impact beyond the completion of research degrees.

9

Research Training in Practice: The Sheffield Experience

Simon Beecroft

In the first few years of the Research Training Programme (RTP) at Sheffield there was a clear feeling amongst supervisors that the RTP took research students away from their research in the crucial initial stages of their study. This viewpoint led to resistance from some supervisors, which was in turn passed on (explicitly or implicitly) to their students. In the ten years since the establishment of the programme the level of resistance from research supervisors and students has progressively decreased, and the benefits of the programme have become much more widely accepted by both research students and their supervisors. In the most recent internal review of the RTP, which was carried out during 2004–05, a number of positive stories were heard about the value of the programme. One supervisor noted that 'in its present state the real value of the RTP lies in the opportunity for students to enhance interdisciplinary and generic skills as well as gain training in high-level subject-specific topics'. Other colleagues agreed that the RTP provides a useful element of structure to the PhD programme and helps students get over problems of isolation in the early stages of their projects. It was even suggested that the RTP helps to establish positive student–supervisor relations, as both student and supervisor are required to engage in a conversation about training and development from the outset of the student's programme of study. This shift in perceptions has emerged gradually during the period that the programme has been in operation and can be attributed to a combination of factors.

The first, and most important of these, has been the University's commitment to provide a formal training programme for research students that aims to develop students' research abilities as well as equip them for life beyond the PhD. From an institutional perspective, this can be described as a commitment to developing high quality researchers, and as a consequence high quality research outputs. It is also an indication of the University's belief in the importance of embedding a developmental ethos into the fabric of the University's research degree programmes.[1] Student performance in the RTP does not form part of the research degree examination process, but it is integral to progress through the degree. Progress in the RTP forms part of the process of 'upgrade' from MPhil to PhD and is also written into the process of annual review of student progress. The twin aims of the programme indicate that whilst a student's successful completion of his/her research project is of paramount importance, of equal significance is the enhancement of that student's potential employability. With this in mind, the commitment of the university's senior managers to the RTP in the early years of the programme cannot be underestimated. Once supervisors and students recognized that the RTP was not going away, it is noteworthy that the white noise of dissenting voices also receded (albeit without ever wholly disappearing).

A second contributing factor to this change in perceptions has been the evolution of the programme itself. This has involved changes at an incremental level to both the structure and the content of the RTP. Over the years there has been a gradual shift in responsibility for the delivery of training units to academic departments. With greater responsibility for delivery has come greater investment in upholding the ethos of the programme and greater awareness of the external imperatives shaping the postgraduate agenda. Anyone who has recently seen an application for research council studentships will be aware that the quality of skills training provision within the institutional and/or departmental setting now plays a key part in determining whether a student/project will be funded. From a purely political perspective, this link to funding provides sufficient evidence to show that the dissenting position is simply unsustainable (although that is not to say that there should not be argument and discussion within individual institutions about the nature of research and skills training provision). Research council funding applications now need to speak the language of research training, and this is naturally achieved to best effect when it reflects a firmly rooted sense of engagement in institutional and departmental training practices and procedures.

A third factor, which has helped to quell the noise of dissenting voices, is the increasing prominence of skills training issues on the national postgraduate agenda. The Roberts report (and the funding that followed) has provided the impetus for all UK HEIs to assess the parameters of their skills training provision and implement appropriate improvements where possible. At Sheffield there is a nice symmetry about this, given Sir Gareth Roberts' presence at the university during the period our RTP was introduced and his involvement in the *SET for Success* (2002) review. In 1994 a Graduate School was created at Sheffield with the purpose of offering an overall framework on issues of graduate recruitment, welfare and training. The introduction of a university-wide training programme for research students was on the agenda early on, and it was strongly supported by both Sir Gareth Roberts (then Vice Chancellor of the university) and Professor Bob Boucher (then Pro-Vice Chancellor for research and chair of the Graduate School, and current Vice Chancellor of the university). At that time, in 1991, the ESRC was driving forward the training agenda (the first edition of their *Postgraduate Training Guidelines* was published in 1991 and the latest edition in 2005 (ESRC 2005)), and the university had an active Social Sciences Research Training Unit in existence. The idea was to extend the training provision across the university both to underpin the specific needs of a research degree and to provide lifetime skills of long-term value. A small programme of generic skills units was piloted in 1994 (offering training in 'information management', 'innovation and project management', 'career development' and 'personal skills'), and a full programme of training was introduced in 1995–96. By 2003, the RTP was already well established and successfully integrated into the fabric of the research experience at Sheffield. Nevertheless, the arrival of the Roberts' skills training funds has allowed us to further enhance aspects of the programme, as well as introduce new skills training activities that complement training provided in the RTP.

One of the reasons Sheffield's RTP has been successfully embedded into the research experience is simply that all full-time doctoral students who intend to submit a PhD thesis are formally required to participate in the programme. This compulsory requirement, which is governed by university regulation, has been in place since the inception of the programme, and reflects a fundamental belief amongst senior academic staff in the value of training for research students. This obligation to participate in the programme may perhaps seem slightly at odds with the notion of students engaging in development activities in order to meet specific training needs and skills gaps. Yet I would argue that it would be highly unusual for a full-time research student not to require any developmental support during the period of his/her PhD, whether it be research methods training in the first year or career development training in the final year. Moreover, given the range of units available in the programme there should be something in the RTP for everyone. The distinction made between full-time and part-time doctoral students is not one based on academic grounds, since both types of students are expected to achieve the same standards in terms of research outputs. Rather, the decision not to require part-time students to engage in the programme is largely due to practical reasons, such as the fact that many part-time students may be based outside Sheffield, many also have full-time jobs (and therefore may already be able to demonstrate many of the relevant skills), and most of the training delivered in the RTP is currently offered in long, thin, face-to-face units. Nevertheless, all part-time students are strongly encouraged to participate in the programme where possible (and happily many do attend courses). In addition, training providers are encouraged to consider more flexible modes of delivery in order to meet the needs of different types of students.

The compulsory participation of full-time doctoral students in the RTP is not the only university requirement that such students must observe. Since its inception the RTP has also always been a credit-rated programme, and as such research students are required to obtain a certain number of credits in order to satisfy university requirements. During the past ten years the exact credit requirement has changed on four separate occasions.[2] At present, full-time PhD students are expected to gain 45 credits in the RTP, where 1 credit is roughly equivalent to 10 learning hours. The programme itself consists of over 400 units or modules, each of which has been formally approved for inclusion in the RTP by relevant faculty officers. Each RTP unit has a notional credit value of 5, 10, 15, 20 or 30 credits. Each unit is also classified against a set of university objectives (see Box 9.1) such that a 10 credit unit might provide 6 credits worth of training in Objective A and 4 credits worth of training in Objective C. In broad terms, Objectives A and B relate to sections A–C and D–G of the Joint Skills Statement (JSS) (RCUK 2001b) respectively. Objective C relates to aspects of section A of the JSS (that is, 'a knowledge of recent advances within one's field and in related areas'), but also arguably goes further than that, since it underlines the value of extending one's subject knowledge in addition to developing new skills or techniques. During the most recent review of the RTP there were mixed views amongst research supervisors on the efficacy of the JSS.

Box 9.1 Key elements of the University of Sheffield's Research Training Programme

- Participation is compulsory for all full-time PhD, MD and DDSc students, and voluntary for all part-time PhD, MD and DDSc students, and MPhil only students
- University objectives inform the ethos of the programme:
  - Objective A: the development of generic skills that contribute to the understanding of research methods, techniques and the context in which research takes place;
  - Objective B: the development of generic skills that contribute to the personal and professional development of a research student;
  - Objective C: the broadening or deepening of subject knowledge.
- University requirements stipulate that full-time PhD students must obtain 20 credits prior to 'upgrade' from MPhil to PhD and 45 credits in total
- Over 400 units or modules, and each unit has a credit value of 5, 10, 15, 20 or 30 credits
- Annual registration onto the programme
- Various modes of delivery ranging from long, thin, face-to-face courses to short intensive workshops and units delivered partly or wholly online
- Various types of assessment ranging from formal examination to certification of attendance
- Regular and periodic evaluation of individual units and the programme as a whole

One supervisor, working within the sciences, indicated that the JSS provided a useful tool with which to present the notion of research training to new students, and against which departments can assess their training provision. Another supervisor, working within the social sciences, argued that the JSS should not determine the extent of the university's research training ambitions, and suggested that the JSS fosters a 'checklist' mentality rather than an aspirational culture of development. The university's RTP objectives therefore sit alongside the JSS, and research students are currently expected to undertake some training in each of the three objective areas (that is, at least five credits per objective area). It is possible for students to apply for a partial exemption from some of the prescribed credits, though exemptions will only be granted on the basis of evidence of prior training or experience. Each student's acquisition of credits is closely monitored during their programme of study at both departmental and university level. Full-time PhD students must obtain 20 credits in the RTP prior to 'upgrading' from MPhil to PhD. Similarly, should a student fail to obtain the prescribed number of credits by the time their PhD thesis has been submitted and examined, then the award would be withheld until such time as the appropriate credits are gained. Thankfully, because of the monitoring that takes place during the three to four years of the PhD, this has only occurred on a very small number of occasions during the past ten years. The supervisors and students involved in such a situation have been both embarrassed and annoyed at the consequences of 'slipping through the net'. Nevertheless, in each case the university regulations have been maintained and the student concerned had to undertake appropriate training units and/or present a very convincing case for a retrospective partial exemption from the RTP.

The process by which research students who arrive at the university at the beginning of the academic session register onto the RTP is almost identical to the process of undergraduate module enrolment. All new research students are provided with a copy of the *RTP Handbook* either before or upon their arrival at the university.[3] In their first week at the university research students attend a variety of induction events, and are encouraged to meet with their supervisor and/or postgraduate tutor to discuss their training requirements. RTP unit choices are recorded on an RTP Registration Form, which is signed by the student, supervisor and head of the department. The student is then expected to attend an RTP Registration Event where he/she will present his/her choices to the relevant faculty officer for final approval. Once approved, the student's choices are then recorded on his/her student record. Following the registration event the student is sent a letter confirming his/her unit choices and encouraged to start attending classes where appropriate, whilst the unit provider is sent a class list, and encouraged to contact participants with timetabling and/or preparatory information. The purpose of holding an annual registration event is that it provides the best opportunity to capture and record in one go those training activities that the new students wish to attend in their first year of study. The value of recording unit choices on the student record is that it supports the effective monitoring and recording of student progress on the RTP, and it allows for the gathering of data on various aspects of the programme. Cross-sessional students are able to register onto the RTP at any time during the academic session, though depending on when they initially register with the university they may have to wait some time for courses to start. In addition, all students can change their unit choices at any time during the course of their involvement with the programme. At the end of each year, all research students participating in the programme receive a Statement of Academic Progress, which provides an update on the number of credits that they have successfully achieved, or are still required to obtain. Registration in subsequent academic sessions for continuing students takes place via post, and students are expected to annually reflect on their development and training needs.[4]

The university's Graduate Research Office administers the RTP (and controls the budget for the programme), whilst academic departments and key support services (for example, the Library, the Careers Service, the English Language Teaching Centre) undertake the delivery of RTP units (see Box 9.2). This separation of administrative and training functions has both positive and negative impacts. On the plus side, the existence of a central administrative team allows for the efficient running of a programme which at any one time involves up to 2000 research students and 300 unit providers engaged in approximately 400 RTP units. It also offers some degree of independence

---

Box 9.2 The University of Sheffield's Research Training Programme within the institutional framework

	Responsible for:
Senior University Committees/Senate	Approval of programme
↓	
Graduate Research Development Committee	Monitoring
↓	
Faculty Officers	Approval of new units and unit choices
↓	
Graduate Research Office	Administration
↓	
Academic Departments/Support Departments	Delivery
↓	
Supervisors	Advice and support
↓	
Research Students	Participation

to the process of reviewing the programme. On the negative side, it means that those responsible for the operation of the programme are one step removed from the programme itself. Whilst the Graduate Research Office has been involved in the commissioning of RTP units, in terms of the development of content and new modes of delivery, the evolution of the programme largely depends on the interests and enthusiasm of academic and other colleagues. It might also be argued that the lack of a central postgraduate training unit has hastened a shift in responsibility for delivery of generic skills training from the faculty/divisional level to the departmental level. In the early years of the programme there was a strong centrist approach to training, and clear expectations about the specific training options open to students from different disciplines. Generic skills training was almost wholly offered at faculty/divisional level. This was to encourage students to work alongside their peers from other or related disciplines, in order to develop a broader appreciation of differing research approaches and contexts. However, over the years academic departments have assumed a greater role in the delivery of generic skills training in the belief that such skills are best delivered closer to the students' subject area. There is of course nothing wrong with this approach. For one thing, it helps to reduce any potential for tension between university training requirements and the demands of the research project. In addition, it ensures that the department can deliver on training commitments made to funding bodies. But perhaps most importantly, it also demonstrates a high level of engagement in the skills training agenda at the local level which, according to Pat Cryer (1998), is vital to achieving a provision that is fully integrated into the research degree programme.[5]

On one level, the embedding of generic skills training provision into departmental practice might perhaps obscure or disguise the real amount of 'generic skills' content available to research students at Sheffield. There is not a core programme of generic skills training courses that all students are expected to attend. Nor is there a single, centrally located, training unit responsible for the delivery of generic skills training. Nevertheless, we remain confident that Sheffield students do receive sufficient generic and transferable skills training to meet the recommendations of the Roberts' review (that is, 'the provision of at least two weeks of dedicated training a year, principally in transferable skills'). This is because the credit rating of each RTP unit is linked to the university's RTP objectives, which means that for each student we are able to closely monitor the amount of training undertaken by him/her within each of the three objective areas. Faculty officers play a key role in this regard, as they approve both the entry of new units into the programme and the unit choices of individual students. In the context of the approval of new RTP units, faculty officers assess whether the unit will provide appropriate training to students within their faculty and can recommend that the content or structure of the unit be amended accordingly. In terms of the approval of research students' RTP unit choices, they assess whether the student has selected an appropriate mix of objectives/credits and can recommend that the student consider alternative training options. Certainly there are units within the RTP that do focus solely on developing the skills associated with RTP Objectives A, B or C. It is more common though that a unit will provide training in support of a mix of objectives, and therefore demonstrate the integration of generic and subject-specific training.

In her article on 'Transferable skills, marketability and lifelong learning', Cryer argues that it is important that departmental training provision is also supported by events run centrally, 'to generate a high profile for the provision and to encourage disciplinary cross-fertilisation' (Cryer 1998: 214). Examples of best practice in generic skills training provision can be found within the RTP at departmental, faculty and university level. At the departmental level, there are many examples of departments devising specific courses or programmes for the RTP that focus on the enhancement of generic skills. In Animal & Plant Sciences, for example, a package of units provides all students with core research skills in literature review, project design and the communication of science research whilst allowing students the flexibility to develop laboratory and field techniques that are pertinent to their individual research projects. In the latter case, students choose a selection of workshops to attend and/or develop advanced training programmes within their own research group and therefore gain training devised specifically to meet their needs. Within the social sciences a more interdisciplinary approach is adopted by a consortium of departments (Politics, Sociological Studies, Geography, Journalism Studies and Law) who collaborate on a broad-based RTP. 'The Generic Programme' begins with a two-day workshop offering an 'Introduction to Research Design' and goes on to cover 'The Research Process', 'Qualitative Methods' and 'Quantitative Methods'. Academic staff from the relevant departments work together to teach and assess each element of the programme, and students from each of the departments benefit from an approach that is invaluable to their understanding of research in the social sciences. The programme is delivered across the academic year and involves weekly lectures and seminars, day schools, poster and oral presentations and computer workshops.

At the faculty level, two units on 'Data Analysis and Computing in Biology' seek to introduce and extend students' knowledge of data collection and statistical analysis techniques within the biological and environmental sciences. The two units are distance learning courses delivered via WebCT Vista where students have access to information about the course, data files that support course activities, links to further resources, a page with answers to frequently asked questions, discussion board activities and both formative and summative assessments. Participants also receive core material in print format. Course participants value the flexibility offered by the delivery of the course by distance learning, and also rate the assessments as being particularly helpful in the development of key skills. In the Arts and Humanities, a very different unit seeking to develop students' awareness of knowledge transfer has been developed, which involves contributions from speakers with experience of taking research outside the academy. The unit involves group work and the preparation of a personal knowledge transfer plan. Feedback has thus far been very positive, including comments such as 'It made me sit back and think about my PhD from a different point of view' and '[it encouraged] me to start thinking in different ways and directions'.

At the university level, students who undertake teaching duties whilst carrying out their PhD can enrol in a 'Teaching Skills for Research Students' unit offered by the Learning Development & Media Unit. This course adopts a blended learning approach involving a mixture of online and face-to-face delivery. Students must attend two face-to-face contact days (part of which involves a microteaching practical), have both a tutor and peer observation of their teaching and complete a portfolio. The portfolio includes materials and feedback relating to the student's teaching and reflective writing by the student about his/her teaching and its development. The online component includes discussion board activities as well as providing information on the course and material, encouraging further reflection on teaching practice. Another course that uses a blended learning approach is the 'White Rose Interpersonal Skills School', which is part of UK GRAD's Local GRADschool programme and is run for the benefit of research students at the Universities of Leeds, Sheffield and York. The course uses a range of experiential learning-based case studies and guided reflective learning to develop key interpersonal skills (for example, team working, communication, time management) in both a face-to-face and a virtual setting. Feedback from attendees has included comments such as 'A great way to spend a few days! Interesting, challenging, thought provoking and motivating. No small amount of fun either' and 'Amazing . . . The informal setting allowed shy individuals to step out more into the limelight'.

In recent years two new university-wide RTP units have been introduced that aim to offer research students more flexibility in the development of key generic skills. The first, the 'Research Student Seminar Series', incorporates a series of short seminars on key research topics, such as 'Good Research Practice', 'Getting More out of Supervision', 'Writing your Thesis' and 'Preparing for the Viva'.[6] Delivered by academic staff, support staff and an external training consultant, these have proved extremely popular (in the first year over 800 seminar places were taken up) and provide a valuable adjunct to the more in-depth training provided in many other RTP units. The second, 'Personal and Professional Skills Development' (which is offered as both a 5 and 10 credit option), provides a menu of training options from which a student may undertake a number of development activities in order to gain RTP credits. Most of the activities are things that many research students would ordinarily do throughout their programme of study, such as 'present a poster at a conference', 'present a paper at a departmental seminar' and 'participate in outreach activities which promote the public understanding of research'. By incorporating such activities within a formal training programme, research students are encouraged to recognize them as training opportunities and are invited to reflect on how their skills have been enhanced through practice. Students are expected to take ownership of their development programme, discuss the choice of activities with their supervisor and report back on learning outcomes to their supervisor, research group or department.

These new university-wide units were introduced into the RTP following the most recent internal review of the programme, which took place in 2004–05. In addition to the annual evaluation of individual units (in accordance with normal teaching quality requirements) and the annual survey of research student views (as part of quality assurance procedures), the university also undertakes a fundamental review of the RTP on a periodic basis (in line with the expectations of the QAA's new Code of Practice). Looking at all aspects of the programme, these reviews have helped to inform the evolution of the RTP during the past decade (see Box 9.3). The reviews have been carried out by a small group of senior academic staff, support staff and research students. The methodology adopted for each review has comprised: (1) the gathering of qualitative and quantitative data from key stakeholders within the university via a questionnaire or written submission; (2) an appraisal of personal experiences of the programmes from research students and supervisors via focus groups; and (3) a survey of practice at other institutions via a brief questionnaire. The purpose of adopting this three-pronged approach is to identify strengths and weaknesses in the structure, content and delivery of the programme and, in doing so, to identify any gaps in provision, to gain a general sense of student and supervisor satisfaction with the programme, and to measure the RTP against other research training programmes as well as external requirements made by the QAA and funding bodies such as the Research Council.

Although the gathering of qualitative and quantitative data is vital for ensuring the academic rigour of the review process, it is the discussions with students and supervisors that are arguably the most useful and interesting part of the review. In the last review the focus group discussions helped to underline much of the raw data that had been collected via the questionnaire. They also served to indicate the real divergence of views across the university about the issue of research training in general, and the RTP in particular. Amongst students, for example, views ranged from those who argued for more training to those who already felt they were expected to undertake an excessive amount of training. Amongst supervisors, there was concern about the apparent increasing formalization of research training implicit in the JSS and yet also a call for greater assistance in the development of students' oral and written communication skills. This range of opinions highlights the need to adopt flexible and innovative strategies for the delivery of research training provision.[7] There will not be a 'one size fits all' solution to the development of research training provision at the departmental, faculty or university level. The key outcomes of the three reviews of the RTP (detailed in Box 9.3) indicate that the reviews themselves have

Box 9.3 Key outcomes of the periodic internal reviews of the University of Sheffield's Research Training Programme

1995–96 Review
- Minor amendment to RTP objectives
- Students no longer required to obtain all credits prior to 'upgrade' from MPhil to PhD
- Cases for exemption must be made against particular University objectives, not individual RTP units
- RTP registration separated from University registration
- Call for earlier provision of programme information to students

1999–2000 Review
- Changes to University credit requirements, and closer link between credits and objectives
- Approval of individual unit choices to remain with the faculty, but recommendations to be endorsed by the department
- Full exemption from the programme allowed for those students who have undertaken a research Masters course
- Unit providers encouraged to reduce size of large units and consider introduction of more flexible modes of delivery
- Call for Information Sessions to be offered to students and supervisors
- RTP registration to take place on a single day for students who arrive at the beginning of the academic session

2004–05 Review
- Recommendation that research and skills training should ideally be spread over all three years of PhD
- Further changes to University credit requirements, and relaxation of link between credits and objectives
- RTP registration to take place annually
- Students expected to undertake an annual training needs analysis in advance of making unit choices
- Full exemption from the programme no longer allowed
- Unit providers encouraged to explore possibilities for implementation of flexible modes of delivery to address issue of part-time students' involvement in the programme

principally brought about what might be termed 'structural' changes to the programme. These have been largely centred on issues of workload/credit requirements, registration, approval, exemption and information dissemination. In contrast, the evolution of the content of the programme has occurred by stealth, as academic departments (and individuals within those departments) have proposed new units that have been approved for inclusion within the programme.

Of course, the UK Government's support for the recommendations contained in the Roberts review has also provided another driver for change in research and skills training provision. At Sheffield, Roberts' funds have enabled the university to increase the scope and variety of training and development opportunities open to research students and contract research staff. Most specifically in relation to the RTP, funding has, for example, been provided to support the development of new units on ethics, research governance and knowledge transfer and to allow for the re-development of existing RTP units so that they might be delivered in different formats. Funds have also been committed to a scheme that aims to support research students to undertake training and development at national and international centres of excellence. The potential benefits of this 'Excellence Exchange Scheme' are many and varied. The scheme allows students to gain practical training in specific skills and techniques that will enhance the quality of their research, but equally importantly it provides participants with the experience of working in different research environments and teams. This will enable students to develop communication, networking and presentation skills, and it will also help them to locate themselves within a wider research community. An RTP Project Officer post has also been employed (located in the university's Learning Development & Media Unit), in order to develop, encourage and share best practices in the delivery of research training units. A survey of RTP unit providers has already been undertaken, and a workshop on 'The RTP and e-learning' has been held. These activities will help to shape the further development of the RTP at Sheffield over the next few years. In 2008–09 another fundamental review of the Research Training Programme at Sheffield will be undertaken. Between now and then, one of the key challenges we face will be to ensure the effective integration of Roberts funded initiatives into the existing framework of research training provision.

Notes

1　The QAA Code of Practice (QAA 2004) suggests that HEIs should seek to embed opportunities for skills development within their research degree programmes.

2　When the RTP was introduced in 1995 research students were required to gain 30 credits of training. This was increased in 1999 to 45 credits and then, following a review of the programme in 1999–2000, reduced to 35 credits due to concerns about the programme being too time consuming. The return to 45 credits was made following the 2004–05 review of the RTP. This latest increase in the credit requirement was made in order to allow for the formal recognition of a wide variety of development activities that most research students ordinarily undertake throughout their programme of study. It is not therefore expected to result in a corresponding increase in workload.

3   The *RTP Handbook* and information relating to RTP units is available on the Graduate Research Office webpages at: http://www.sheffield.ac.uk/pgresearch/students/rtp.

4   This is in line with the QAA Code of Practice (QAA 2004), which highlights the need for research students to have opportunities 'to reflect on their learning' on their development, and also links to the ESRC's *Postgraduate Training Guidelines* which sees 'self-assessment of skills and potential training needs as a routine element in reviews of progress'. The university has an online personal development planning (PDP) system that research students can use on a voluntary basis in order to keep a record of this process.

5   'To attract large numbers of students, the provision needs to be integrated into their research degree programmes, so that supervisors, postgraduate tutors and heads of department are all seen to regard it as mainstream rather than peripheral, and so that the training in the development of skills for success in the research degree can be integrated with training to identify and recognise developing skills which will be useful for future employment. The main initiative would thus best be at departmental level' (Cryer 1998: 214).

6   Further information about the seminar series can be found at: http://www.sheffied.ac.uk/pgresearch/grc/seminarinfo.html.

7   This message is particularly evident in the latest edition of the ESRC's *Postgraduate Training Guidelines*, in which flexibility and innovation are repeatedly signalled as key elements of the developing training agenda. See, for example, the 'Chief Executive's Foreword': 'Increased emphasis … is placed on two areas which are considered key to better training provision: flexibility and innovation.'

10

The Social Sciences Research Training Programme: Ten Years of 'Going Over the Top' at Bradford

Judi Sture

Introduction

National background context

The national trend towards taught research training (RT) as part of higher research degrees, combined with the relatively small size of the University of Bradford, has led us to provide centralized training for our PhD students. This is not always easy, as generic provision goes against the traditional model of research in higher education.

Under this model, disciplines are autonomous, with academics responsible to their peers, and collegial decision-making is common. Quality assurance (QA) of research is by intradisciplinary review. There is a belief within this model that 'increasing quantity equals reduced quality', and resistance occurs to any centralizing of academic expertise (ESRC 2005).

We are now confronted with a research council-led economic approach to higher education, one which is traumatic to those of us still walled up in self-cleaning ivory towers. Funding is connected to performance, and we must emphasize economic as well as academic output, which concentrates the mind wonderfully. As has been noted in various reports and papers, we can no longer rely on our peers to review us, or on traditional approaches to getting PhD students to the viva (OST 1994; Harris 1996; Metcalfe et al. 2002; QAA 2004; ESRC 2005; Green H. 2005).

Central, shared provision is a useful way to achieve survival. But getting several disciplines to agree on a common programme of RT when they cannot even agree on the relative values of quantitative and qualitative methodologies is something of a challenge. When we *can* get agreement without the facilitation of a peace-keeping force, we can provide generic training programmes that enable us to more easily track and record students' acquisition of the transferable skills that can support them in the real world. As Green H. (2005) and others point out, standardized provision of RT makes us attractive to Research Councils, the QAA, Research Charities and the UK Government. Above all, shared, centralized RT prevents 'doubling up' and makes QA easier to manage.

The Bradford context

The University of Bradford is relatively small. It recruits around 150–200 MPhil/PhD students each year, which makes institution-wide RT more practical than it would be in a large university. The University offers an ESRC-accredited programme, the Social Sciences Research Training Programme (SSRTP), which leads to the degree of MRes. A programme of Short Courses for Research (SCR) comprises a range of half-day to two-day courses in transferable skills, including supervision training for academic supervisors (as highlighted by Johnson et al. (2000) and Pearson and Brew (2002)), as well as Graduate Teaching Assistant training for postgraduates. There is shared provision of some sessions between programmes. This chapter focuses on the SSRTP.

The SSRTP began life as the Doctoral Training Programme (DTP) in the Faculty of Social Sciences in 1996–97. Coverage was both qualitative and quantitative from the beginning in order to train students in a broad spectrum of research methodologies, thereby equipping them for a career in research (as many skills are transferable), not simply in 'how to do' their own PhD. In 1999 the university-wide Graduate School was formed. It renamed the DTP as the SSRTP, and rolled out its RT provision to include other schools (see Figures 10.1–10.3).

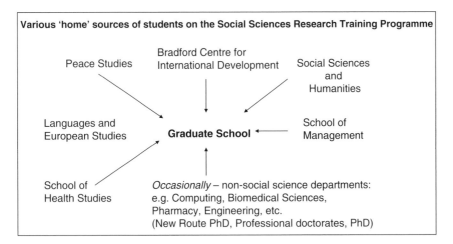

Figure 10.1 Students registered for MPhil–PhD in 'home' departments who come to the Graduate School for their research training

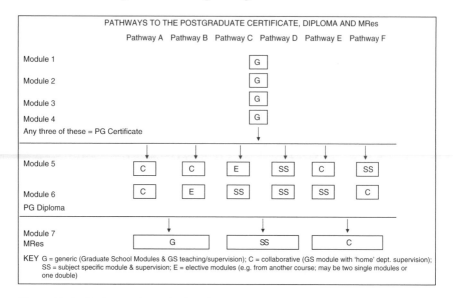

PATHWAYS TO THE POSTGRADUATE CERTIFICATE, DIPLOMA AND MRes

Pathway A   Pathway B   Pathway C   Pathway D   Pathway E   Pathway F

Module 1 — G
Module 2 — G
Module 3 — G
Module 4 — G
Any three of these = PG Certificate

Module 5 — C   C   E   SS   C   SS
Module 6 — C   E   SS   SS   SS   C
PG Diploma

Module 7
MRes — G   SS   C

KEY G = generic (Graduate School Modules & GS teaching/supervision); C = collaborative (GS module with 'home' dept. supervision); SS = subject specific module & supervision; E = elective modules (e.g. from another course; may be two single modules or one double)

Figure 10. 2   Pathways through the SSRTP to the PG Certificate (60 core credits), Diploma (120 credits) or MRes (180 credits). Pathway A is the usual route, with pathways B–F offering subject-specific variants leading to named specialist degrees

The rationale for centralizing RT was largely that of 'critical mass' and value for money, as promoted by the Research Councils (ESRC 2005). Since the 1990s, as shown by Delamont et al. (1997) and highlighted by the government, the provision of quality, standardized research skills has been recognized as a key factor in QA and raising the standard of our research capacity. Green and Powell (2004) and Green H. (2005) have highlighted the strengths of this, while emphasizing the long-term benefits of the costs incurred. By providing centralized RT, we have been able to support students in overcoming common research problems as identified by Wisker et al. (2003). We have not, however, been able to overcome the initial antagonism to RT shown by many students in the early stages of the programme. Figure 10.1 shows our 'client base'.

The Social Sciences Research Training Programme

So, how does our SSRTP work in practice? Our client departments send us their MPhil–PhD students for their first year to complete the PG Diploma in Research Methods (120 credits). Figures 10.2 and 10.3 show how the SSRTP is delivered. Each student belongs to a 'home' department and has to pass the PG Diploma in order to transfer from MPhil to PhD registration. When the student successfully completes the PhD, he/she then receives the PG Diploma as a bonus. We offer the Diploma as an 'added extra'

ACCREDITED COURSES OFFERED IN THE GRADUATE SCHOOL

The Postgraduate Certificate	**60 Credits (used as an exit qualification)**
The Postgraduate Diploma	**120 Credits**
The MRes (Masters In Research Methods)	**180 Credits**

Some students take subject-specific modules in place of these versions of Modules 5 and 6 (pathways B–F).

Module 1: Research and Scholarship Skills (20 credits)
To introduce research students to the distinct nature of doctoral level research and how to manage a research project. Also, to introduce students to library databases and how to communicate, both in writing and verbally, to likely audiences for their research.

Module 2: Data Collection Skills and Techniques (20 credits)
To enable the student to design the various stages of a research project in order to address the basic research questions and to achieve the research objectives of the project. We also offer a 10-credit version of this module.

Module 3: Philosophy of Research in Social Sciences and Humanities (20 credits)
To enable the students to critically examine their assumptions and methods of research and to locate these within a wider framework of the philosophy of science as specifically related to the social sciences and humanities.

Module 4: Quantitative and Qualitative Data Analysis (20 credits)
To enable the students to critically examine their assumptions and methods of research and to locate these within a wider framework of the philosophy of science as specifically related to the social sciences and humanities. We also offer a 10-credit version of this module.

Module 5: Preparation of Research Proposal (20 credits)
To produce a research proposal as if applying for a grant or a postgraduate research position.

Module 6: Preparation of Research Review and Report (20 credits)
To prepare and write a major conceptual paper related to the specific research question of a thesis and to make a verbal presentation of the paper to a departmental review group/upgrading committee.

Module 7: The Dissertation
To apply the knowledge, understanding and skills gained in the core generic modules 1–4 and other subject-specific training to carry out a substantial piece of research on a subject primarily oriented towards the evaluation or development of a new or existing research methodology or method(s).

Figure 10.3 The Social Sciences Research Training Programme: modules leading to the degree of MRes

with the PhD fees. Only if the student withdraws from the PhD do we charge for the Diploma. This is quite an incentive to do a PhD at Bradford, as the Diploma is ESRC accredited and helps with recruitment.

Tuition is based on lectures, discussions, small group work, practicals, project work and a lot of personal reading. This gives students the opportunity to pursue subject-specific reading to complement the generic classes.

We offer tutorial support to students and find that this is more commonly required in some modules than others and varies between disciplines. For example, the philosophy module panics students until they grasp the content and unfamiliar terminology; we also find that the modules on data collection and analysis generate many tutorial requests from certain disciplines. Group work in class is designed to address this but never completely covers the ground.

We devise assessments that fit into students' projects in response to student evaluation comments (see Figures 10.3 and 10.4). This ensures better engagement, as students recognize that assignments can become the foundation of a thesis section. We require students to address why they may *not* be using certain methodologies, ensuring that they have made a critical decision, rather than simply concentrating on their own preferred approach. Some students have to be strongly encouraged to do this.

All students have a Research Training Record, which must be signed off on completion of all RT courses. This forms a record of training in transferable skills that they can take with them when they leave the university. It involves a large element of self-direction in the identification of training needs, as Johnson et al. (2000) and Pearson and Brew (2002) have noted.

We provide supervisors with assessment feedback and regular communication. It is not uncommon for supervisors to be astonished when a student fails an assessment, and there can be pressure on tutors to revise their opinions. This is a difficult situation, but it can be resolved by open discussion and agreement to follow university academic policies.

How is the SSRTP staffed? We have a full-time Programmes Director who gives academic leadership to the SSRTP. A range of part-time tutors (25 per cent full-time equivalents (FTE)) are seconded internally to deliver parts of the programme. They are supported by visiting speakers who offer sessions on specific elements of expertise. We pay visitors an hourly lecturing rate. By seconding tutors we share their salary load with their home departments, which benefits everyone.

How often do we deliver the modules? Three times a year – to one on-site cohort every Monday, and to two distance learning cohorts in the UK and overseas (Europe) on a one-week workshop basis across the year. This is a heavy teaching load and requires several tutors to support it effectively.

Issues and responses in practice

Learning and teaching

We cannot represent all disciplines on the tutor team. As the programme is generic in nature, this need not be an issue, but, as Pole (2000) says, it has an impact on student satisfaction and what they see as the 'appropriateness' of their tuition. Lindsay et al. (2002) note this, and we believe it is a widespread experience of generic RT providers, which is aided by tutors

---

Exemplar assignments

1. Give a short (one page maximum) introduction to your research project (10%). Discuss the ethical issues that will arise in your proposed research (40%) and show, explicitly, *how* you will address these in your research planning (50%). (The emphasis in this essay is on identifying the *relevant* ethical issues and showing *how* you will deal with them at the planning stage – what will you plan to *do* to meet your ethical responsibilities?).

2. Write a critique of the journal paper 'xxxx' *Journal of XXX, 2001*. You can obtain copies of this paper from the tutors. You should use the accompanying guidelines on critiquing literature.

3. Choose the data collection method(s) that you consider to be appropriate to your research.
   (a) Explain the *methodology* within which you will use these methods of data collection. Why are you taking this approach? Explain why you are *not* using other methodologies (30–40%).
   (b) Describe how you will implement the appropriate *methods* in the context of your project, with examples. If you do not know exactly what data you will have, give hypothetical examples (40–50%).
   (c) Reflect on how you will develop or acquire the interpersonal and technical skills needed to carry out your plans effectively, and explain how you will go about achieving these goals (10–20%).

4. Critically discuss epistemological issues by examining the claim to 'truth' of a specific author (or series of authors in one school) whose work is relevant to your own research topic.

5. 'If parts of society exist, but are being constructed and reconstructed through social interaction, how do you assess the meaning of interview data or other primary social data?'
   Critically discuss the potential problems with reference to your own research topic

6. Discuss the methods of **data analysis** that you plan to use in your research project.
   (a) Provide a rationale justifying your choice of methods of ANALYSIS, and your reasons for the exclusion of others (20%).
   (b) Demonstrate how you intend to apply the chosen method/s of ANALYSIS to your data set, with examples (hypothetical if necessary), and show how you will display your results (60%).
   (c) Identify the skills, knowledge and types of data that you need to acquire in order to present your findings effectively, and show how you will go about addressing these needs (10–20%).

We also require a statistics portfolio and an annotated bibliography from all students.

Figure 10.4   Exemplar assignment questions

being active in research. Tutors must be thick-skinned and good at taking criticism – hard hats are provided. Coate et al. (2001) looked at the relationship between research and teaching and found that new ways of managing these should be considered; we believe that it can be enhanced usefully in the RT scenario.

Many academics believe it is impossible to teach *generic* RT skills in interdisciplinary classes covering many *specialties* (Gilbert et al. 2004). Our experience shows that this is not the case, but it can be a painful process for students and tutors (hence the hard hats). Our response to this is to provide examples from several disciplines when teaching, just as Neumann (2001) described interdisciplinary variation in learning styles, which is ubiquitous. Students then feel that they get some recognition of their own area in class. Unfortunately, each area feels that it is getting fewer relevant examples in class than the others. It is impossible to please all of the people all of the time! This is inevitable in cross-disciplinary teaching. Most research students have only been exposed to relatively narrow research traditions within their own disciplines. Put bluntly, they do not know 'what it is that they don't know'. The same goes for some supervisors, many of whom have not had formal RT themselves. Our task is to show students the whole range of research options available and to listen when they tell us their needs. For example, student feedback led to us changing the delivery order of the modules 'to make more sense', which has proved successful. We have also introduced software training introductions to the syllabus at student request, now including SPSS and Nvivo classes.

Our syllabus encourages students to appreciate the value of both quantitative and qualitative perspectives. We develop, or in some cases, institute, a critical approach to research in our students. Each year begins in class with the 'quant' camp at one side of the classroom (Management students), the 'qual' camp at the other side (Peace Studies, International Development, Social Sciences, Languages) and Health students somewhere in the middle, with clinical trialists talking to managers, and 'touchy-feely' (a student's own term) mental health or patient-oriented professionals talking to the Peace Studies contingent. Within weeks, this academic iron curtain dissolves, and the groups interact, as they recognize the benefits of the approach of the 'other side'. We see this interdisciplinary suspicion every year amongst the new students; unfortunately, it is perpetuated by supervisors, but life goes on and the hard hat proves its worth. One colleague put it well. He was about to deliver a lecture on the uses of quantitative data to a predominantly qualitative class, and stopped, hand on the door, with a strained look on his face, saying 'Wish me luck – I'm about to go over the top'. Take note.

Despite this annual challenge, peer-learning between students is a highly valuable mechanism that should not be underrated, and we encourage it as much as we can. We use discussion regularly in class, with students sharing their (often entertaining) experiences in research. This openness between disciplines stimulates students to consider their own positions, and to consider other ways of approaching their own research, as well as supporting each other along the way. Real world anecdotes are vital.

Should we insist on compulsory attendance? We notice a generally positive relationship between attendance and assessment outcomes. Supervisors expect good results from their students, and they expect us to deliver them (as their departments are paying us), but if students do not attend classes and do not do well in assessments, who is at fault? There are already varying PhD-work demands between departments in the first year. When students discover this, the heavily worked ones become frustrated and this causes us problems, as they mistake the problem for a Graduate School issue. This happens because students mix far more between disciplines than has previously happened. Another issue that impacts attendance is the provision of Web-based learning materials. In 2002, student requests led to all learning materials being available via Blackboard (not just to distance learners), but an unintended outcome of this has been that some students choose to miss classes in favour of using Blackboard to prepare them for assessment. They lose the vital part played by peer-group learning and face-to-face tuition. We have not yet resolved this issue, but are looking at the work of Barry (1997) to find ways to improve student appreciation of the uses of e-based materials.

We occasionally take students from non-social science areas. These students have all been successful, but they have all been disadvantaged by 'culture shock'. Deem and Brehony (2000) noted issues of research style in this scenario too. Compared to sitting in a safe laboratory or working in the field, the average scientist finds the experience of being shut in a roomful of social scientists once a week extremely unnerving. It is not often we see scientists quivering, but put them amongst a bunch of social 'scientists' and see what happens. We recognize that most science students come from a quantitative, positivist background, but social science classmates can consider positivism to be the work of the devil. Scientists in class want to measure everything, and when they cannot quantify 'feelings' they become alarmed. Used to accepting that a broken light bulb is a broken light bulb, scientists find it worrying to be told by postmodernists that the concept of brokenness is culturally relative and carries connotations of social, scientific and ontological superiority that may be inappropriately associated with, and not recognized by, the light bulb. QED.

The result of this is that tutors have a heavy load of 'nursing' (extra tutorials, desperate phone calls) in order to get demoralized, intimidated scientists through the modules. So, we have developed a number of 10 credit modules based on the core 20 credit versions. Science students now attend only some of the 20 credit classes. In those classes we try to avoid getting into animated critiques of 'science', leaving those for days when the scientists are safely back in their labs. This does not mean that scientists are protected from all critique – far from it. But, we do try to limit it occasionally in the interests of interdisciplinary harmony and the sanity of tutors. This has been successful to date, with less tutorial time needed to support the students in question. We have also found that science students enjoy and benefit from sitting in on research philosophy lectures. This works wonders in getting them to understand the social science worldview, and we would recommend it to anyone trying to grasp this nettle (it would also be good for social science students to appreciate that there are research benefits in positivism and quantitative approaches, although it would require a brave soul to try).

Finally, under learning and teaching, the English language skills of international students must be addressed. Put bluntly, more international recruits today cannot speak and/or write adequate English on arrival. I would say this to central RT providers: get a cast iron language testing policy in place across all recruiting areas. Preferably with tests that include photographs of the student. It is insufficient to require language testing on arrival. Having identified weak students, we must then insist they take language classes before proceeding with the PhD. This should save delay, failure and possible litigation later. Poor English skills also cause problems for the rest of the class and the tutor. Supervisors often do not believe us when we point out that their star arrival cannot understand classes. This has led to some interesting exchanges that only cease with the arrival of their student's assignment results. We also act as an unofficial filter for supervisors in highlighting other problems, often uncovering difficulties with proposed projects, ethical issues and even domestic issues that may be impacting a student's progress.

Management

Communicating effectively with all the staff associated with a student is vital, as interdisciplinary RT incurs a vast amount of accountability. We hold an annual meeting in May for the PG secretaries of all our clients, at which we provide the dates and changes for the coming session, including dates for registration and induction, teaching sessions, assessment submission and so on. These are then sent out with letters to new students when they accept a place. For supervisors, the Programmes Director goes on a tour each October to explain the workings of the Graduate School in each client department; also, each of these has a representative on our assessment committee, exam board and governance team. This enables all clients to have a say in the development of the programme. Our committees report to higher committees up the university ladder, and this enables us to get recognition and ask for help when we need it.

Delivering the programme to different cohorts each year requires a lot of flexibility. It is taxing on tutors as adaptation is needed for each cohort. This is a major workload issue, and it should be considered by anyone planning multiple delivery of an RT programme. It is not as simple as to say that distance learners require more e-mail or Web-based support than on-siters. Both types of cohorts require this, and in our experience the amount and content of support needed depends more on the background, academic and language ability of the student rather than on the mode of registration.

Standardization of modules for QA purposes is vital and is best accomplished by the programme leader having a hand in the devising of any programmes to which the RT modules contribute. If the same tutor team can be responsible for most of the teaching for all cohorts, this makes standardization easier. If this is not possible, the programme leader needs control over the content of the teaching and an input to other modules in order to avoid clashes of approach that may confuse students and impact assessments.

External accreditation of RT programmes is useful as it seems to both enhance recruitment and give a stamp of quality to the qualification. It brings in a valuable income strand via quota studentships and successful open competition applications. Our SSRTP requires re-recognition by the ESRC every four years. By working closely with the governance committee, the Programmes Director is able to manage this exercise much more easily.

Funding is a major issue for any RT programme. Despite assertions of brotherly academic love, all departments want us to teach only what is 'useful' (that is, traditional) for their students. Our approach, with 25 per cent of tutors covering a range of academic areas, helps, but is not perfect. This is an area that needs ongoing review and adaptation to the needs of the university. Each student is paid for by their home department on an FTE-transfer algorithm into the Graduate School. Universities considering centralized RT provision should think hard about this issue from the start and consider centralized funding to match it. This should save on academic civil unrest.

The SSRTP is subject to the usual annual monitoring process (of which student evaluation is a large component) and other university QA processes. This is an area that needs special note by those wishing to set up an institution-wide programme. It is insufficient to assume that the central programme will 'fit' into the normal processes – it will not, neither the finance, the QA or the staffing models. Generic RT requires relatively more staff hours than other programmes and will struggle without adequate resources – financial and human. It is a service provision, not an academic department, and recognition of that is vital for those who are managing it, as well as for the understanding of it by stakeholders who only see their own students' viewpoint. This makes for a huge administrative load.

General

Rising student numbers brings a much greater rise in administrative, pastoral and development responsibilities, and these should not be underestimated. Not only do tutors have to deliver to larger groups, but the style of teaching has to be adapted accordingly. A rise in international student numbers is particularly hard due to language issues. Cultural awareness in teaching is necessary – we use a variety of inter-cultural research examples, but this takes time to develop. Some cultural groups come from backgrounds where the academic system is significantly different. Adjusting to the UK grading system which uses 70 as a distinction is humiliating to those who got 90+ at home. Some overseas male students are unhappy with female tutors and, in some cases, are reluctant to take critical comment from them. We have dealt with issues like this by taking advice from our Equality and Diversity Officer, but again, it is time consuming and can be frustrating for the staff concerned.

Managing student and supervisor expectations is an ongoing concern that will not disappear, given the nature of postgraduate training and the various disciplines from which our classes are drawn, as McCormack notes (2004). Often, ideas of RT do not match up between students and the university. No matter how much information we give to supervisors each year, most still expect the RT to consist of us telling their students how to do their own PhD and no more. Supervisors often contradict class materials with which they are unfamiliar. Many students do not wish to know about methodologies which are unfamiliar to their own discipline. Most begin to recognize the benefits of broad-spectrum training by the end of the core modules, but many do not and simply take away their 'own bit' and go through the motions with the other elements of the programme. But, we do not know how many of these go on to benefit from 'the other bits' in later years.

Many students are unhappy at having to take a course that they think gets in the way of their PhD. Interestingly though, we receive regular comments from final year students who tell us that it is not until the later stages of their PhD that they truly appreciate the long term benefits of the programme (Cryer 1998; Pole 2000).

Summary

There are strengths and limitations to cross-disciplinary RT. The generic/specific issue will never go away and must be handled sensitively, with an awareness that it is impossible to please everyone at the same time. A central model is economically and academically appropriate and effective, but it does not remove the need for smaller-scale, subject-specific RT within individual departments/areas.

The management of student and supervisor expectations is of paramount importance if problems are not to get worse. We need to make clear that the RT programme is not simply a course focussing on the student's own PhD or piece of research – it provides transferable skills for a career in research.

We must take into account the differences in academic culture between the various disciplines served, as tensions will arise (as recognized by Delamont et al. 1997; Green H. 2005). These are largely philosophical in nature, underpinning different perspectives and traditions, but they can cause problems to students and tutors if not openly addressed and fairly discussed in class.

Funding should, if possible, be centrally sourced in order to avoid interdisciplinary clashes of expectation with perceived or actual input. This is a source of frustration between disciplines if not handled carefully, but it can be relieved by sharing tutors across disciplines from an early stage.

There are differences between disciplines regarding the academic development of Postgraduate students when they arrive for their RT. Some disciplines clearly develop a critical attitude to research during the undergraduate period far more effectively than others – a very delicate situation to address.

This means that certain disciplines tend to be more open than others to take on new ideas when they embark on postgraduate RT – tutors must handle this in ways that allow all disciplines to benefit from the RT equally.

All these issues may be summed up by saying that generic, cross-disciplinary RT cannot keep everyone happy all the time. The conflicting demands of each discipline have not been sufficiently recognized by those driving higher education policy (Delamont et al. 1997), yet the trend to 'share' continues to grow in relation to the increasingly economic view within the sector. However, our experience at Bradford shows that it is possible to provide generic RT in a way that sets many students from diverse disciplines on the path to success. One of the most positive outcomes of this has been, from the students' own comments, the interaction and subsequent learning between students from different disciplines that would never have taken place had a generic, cross-disciplinary programme not been in place.

Overall, centralized RT, supported by localized specific training, does avoid 'doubling up' and helps standardization. It requires students to join a broad learning experience that enhances their personal development through seeing other research options in practice. This can only serve to support the trend towards inter- and multidisciplinary research.

Ultimately, leading a mixed bag of research students into an understanding of what research really is and seeing them blossom is fantastic and gives us all a buzz. There are few things as satisfying as seeing your students go out all over the world doing research that you set them off on . . . but do not forget that hard hat.

11

Professional Learning through Reflective Practice: The UEA Experience

Imelda Race

The notion of professional learning through reflective practice

The challenge for research institutions in this post-Roberts era is to successfully embed professional skills training as an integral part of the research postgraduate curriculum. This will inevitably require a culture shift within the academic research community, as discussed in earlier chapters. The key to successful implementation is to make overt and tangible the added value of generic skills training to both the postgraduate students and the research institutions, not only in the longer term, by enhancing employability, but also more immediately, in terms of the overall quality of the postgraduate experience, resulting in improved retention and completion rates, more efficient researchers and an increase in the quality of the research. Ongoing educational research has a role to play in capturing and evaluating current practice, as it is through such evidence, and over time, that the true effect of today's measures can be gauged and subsequently valued.

Importantly, in this climate of rapid change, practitioners should continue to actively disseminate and share good practice across the wider research community.

Therefore, in the spirit of sharing developmental experience I include an insight into the professional skills training programme at the University of East Anglia (UEA) and elaborate on 'lessons learnt'. The search for an appropriate and effective curriculum design for the professional skills development of novice researchers at UEA has been a challenging and, as yet, incomplete journey. Curriculum design and innovation is a dynamic process, continually being informed by experience, feedback and evaluation. It is clear, however, that a sound educational framework is emerging that underpins our training programme. The programme is built on the notion of ongoing professional development through experiential learning and reflective practice, with the firm belief that proficiency in these processes can be taught.

The significance of reflection within professional learning is emphasized by Schön (1983, 1987). These works explore the process of reflection and how it can be developed and coached within students. Subsequently, several models of reflection in the professional learning context have been proposed. For the practitioner, notable work in this field include Boud et al. (1985), Boud and Walker (1993), Wildman and Niles (1987), and, for interpretation and practical application, Moon (1999).

Much of the continuing professional development of the researcher is based within practice. Therefore, novice researchers should be exposed to this approach to learning during their formal training and encouraged to develop the skills underpinning effective experiential learning, in particular the skills of reflective practice, at an early stage. This logic for a training model is reinforced by Boud et al. (1996: 55): 'If professionals are to develop skills in reflective thinking it is important that they be encouraged to do so in their initial training.' Furthermore, this leads to strengthening the recognition of research as a profession 'with researchers recognised as well as recognising themselves as professionals' (Kane 2005).

Therefore it is, I believe, important that reflective practice and experiential learning are at the heart of the postgraduate training programmes that are emerging in this time of substantial culture change surrounding the way researchers are perceived. It is, indeed, the nature of experiential learning in the context of generic skills development, its role in higher education and the implication for research postgraduate skills development programmes that I wish to focus on in this chapter.

The Professional Skills Training Programme at the University of East Anglia

During its years of development, postgraduate research (PGR) skills training at UEA has moved from a collection of isolated taught skills courses for science postgraduates to an eclectic programme available to all research postgraduates across all disciplines and years of study and embedded in the UEA staff culture of continuing professional training and development. The pace of development has accelerated since 1999, at which time a coordinated training programme was launched across the physical sciences. This programme provided the basis for current developments triggered by the Roberts report (2002). At the heart of this development has been the notion that the whole postgraduate experience is an 'apprenticeship' for the professional researcher, in terms of academic knowledge, research methodology and personal and professional skills development. Over time and through experience, successful and otherwise, and aided by feedback and evaluation, a programme of generic skills training has emerged which embraces an embedded skills value that goes beyond the explicit formal taught framework.

The impetus of the Roberts report (2002) and related developments in funding led to a redefining of UEA postgraduate skills provision, with the emergence of the current Transitions Programme (see Figure 11.1) in the academic year 2004–05. The Transitions Programme focuses on the notion of 'transitional change' in professional development needs from first year postgraduate through to postdoctoral researcher, as well as on supporting individuals through the process of change and continuing development. This conceptualization is in keeping with the emerging theme, both in the UK and across Europe, as reported at the 2005 Conference on the European Charter for Researchers and the Code of Conduct for their recruitment, that there is a need to create a positive environment in which researchers from the outset are perceived as members of a profession who are effectively supported and managed to fulfil their potential. To reinforce the notion that, within the research profession, professional development is a continuous process supported by the research institution, the concept of the Transitions Programme at UEA is extended to include early career researchers. Furthermore, the programme has been embedded within the university's staff development unit.

The UEA Transitions Programme contains three core elements, corresponding to key transitions in the process of personal development as an apprentice researcher:

Transitions I – Getting started on the professional path
Transitions II – Constantly improving your skills base
Transitions III – Developing your professional career
Transitions IV – In-service development for postdoctoral researchers

A selection of training modules is available to support each stage of transition. The menu offered goes beyond the traditional taught skills courses and includes a strong element of experiential learning. Although there is a compulsory core of training required by all postgraduate researchers to ensure a basis of common standards and achievement, there is flexibility in the programme, based on a formal assessment of training needs conducted by the student and the supervisor at regular intervals. This ensures that individual needs are met and that training appropriate to potential future career trajectories is provided. Experience has shown that where there is an element of compulsory attendance, this needs to be balanced and offset against components involving choice and the opportunity to tailor to individual needs.

A characteristic feature of the first year of the Transitions Programme (Transitions I) is that it is prescriptive and consists of taught courses covering a range of skills from the Research Councils' Joint Skills Statement (JSS), including working with others, time and project management, academic reading and writing, presentation skills and interpersonal skills. All first year training is framed in the context of the immediate needs of apprentice professionals embarking upon independent postgraduate research, since experience has shown that it is this rationale which 'buys in' students (and

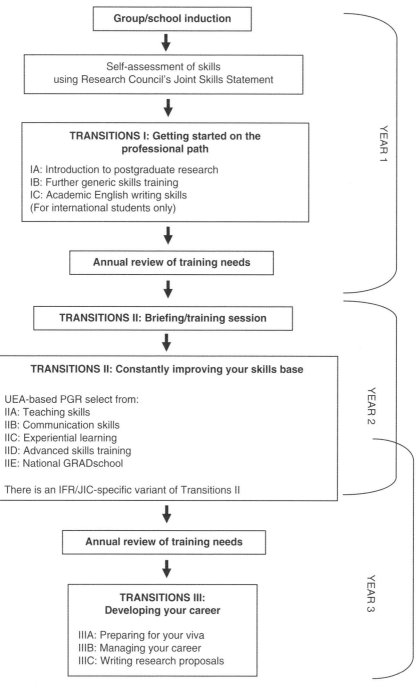

Figure 11.1 Schematic of the 'Transitions Programme' of the University of East Anglia

their supervisors), rather than the longer-term aim of employability. For example, the teaching of time management skills focuses on the PhD as a time-bound project which needs managing from day one, involving objective-setting, prioritizing and a whole range of effective time management strategies. The teaching of interpersonal skills is set in the context of building and maintaining an effective supervisory relationship. This prescriptive 'taught course' approach ensures that all research postgraduates starting out on the professional path become engaged in a core of generic skills development pertinent to their immediate needs in their new research environment.

The 'taught course' approach has the added advantage of creating a sense of cohort amongst the teaching groups (30 or so peers). This has proved to be a valued feature of the taught programme from the perspective of both the postgraduate researchers and the institution, and it helps tackle the potential issue of isolation, particularly among Arts and Humanities postgraduates. The degree of support this provides may ultimately contribute to increased retention rates.

The opening module of the taught element of the Transitions Programme is delivered to all research postgraduates within three months of registration, in line with 'transition' being the basis for the training. It is hoped that the orientation and focus this provides may be a factor in improving completion rates and, as evaluation has shown, is a particularly important and valued element for both part-time and international students. Research conducted at UEA (Aspin and Aspin 2006) on the early stages of development of a professional skills programme has revealed high embedded value expressed by participants in terms of the networking opportunities, support, reassurance and confidence provided by the early taught elements of the programme, beyond and, often, well above their perceptions of the value of the programme content in terms of skills development. This is an aspect of the postgraduate training agenda which is in danger of being overlooked and underplayed.

Whilst the first and, in part, the final year 'taught course' phases of the programme assume there is an initial core of generic training based on the Research Councils' JSS, in contrast, the middle phase of the programme, Transitions II, is concerned with meeting individual needs and can, therefore, be tailored. A flexible training framework is provided from which PGR students can select a suitable menu of provision to build a programme that meets both the requirements of the Roberts report (2002), that is, a minimum of two weeks engagement in skills development, and their individual training needs in the area of generic skills. This act of selection, itself, evidences 'personal effectiveness' under section D4 of the JSS 'to be able to demonstrate self-awareness and the ability to identify own training needs'.

At this stage of the programme, there is a major focus on the development of skills in context through experience-based learning, or experiential learning, beyond the taught classroom environment. Individuals select personally challenging activities, above and beyond those that they would normally encounter day to day during their research degree studies, that would allow them to develop a range of generic skills identified from the

Research Councils' JSS and thereby meet their individual training needs. The postgraduate researchers negotiate, arrange, seek approval for organize and manage all aspects of the activity. Should finance be required, the student submits a budget for consideration and engages in follow-up negotiation, if necessary. The skills underpinning these organizational aspects are, themselves, generic and are an integral part of the whole learning experience. The experiential learning element is a mandatory requirement for Roberts-funded PGR students and highly recommended for all as part of their ongoing personal and professional development.

During a briefing session, the postgraduate researchers are provided with some suggestions of the types of activities they might like to consider undertaking using this training methodology. These range from the large-scale national schemes endorsed by various research councils such as the *Researcher in Residence* scheme, the *NOISE Scheme for Science Role Models* or *Knowledge Transfer Partnership* schemes, to more local or smaller-scale initiatives. For example, the Norwich Research Park has an excellent local Teacher–Scientist Network that encourages teachers and researchers to work in collaboration. The university is involved in many widening participation projects, such as the HEFCE Aimhigher Programme, that provide ample opportunity for PGR students to test out and develop their communication, interpersonal and other personal effectiveness skills through mentoring or teaching. The university has its own 'Volunteers scheme' brokering a variety of mutually beneficial relationships and, like other universities, the local 'Knowledge Transfer' (KT) agenda has many schemes to offer opportunities to postgraduates striving to develop their skills base through experience. Indeed, there may be further merit in developing the awareness of KT activities amongst novice researchers, as current trends indicate an increase in the significance of this element of the professional researcher's role. PGR students are encouraged to consider any level of involvement, from an activity which might take a few hours to one that may happen over several days or weeks. The activity must, however, incorporate a significant personal challenge that will test and stretch the student's abilities in specific areas.

The role of experiential learning

The quotes throughout are extracts from the experiential learning final reports submitted by students on completion of their selected activity.

Experiential learning is a significant and important feature of PGR training, since much of the professional development of researchers is embedded in practice. The style of teaching on the taught courses is distinctly biased towards experiential learning. In some courses this is more marked than in others. For example, the content of the teamwork module is structured around the learning cycle devised by Kirk (1987) and developed from the Kolb model (Kolb 1983). In this module, activities are selected which provide a collective experience for the participants, and this is followed by the opportunity to review events collectively in small peer groups or individually.

This review leads to the formation of abstract concepts and generalizations (the 'learning' stage). The final stage of 'applying and testing' the new learning, usually, but not always, occurs beyond the taught environment. In a similar way, academic writing and presentation skills are also developed using experiential learning, in that the postgraduates 'do' some writing or a presentation following a series of inputs to stimulate good practice, engage in peer 'review', use the feedback to 'learn' from the experience and go on to 'apply' their learning in future practice. The Transitions Programme structure seeks to build on the experiential mode of learning established in its early taught elements and use this as the foundation for the training in the second and subsequent years.

I maintain that the application of the experiential learning approach to skills acquisition requires deliberation and structure in curriculum planning if it is to be a successful and effective learning methodology. There is an assumption that skills acquired by experiences in context are merely 'caught', not 'taught'. Some believe that the most effective experiential learning 'just happens' (indeed, it is this philosophy that justifies the historical model of PGR training through the sole vehicle of conducting a supervised research project). I propose that the situation is far more complex and that learners can, in fact, be trained or coached (Schön 1983, 1987) to become more proficient at consciously and deliberately developing their competence through reflecting on experience. For this reason, a training session in reflective practice forms a compulsory prerequisite to the experiential learning element of the Transitions II programme. The training workshop is based on the work of Honey and Mumford (1992) on learning styles and the 'BBC for Business' training material on the learning experience, produced by Peter Honey (1998). The session examines the learning process through analysing its stages, identifies learner personality types and explores methods that enable individuals to harness their full learning potential. It emphasizes the importance of reflection and making learning a conscious and deliberate process in order to maximize learning from experience. This builds on the classroom-based experiential learning within the taught element of the Transitions Programme and encourages researchers to consider reflective practice and learning from experience as ongoing processes which are integral to their continuing professional development.

The role of reflection in experiential learning, using Kolb's model (1983), is to make conscious the process of re-creating or constructing learning which leads to improved action. Using the interpretation of Eraut (1994), reflection is required to take action and observation (experience) beyond the level of impressions and assimilate it into existing schemes of experience or induce those schemes to change in order to accommodate it. The result is to consciously deepen and improve the learning. The quality of the reflection is crucial in ensuring that the learner progresses in their learning. This highlights the need to develop the postgraduates' competence in reflecting on experience and to consider ways of creating a 'reflective learning' culture amongst researchers. Furthermore, experience cannot be developed into appropriate learning if the learner does not intend to learn (Eraut 1994). Hence, the experiential learning 'training workshop' overtly puts the learning process on the conscious agenda. Kolb's cycle is used to guide the reflective process. The identification of learning styles in relation to stages of the cycle helps the students focus their development needs en route to competency as efficient learners from experience.

To encourage reflective practice, the experiential learning element of the second phase of the Transitions Programme requires all participants to submit a brief report detailing their improvement in generic skills as a result of the learning experience and their engagement in reflection on it. Sample extracts are presented throughout this section to illustrate the students' perspectives on their learning. For example, the following environmental science researcher arranged to present his research to Y13 students at a local school and placed great value on the role this played in developing his communication skills and his ability to communicate to an audience outside his academic peer group:

> As a PhD student, there is a tendency to present at a very high level of subject matter to your peers and senior members of staff. Inevitably this leads to getting bogged down in very specific details and sometimes overlooking the big picture . . .

> This activity is definitely one for developing communication skills; it pushes the boundaries a bit beyond what would normally be expected in a university. It has obviously helped me to think about presenting in a clear and appropriate style to the purpose and in doing this I have definitely contributed to the public understanding of some of the research that is carried out in environmental science.

The experiential learning final report forms the basis of a short informal interview with the supervisor or supervisory panel during which the PGR student articulates those skills that have been developed and explains how they know they have successfully improved their competency. In this way, the Transitions Programme methodology at this stage provides the opportunity for postgraduate researchers to develop the skills of self-awareness, self-evaluation and self-learning. This is further illustrated by this extract from a student who delivered a presentation to A-level maths students about PhD research and studying maths at university:

> I chose this activity as my experiential learning activity because during the training session for developing reflective practice, the learning styles questionnaire had identified that I was more of a reflector and that I needed to develop my activist style which was clearly my weakest. Hence the opportunity to give a presentation to an unknown audience seemed like a good way of developing this . . .

> This experience of giving such a presentation has taught me many things. Firstly, with regards to giving a talk, it has given me a great deal more confidence to stand up and talk about my research in front of a group of people. Also, in having to adapt my talk to make it suitable for the audience, I have had to think more about how my research can be made accessible to a general audience . . . I have had to look at my research from a different angle.

Indeed, identifying needs, monitoring improvement and articulating achievement are key characteristics of professional learning. This also helps address the issue, identified in the Roberts report (2002), that employers felt that not only did the interpersonal skills of researchers need improving but also their awareness of these abilities.

> It (the experiential learning opportunity) has also provided an insight into the transferability of my research skills to different activities and the requirement for continuous professional development.

The involvement of supervisors at this stage is also a key factor in the awareness-raising needed to underpin the emerging culture change in the professional development of researchers alluded to earlier.

Ongoing challenges

One of the major challenges with the experiential approach to teaching and learning lies in convincing postgraduate researchers that learning from experience is a process that one can deepen and develop, that it is not wholly intuitive and not just commonsense and that it is a valuable skill, transferable across contexts and core to effective ongoing professional development. This is why the initial training session is an important and essential element of the experiential learning experience at UEA. Indeed, it is why the notion of experiential learning is presented during the first session of the Transitions Programme as an intrinsic characteristic of professional practice. Much work still needs to be done, though, on 'selling' this rationale to both students and their supervisors.

A further challenge for skills development practitioners is convincing supervisors that generic skills development emerging from engagement in a wide range of activities outside academia will provide added value to the research itself, as a result of the student becoming more competent. This extract from a postgraduate who took on the role of foreman for a Morris dancing group as an experiential learning opportunity illustrates the rich vein such engagement can yield:

> Personal effectiveness . . . I have had to learn that I have responsibility to the side and have to assert myself . . . previously I have always accepted

other people's opinions and I have not tried to become involved in any controversial decisions . . . I am now finding myself having to lead these discussions and come to a decision based on the other members' points of view . . . I have had to develop more assertiveness so that during meetings I can make sure everyone's opinions are taken into account.

The experiential learning reports, submitted by students completing Transitions II this academic year (2006/2007), are providing a valuable source of information with regard to benefits to the research process and the research institution, as this extract from a student who helped to set up a wildlife conservation exhibition shows:

> Through setting up this display with staff members who are experienced in environmental education I have learnt a great deal about how to convey knowledge and information in a way that grabs people's attention and hopefully change misconceptions. Although the issue is one that I am knowledgeable about, as it is the subject of my PhD, communicating this information effectively is key to allowing this knowledge to be of use and to create beneficial change.

The nature of experiential learning and its significance in the context of postgraduate research skills development programmes is an emerging picture. Reflecting on the UEA experience here in this chapter is the starting point for my personal exploration of this process. It is my future intention to conduct ongoing action research at UEA in an effort to add to our understanding of the role and potential of experiential learning and reflective practice in this context. Further research needs to focus on identifying the conditions necessary to bolster reflective learning among novice researchers. The work of Wildman and Niles (1987) on developing reflective practice in experienced teachers, for example, concludes that support, time and space and a collaborative environment are the required conditions amongst this group. Are these findings transferable? It may be necessary for us, as a community of practitioners, to consider further the nature of an environment conducive to reflective learning, and the subsequent implications for the kind of learning environment needed to support the training and development of postgraduate researchers. Moon (1999), in her book *Reflection in Learning and Professional Development,* makes some interesting suggestions for trainers to consider, including employing 'facilitators of reflection', using reflective learning journals and making use of 'learning sets' for group supported reflection. The educational psychology of learning provides a potentially significant framework for innovative curriculum design in the context of the professional development of researchers, making this an exciting time to be involved in researcher training and development.

Part 3

The Future

12

Getting Beyond Supervision

Julie Reeves

Introduction

According to trainers, one does not have to be involved with the skills training agenda for long to realize that the most substantial obstacle to any successful programme is 'the supervisor'. In the view of those tasked with programme delivery, it is usually 'the supervisor' rather than 'the student' who is seen to present the most difficulty.[1] While traditional thinking maintains that a PhD researcher requires the stewardship of at least one supervisor, this particular difficulty looks set to remain for trainers. However indisputable the supervisory role appears, the changing environment and the questioning of 'What is a PhD for?' (Park 2007) inevitably raises the issue of how necessary the supervisor is to the process of a PhD. This chapter explores if, and in what ways, the skills training agenda presents a challenge to the traditional supervisory relationship and what the implications of this are for the existing PhD model.

What follows is a largely theoretical discussion of the commonly perceived problems with the skills training agenda as defined from the deliverer's perspective. That is to say, this is an exploration of the assumptions currently inherent in the Roberts agenda by those charged with its advancement. The chapter is divided into three parts: firstly, common problems are identified; secondly, conventional solutions are examined which reveal some problematic and underlying conceptual assumptions; thirdly, an alternative to the traditional model and assumptions is entertained. The chapter concludes with the suggestion that the skills training agenda not only challenges the substantive experience of doing a PhD (that is, what a student does during their programme of research) but, moreover, it presents an epistemic challenge that requires a conceptual shift in the way we view and support the process. This conceptual shift is required by all those involved in research development programmes – the postgraduate researcher, the supervisors and the skills trainers.

The problem with skills training is . . . the supervisor

Fairly or otherwise, there is a general view among skills trainers and administrators that the most problematic element in the skills training agenda is the supervisor. The supervisor is seen by administrators and trainers as the elephant in the corner of skills training 'sabotaging', as one trainer put it, every effort from training courses and skills audits to personal development planning (PDP).[2] Clearly, many academics are very supportive of skills training, but experience in the field has led to a number of problems being directly attributable to the negative influence of supervisors on students. Four common complaints regarding supervisors are: their outright rejection, their mild to chronic forms of indifference, the tendency to blame external (non-academic) bodies and 'the janus-faced' attitude towards skills training.

First, although few supervisors deliberately sabotage the training agenda, one does hear of the occasional supervisor declaring that any form of skills training is 'a complete waste of time'. A myth perhaps, nonetheless this view fits neatly with the belief that PhDs are trained for an academic career and this is the main reason for embarking on the project in the first instance. Contrary to this view, the growing majority of PhDs find employment elsewhere, as the *What Do PhDs Do?* (Shinton 2004) survey found. Moreover, PhDs are actively seeking alternative careers. It has been noted that supervisor's views pass easily to students as 'Doctoral education is as much about identity formation as it is about knowledge production' (Green B. 2005: 153), and it is common currency among trainers that the negative attitudes of students can be attributed, frequently, to those supervisors who are well known for their obstructive attitudes within their institutions. 'The chances are', one trainer stated, 'that when I come across a student who says training is a waste of time and I know what subject area they are in – I have a very good idea exactly who their supervisor must be. And the terrible thing is I've never been wrong about that yet!'[3]

If the open saboteur is a minority figure, there are also ways of undermining the efforts of trainers and administrators with an attitude of indifference. This is expressed as a diluted version of the 'it's all a waste time' attitude, but proves equally damaging. Indifference can appear as a chronic or a mild case, but generally the view is expressed that training has little or nothing to do with thesis supervision. The supervisor is only there to supervise the research and not to administer personal development planning or give career advice. At first blush this does not appear an unreasonable point of view. Supervisors do not openly reject the training programme, but failing to actively support it proves a serious source of difficulty within the current, traditional, PhD model. The stance still undermines the student's commitment and enthusiasm for training because of the influence the supervisor enjoys. For example, a student who had kept very good logs and details of training courses in the first few weeks of her research degree accounted for the subsequent dramatic drop-off in records by saying, 'my supervisor never asked me about it – so when the introductory training was over, I stopped filling the forms in because he never mentioned it or checked up on it'.[4] This student expressed regret for not continuing independently when discussing her experiences towards the end of her programme, but this informant begins to reveal the level and range of student dependency on the supervisor in the PhD process – what Green calls 'the social dynamics of power and desire' (Green B. 2005: 153).

The indifference of supervisors can be the result of a lack of up-to-date and appropriate knowledge regarding the PhD researcher's expectations and aspirations. Most would agree that the PhD is no longer a 'life's work', it is a project to be completed within a determined amount of time, and although many may lament the demise of the good-old days when academics could be trusted financially and intellectually to get on with it and take as long as they liked, the current tax payer is more exacting. Moreover, the competition for jobs, including academic ones, is global – not even the students want to hang around for ever on a project (especially if they have debts to repay). In view of the competing demands on and of students, the onus is on institutions to prepare them the best they can for the future. The contemporary reality for a newly qualified PhD is very different from someone who has been in post for a few years and has publications under their belt, whilst the demands of employers (including HEIs) means they will brutally sort between candidates. Certainly, students are going to be disadvantaged where the supervisor does not have a current and realistic grasp of the nature of the job market, and publishing is one area where some supervisors can damage a student's career prospects by failing to recognize that most students need to be published if they wish to be considered for an academic post.

The problem lies not just with the lack of up-to-date information, but often with the assumption that non-academic staff have nothing to offer the PhD. Non-academic talk of PDPs, training needs analysis (TNA) and generic skills training are deemed peripheral matters (an add-on) to the traditional university structure, which renders them 'other' and second rate (see Simmonds 2003/2006: 5–28).

Thirdly, there is the supervisor who appears to support the training agenda but undermines it by designating it an imposition from outside the institution (that is, by the government) or worse still, an imposition from within (that is, by administrators). It is easy to blame the government for imposing training requirements that appear dominated by financial concerns, that is, 'if we don't go along with the training agenda, the institution will lose money'. However, this has the effect of conveying to students the view that training is something they have to do because they have been told to and there will be (indirect) financial penalties if they do not. The message is one of money being more important than student development. Where training is associated with internal imposition, the situation is much more divisive.

Under these conditions training is merely seen as an extension of a deeper problem, namely that universities 'are being taken over by bureaucrats and administrators', which is inevitably seen as a degenerate development.[5] This appears to place trainers and academics at odds with one another. As one senior academic complained, 'what does an administrator know about a PhD?' Comments such as these demonstrate little awareness of either the standard of qualifications administrators possess or that previous PhD experience can be a major motivating factor in the role. Whether the imposition of training requirements is perceived as coming from external sources, in that it is seen as government imposed, or from inside the institution itself, the net result is the same – students remain distanced or worse, alienated from training, frequently failing to see the point of it.

Finally, there is the janus-faced supervisor; the supervisor who supports the idea of training in theory but who undermines it locally with their personal agenda. This supervisor says that training is an excellent idea, that they wished they had had the opportunity in their day but then declares that 'all training courses are crap'.[6] This may raise a few laughs in a lecture theatre but it probably has little relation with actual experience of courses and neither does it encourage students to take training seriously.

The cumulative effect of negative statements, the mild to virulent indifference and the political utterances about training programmes (no matter how off the cuff) is highly influential among students and damaging for the promotion of the training agenda. Many supervisors are welcome and enthusiastic supporters of the skills training agenda; however, negative reactions and statements can serve to undermine effort all around. In view of this, it is, perhaps, unsurprising that the supervisor is perceived to be the biggest problem in the skills agenda, while the key and perennial question concerns what to do about them.

The conventional solution is . . . rehabilitation

The conventional answer to the supervisor problem is, rather predictably, that supervisors need training and most, if not all, universities offer their supervisors some form of training and information on the Roberts agenda. Beyond this, there is an assumption among trainers that specific and additional training in the skills programme is required. An undercurrent of opinion exists that believes supervisors ought to be put through some kind of rehabilitation programme to cure them of their 'sabotaging' ways and to endear them to the spirit and aims of the training agenda. Although liberal in intent, it is based on the belief that there is a good and proper standard of training, one stuffed full with admirable intentions, and all that is required is some minor (or major) attitudinal adjustment to bring the supervisor around to the right way of thinking. Numerous strategies are discussed – bringing champions on board, or using supervisors known to be sympathetic to the cause as local ambassadors; newsletters to spread the word; the offer of exciting training opportunities for staff; briefings by experienced trainers in useful and relevant topics; informal discussion sessions, working lunches and so on. Ultimately, and in view of the acknowledgement that there are always a few hardened nuts to be cracked, the argument always turns towards compulsion with directives issued from the top-down, from the Vice Chancellor, Pro-Vice Chancellors or Deans. However, knowing that academics tend to resent directives of this order, trainers are currently resigned to 'plug away' at the problem while harbouring their own grievances over being undermined by colleagues.

Although the basic concept of rehabilitation is viewed as a worthy cause, a number of problems arise. There is the obvious problem of getting supervisors to embrace training. One institution acknowledges that the term 'training' has negative connotations amongst supervisors, which has led to anything that resembles it being re-labelled as 'awareness'. Two difficulties occur in addition to problems with terminology and the natural resistance of some supervisors to training; first, instead of being in the business of training one group of people (the students), trainers are now faced with the task of training two groups – supervisors *and* students. This problem can double the workload and the costs, whilst requiring alternative strategies appropriate for staff and students. Whereas a trainer in careers can train students without question, the problem with training supervisors is that it requires other academics to do it because academics are often reluctant to accept expertise in people other than themselves. Green (2005) sees that both supervisors and supervisees are subject to a 'field of identifications', implying that boundaries and hedging of all kinds are necessary to protect some sort of frightened herd. This presents difficulty in terms of provision and locating people with an appropriate level of knowledge, skill and academic respect required to carry out the training of supervisors. This practical problem aside, a second difficulty remains; this approach is still premised on the very large assumption that supervisors are willing to be reformed and are capable of carrying any reform through to their students, which is the basic flaw in the rehabilitation strategy. The difficult question is not one of addressing the reluctance of supervisors to be trained (they could be compelled to do so) but rather concerns the central issue of defining what the supervisor's role should be in the PhD and of determining where the boundaries of responsibility reside.

The notion of training supervisors and winning them over to the training agenda is predicated on the belief that supervisors want to be trained, that they will accept the benefits and that they are willing to promote this among students. An awkward question is yet to be entertained by the training community; what if supervisors do not, will not and cannot do this? How will trainers overcome the fundamental contradiction in their approach – that the perceived solution to the problem may actually be the problem? Perhaps we need to rethink 'the problem' more sympathetically.

What do supervisors want? Generally speaking they want to do their own research, to guide and advise research students and to have time to write and publish. Supervisors might also teach, worry about the research assessment exercise and work to establish their reputations. What they do not want is an increased workload. Unfortunately, the average PhD student can be a high-maintenance creature, expecting a wide range of services and expertise beyond the academic role. Supervisors are expected to be project manager, human resources manager, counsellor, confidant, motivator, financial manager, careers advisor and now it seems skills training coordinator. The problem is that not all supervisors are equipped to take on these roles; they are not all experts in careers, counselling skills or PDP, and they may not want to be. It may even be an institutional irresponsibility to assume that they can be expected to want to take on these roles. Although the dispute and assessment boycott in 2006 focussed on pay and grade restructuring, in the background were high levels of discontent over fixed-term contracts, stress levels, workloads and the volume and range of duties staff have to deal with (Crace 2005).

There may be some objection that supervisors are not expected to take on the training agenda, but are merely required to support it. Yet, if we are honest as trainers then we do expect supervisors to take on a more active role and responsibility than to simply pass on the message that training is a good thing. There is a tacit assumption that supervisors need to be as engaged and interested in the agenda as we are. Indeed, to actively promote the training agenda supervisors would have to regularly enquire about student engagement, which necessarily requires in-depth discussion about the training programme and inevitably will result in offering advice on what to do. All of which assumes a good deal of *a priori* expertise and regular updating of interest. In view of the fact that students already hold high expectations of supervisors, it would not be unreasonable for them to expect supervisors to also provide them with developmental and career advice. Moreover, if this involvement in skills training is of insufficient quality and pertinence, it could provide additional grounds for student complaint. Far from expecting supervisors merely to support the training agenda and to cease undermining it, as trainers and administrators we require them to work alongside us in its active delivery (and of course many do). Yet, the success of the skills programme rests on the continued, and high level, input of supervisors; the question is whether this is a reasonable and sustainable expectation or a viable and realistic assumption. Moreover, these assumptions do not challenge the traditional academic power structures but merely seek to accommodate themselves within it, a point I return to below.

Some PhD students have a high level of dependency on the supervisor, notably international students, and thus look for the supervisor to be interested in activities and progress beyond the thesis (see Rose 2002). This would seem to undermine the central notions of students taking ownership of their professional and personal development that compose the underlying rationale of the training agenda. In short, there are a number of dependencies and inherent assumptions held by students, supervisors and trainers alike that ought to be questioned by the training agenda and are reinforced by the expectations surrounding the traditional PhD model.

The Roberts agenda, the needs of students and the demands of the economy push us to move beyond the usual boundaries of what a PhD is and to take a more radical approach. Indeed, the push seems to be towards a fragmented, de-centralized and modularized PhD experience, where new roles are made explicit and students have a range of options to choose from.

Beyond supervision?

As HEIs move towards performance management and increased professionalism, the boundaries of PhD research are being redrawn with specific reference to issues of involvement and control of the process such as the role of the supervisor within the realm of skills training.

Successfully meeting QAA precepts, RCUK requirements and fulfilling the aspirations of Roberts would seem to involve supervisors in a large, if largely assumed, role in the skills development agenda. Even students believe that their personal and professional success resides with the supervisor prompting or promoting skills training, which indicates a level of dependency that may not be entirely healthy. What is most surprising is that many trainers seem to subscribe to a similar view that supervisors are central to the success of the skills programme. Ironically, for all the complaints from trainers of lack of supervisor support and views of the skills training as alien and threatening to the academy, the training agenda has not recognized its radical potential but instead has simply sought to accommodate itself to the established discourse. It may appear that a quiet battle is being raged in HEIs with the volume of problems and complaints, but it might be better described as a storm in a cup; the real (and political) site of contestation is over definition. Yet, in this respect, the skills agenda presents more than a challenge to the time and space of a PhD (that is, the time it takes to engage in training and the mental intrusion the agenda makes in the intellectual space belonging to the student–supervisor relationship); rather, the challenge that skills training presents is one that requires an epistemic shift.

A guiding maxim in training is that provision should be user-driven, not provider-led; therefore, the obvious place to begin an examination of the supervisory role would be with PhD researchers and their employers. What do the researchers want?[7] They want their PhD, but they also want more supervisory support than they usually get and on a wider range of matters than academic ones, such as those affecting career, financial and psychological issues. Frequently, they expect more supervision than they actually receive, for example and in the extreme, a few expect to see their supervisor every day, and institutional requirements are often not quite the level of supervision students have in mind.[8] Students expect their supervisors to be 'available when required' and many believe supervisors will lead the research more so than perhaps supervisors anticipate.[9] Whilst general knowledge and studies of international students indicate mismatches in the expectation and perception of the supervisory role by students in comparison to the reality (Wu 2002), most students tolerate the situation without public complaint.

On the post-PhD side, employers bemoan the 'lack of commercial awareness' (EMPRESS: November 2005) as well as the lack of leadership, communication and interpersonal effectiveness (ESRC 2006) among the PhDs they employ. Former PhDs, however, recognize 'deficiencies' in research methods training that could have been useful in subsequent employment (ESRC 2006).[10] If the current system of supervision does not meet student expectations during the PhD (and perception is a crucial aspect of a successful experience) and fails to adequately equip them for future employment, then the answer may not be to increase the burden of the supervisor but to place responsibility where it is best fulfilled. This requires transforming the way PhD research is handled and conducted as an overall process. The idea of a 'PhD programme' takes on a more pertinent meaning and one whereby the notion of a programme implies a series of specific and managed events. The establishment of clearly identified and agreed milestones relevant to each researcher would seem vital and necessary.

In short, this points to a modularized approach where students can receive the best training appropriate to their needs, whilst, simultaneously, the responsibility for the PhD as an experience and outcome becomes more heterogeneous and dispersed.

Many HEIs are already moving in this direction in one form or another. The modularized approach is already discernible in HEIs where training is offered as part of a 'path-way', credit-rated and/or compulsory. However, simply modularizing training and offering students a greater range of courses may be insufficient to lift the burden of responsibility from supervisors. Indeed, without a fundamental transformation in the nature of PhD management and its conceptualization, such an increase in the number of courses and options available to students may exacerbate existing problems in so far as the supervisor is still expected to provide advice and to prompt the student. A re-conceptualization of the PhD depends entirely on thinking about the process in alternative ways that befit the skills agenda.

Where the traditional model of the PhD is hierarchical, the skills agenda demands a flatter, more dispersed and democratic structure; a structure that would, incidentally, fit a feminist framework very well, particularly as the skills agenda offers a 'different voice' to the existing model.[11]

One emerging alternative to the traditional model of PhD management is to locate PhD researchers in small teams. Chris Park (this volume) envisages the demise of the 'lone scholar' and a general move towards larger teams of researchers in the future. In some HEIs the notion of a supervisory team is already the norm and increasingly a second or co-supervisor is seen as elemental (if only to protect the student or, within a litigious environment, the institution), while the promotion of the idea of a broader supportive structure for the PhD process is also beginning to be articulated.

The natural sciences already operate this model to some extent, where teams of PhD researchers work on specific projects. This is a more radical approach to PhD management than that in the Humanities and Social Sciences, but even in the natural sciences students still risk being exploited by academics who may not be wholly equipped for people management and may have never been trained or assessed for the qualities and skills required. Frequently, such teams come under the guidance of postdoctoral researchers, barely out of PhDs themselves, who are often inadequately prepared to direct teams and are lacking in leadership, teambuilding and communication skills. This team-based approach maintains the 'traditional' model with its inherent hierarchical relationship and serves to perpetuate all of the problems students and employers complain about.[12]

However, the foundations are already there and an evidence is found in Chiang's 2003 study of the differences between the teamwork model of Chemistry research students and those in Education where a more individualist approach is adopted. The subject areas traditionally lend themselves to different methods of supervision, but Chiang found significantly higher, levels of satisfaction amongst Chemistry PGRs than Education. Chemistry is seen as 'training focussed' (Chiang 2003: 6) and more vocational, their 'way of interaction' is 'collegiality' and 'not hierarchical', as opposed to Education, where there is 'sense of distance' and 'formal[ity]' (Chiang 2003: 19). In other words, the working arrangement of science 'teams' already has the basis for the structure of a new episteme as it is training focussed and there is no reason why it should not be applied to areas where the individualist approach is supreme such as the Arts and Humanities and Social Science.

There is a view that the skills agenda is being driven by the commercial sector and certainly Roberts (2002) and the Research Councils are concerned with advantages to the UK (knowledge) economy. Yet, since few employers actively seek PhDs (chemical and engineering employers are areas of exception) and acquire them by default, perhaps the assumption is slightly misplaced. It is ironic that there may be insufficient commercial input and that to operate successful training programmes we need to manage them in similar ways to the business world. For those in skills training who suffer from substantial numbers of PhD researchers who fail to turn up for events and who lack the courtesy to notify the organizers, there is an obvious attraction to importing the professional attitudes of business; particularly attractive are the requirement to meet deadlines, to keep appointments, to respect others and to be self-aware.[13]

Work outside academia is increasingly project based and it would not be difficult to replicate the model within the university system, redrawing the boundaries of the PhD in line with spheres of expertise relevant to students needs. The key components of PhD research such as project management, time management and performance management can all be instilled and managed by someone who is professionally trained for the role. Although the content of PhDs vary, the actual process of academic research is no different from research or projects conducted elsewhere; so there should be no difficulty for someone who has expertise, not so much in the specific subject area but in the process of completing a large project in a professional and timely manner, in overseeing the process to completion. Moreover, if brought together as small teams under the direction of a dedicated project manager, not only could the problems of isolation that PhDs suffer from be dealt with but, additionally, all the other requirements of professional training could be met. It would be the project manager's responsibility to ensure that each team member developed their personal effectiveness and communication skills; to manage opportunities for leadership and networking, experiences of team-building and strategic/operational thinking, and to ensure that all of this occurs in a structured and meaningful way. Additional expertise in career management, personal well-being, publishing, grant applications, health and safety, diversity and equality, coaching and mentoring could be drafted in when required as part of the programme.

It is in the interests of the institution not to overburden the supervisor or to provide a second-rate service to its students. In the last resort, students want supervisors to read their work and to pass intellectual comment on it. Taking unnecessary burdens off supervisors entirely (and following the logic of the argument for professionally provided service to an end) there is no reason why an academic cannot perform the role of intellectual advisor on projects. In view of the expectation by students that supervisors ought to be concerned with more aspects of the PhD, perhaps a name change would be beneficial. Where there is a 'supervisor' there will be, always, a 'supervisee', whereas, a 'researcher' may have a network of professionals to call on. Instead of 'supervisors', academics could be contracted as 'intellectual consultants' to the project, in the same way that external examiners of theses are engaged. What is certain is that a wider range of professional expertise is increasingly required to provide support to PhDs. Individual students and projects can be supported by a broad team of professionals whose expertise and service is targeted towards needs. Professional guidance may include mentors, trainers, counsellors, financial and careers advisors in addition to the 'traditional' intellectual guidance from an expert individual in the field or a panel of academics (formerly) known as 'the supervisors'. Indeed, if early career researchers are so important to HEIs and the UK economy, it can be argued that they should be handled with a recognized level of seriousness, which is to suggest that small teams of researchers ought to be managed by a dedicated project manager.

In terms of delivering the training agenda, re-instituting 'the supervisor' as an academic consultant focuses resources precisely where they are required, that is, firmly on the training for students. Instead of thinking of more elaborate ways of getting supervisors on board, it may be preferable to instil in students from the outset that doing a PhD means being part of a team.

Final remarks

Why do we need to get beyond supervision? The short answer is that it is in the student's interest, both for the PhD experience and in the professionalization of the outcome, in which the student can be viewed as a potential employee for industry and academia. Advocating re-training 'the supervisor' may be insufficient to contend with current realities and demands on staff time and expertise. Moreover, this strategy reinforces the status of the traditional PhD model and supports the existing epistemological assumptions. Conversely, the democratization of knowledge with its widening participation, lifelong learning and international recruitment suits the skills training agenda, but it also demands the displacement of traditional relationships and the re-conceptualization of the place of the postgraduate researcher within their research and institution.

It is widely acknowledged that the world of the PhD student is changing. The changing nature and climate of the PhD raises questions over what a PhD is for and who should be involved in it. The student is at the centre of the PhD process and this should be stated strongly, not because there is a bureaucratic, financial or capitalist imperative to do so but because we need to be realistic about what serves our students best of all. The current generation of PhDs will have to be faster and slicker in the way they communicate, compete in global markets, and present their ideas, whilst also being able to adapt and present themselves to suit the demands of changing audiences. The PhD experience should result in a portfolio of skills for life, not simply a hard-bound manuscript that sits in a library. The skills agenda presents not just a physical challenge but an epistemic one; a modularized approach seeks to displace the centrality of the supervisor in the research project with a move towards shared responsibility and a broad-based approach to individual development. Under more radical terms, such an approach even displaces the PhD project itself by placing the individual and their overall development at the heart of the postgraduate agenda. This is more than a moot point; the skills training agenda presents a serious conceptual assault on many ingrained assumptions about PhD students and their relationship to the supervisor. Yet, as postgraduates learn to navigate their way around 'needs based' and 'personal development' approaches, they will, undoubtedly, become more discerning of expertise and therefore more demanding of what is available to them. It is unlikely that even the most knowledgeable and committed of supervisors (or trainers) will be able to supply all of the services postgraduate researchers will demand in order to simply survive. Ultimately, it may be the students rather than the skills trainers who force the re-conceptualization of the PhD and vote with their feet by choosing institutions that can deliver the range of skills an individual requires to operate in the twenty-first century.

Notes

1   Information has been informally collected from trainers, administrators and academics during 2005–06.
2   This phrase was expressed by a trainer in reference to the resistance of supervisors to PDP (November 2005).

3   Experienced academic and trainer at a large HEI (March 2005).

4   Third-year computer science PGR student (North West HEI, February 2005).

5   View expressed at an academic conference (November 2005).

6   Academic comment at conference (November 2005).

7   The following information comes from exercises conducted on PhD expectations at the University of Manchester in January 2006 and October 2006, involving approximately 140 students.

8   Certainly, there is less physical accountability for PhD researchers than for more typical employees outside academia whose every form of absence must be accounted for (even if you are working from home colleagues must be informed). Outside academia, it is normal for longer periods of absence to be followed up and pursued by line managers.

9   This view was regularly expressed by first-year students during an induction exercise on expectations (January 2006).

10   The ESRC report also notes 'that supervisors had colluded in students' resistance to research methods training that they [the students] did not see, at the time, as very important in terms of their own project training needs; resistance which, with hindsight, several [PhDs] regretted' (ESRC 2006: 51).

11   See Gilligan (1982). Gilligan wrote *In a Different Voice* 'to bring women's voices into psychological theory' (p. xxi) and to create a place in theories that 'eclipse the lives of women and shut out women's voices' (p. xiii). Interestingly, Gilligan pointed out that not only 'were men leaving women out, but women were leaving themselves out' by adhering to the dominant discourse (p. xiii). The skills training project is excluded from the discourse and theories of the traditional model, but similarly fails to recognize that it has its own voice and offers a different approach to the concept of a PhD.

12   ESRC (May 2006).

13   See the Research Council's Joint Skills Statement, section D4: 'demonstrate self-awareness and the ability to identify own training needs'.

13

A Framework for the Future of Doctoral Study: Resolving Inconsistent Practices and Incorporating Innovative Possibilities

Stuart Powell and Howard Green

Introduction

As Park earlier in this book illustrates (Chapter 3), transferable skills training is just one aspect embroiled within the changing UK doctorate. In this chapter we explore in some depth the variations in doctoral practice in the UK. We provide a doctoral framework that gives clarity for the future within which we consider the implications for transferable skills training.

Currently, there is a profusion of research doctorates, in addition to the traditional MPhil/PhD (for example, practice-based, New Route, European and 'by published works'), that challenges the vision of a level of standardization put forward ten years ago in the Harris report (Harris 1996). Add to this the large range of professional doctorate titles (see Powell and Long 2005) all with their own idiosyncratic structures and greater or lesser involvement with kinds of taught delivery, and the doctorate may seem to have taken on a complexity over the last ten years similar to the Masters in the mid-1990s. We are aware that various groups, most, if not all with no authority to make pronouncements, at a global, European and national level are investigating the position of the doctorate (see, for example, CIRGE 2005; EUA 2005; Park 2007). We suggest in this chapter that there is an urgent need to pull this diversity into some kind of coherent structure if students and employers are to fully comprehend what they are dealing with and if we are to establish a credible baseline from which to develop the award internationally. First, we set out some of the issues and then – somewhat in the style of a polemic – we put forward a framework for the development of the UK doctorate.

Real innovation in patterns of doctoral study?

Innovation or change?

Ten years on from Harris, we can document a large number of changes which have taken place in doctoral education (Green and Powell 2005). These can be categorized, for example, as organizational, the rise of the graduate school (UKCGE 1998), the QAA and its code of practice (QAA 2004); as funding related (Roberts 2002; HEFCE 2004); and as matters relating to training, including the development of the UK GRAD Programme (HEFCE 2003a; RCUK 2001b).

Whilst these developments are of interest, not least because they have become requirements of the funders, they add little to the award itself and more importantly to our understanding of its structure, content and purpose. In a sense, we have spent a considerable amount of time and effort looking at change without examining that to which change is being administered! It is vital to examine some of these changes to assess whether they are simply short-term expedients, whether they have significance for the doctoral award and ultimately whether they challenge the award itself.

The 'New Route PhD'

The so-called New Route PhD is an excellent example of incremental tinkering to address specific requirements. It has added an additional year to the normal PhD programme in order to incorporate extra elements directed towards a specific market. But what is not clear is whether or not these elements are a part of, or are an addition to, the doctorate itself. If they are such a part, then it is legitimate to ask where the assessment of them takes place. If on the other hand they are elements that are somehow in addition to the doctorate itself, then they should be interpreted as a precursor to that level of learning rather than at the doctoral level. In all of this it is hard to see where the 'newness' of this route lies. There is nothing new in front loading elements of taught courses in research methodology to doctoral programmes (neither in the UK nor elsewhere). For the route to be accurately describable as 'new', it would need to involve pathways that do not exist in the 'traditional' doctoral programmes, and this is not evident. All that *is* new is the marketing and branding of the award and collaboration between participating institutions in these respects. This is itself, however, a significant move forward given that the marketing of doctoral programmes is often an ad hoc activity, which at the institutional level is frequently separate from mainstream marketing, and that interinstitutional collaboration is rare.

Practice-based doctorates

Some institutions separate out doctorates in practice-based areas for special regulatory consideration, and the question arises then as to whether such 'practice-based doctorates' are simply doctoral level awards within research paradigms that differ from the 'traditional' with outcomes expressed in different ways, or whether they are fundamentally different kinds of academic endeavours. It seems to us that what is at issue here is that such awards involve research defined in specific ways that do not conform to what may be characterized as traditional, science-oriented ways of operating. Any deviations from this traditional characterization in terms of teaching methods or assessment procedures arise from paradigmatic differences in the relationship between knowledge, contributing to that knowledge and ways of making judgments about such contributions.

In essence, the doctoral product remains the same as in other doctorates across the sector and across disciplines in as much as candidates need to demonstrate their ability to contribute to the field – the doctoral awards are simply recast to address the particular demands of the disciplines concerned (again, in terms of the relationship between kinds of knowledge and ways of making a contribution, etc). Within this constancy with the 'traditional' PhD model, however, the practice-based doctorate may challenge the conventional submission particularly in terms of appropriateness in demonstrating research capability and outcomes. We suggest that this challenge is a healthy one, and that the 'practice community' puts its own creativity at risk with any emulation of a science model of doctoral research where that is not appropriate. What is needed is an analysis of the inherent intellectual structures within particular domains rather than any slavish intention to emulate (inappropriate) structures from others (see Biggs 2002).

Professional doctorates

Professional doctoral awards have proliferated in the UK in recent years and there are now at least 52 differently named awards (Powell and Long 2005); this is more than in any other country (see Powell and Green 2007 for a review). We suggest that what is required here is an examination of the research demands of the professions and how competences and advances in these areas should be evidenced, rather than inventing new named awards, which suggest but do not necessarily mean any kind of new route. Certainly, the notion of 'contribution' may need to be revisited to accommodate a new interpretation of the boundaries of an intellectual field where, for example, differing traditional academic disciplines may be brought to bear on specific, professional, decision-making contexts and hence, by implication, the ways in which those fields can be progressed. In this sense, 'contribution to knowledge' is redefined. But reifying a concept of professionally oriented research, as somehow wholly discrete from academic research, may give rise to a false dichotomy. The sole issue to be considered is the way in which a contribution can be claimed and the kinds of evidence that may be presented legitimately to support it.

The innovative possibilities of electronic submission

The development of electronic submission and storage has major potential for the development of the doctorate and the bringing together of the various doctoral forms as it enables a focus on a single form of submission for the diversity of disciplines and their traditions. The interactive potential of electronic submission will, for example, permit both musician and chemist to demonstrate their competences in performance and experiment, respectively, and potentially will offer an entirely new approach to the presentation and testing of evidence. Electronic submission will also, of course, enable wider and quicker access to doctoral submissions, thus benefiting the knowledge base and the transparency of standards.

The innovative possibilities of the personal development plan (PDP)

Following Dearing (1997) all students in UK HEIs should develop a transcript recording their achievement and a means by which they can monitor, build and reflect upon their personal development. Subsequently, QAA has developed policy and practice in this area (QAA 2001b). However, there is a growing concern in relation to PDP about what the subject of the final assessment of the doctorate should be. As students are now expected to include the PDP process within their doctoral programme, it is reasonable to expect that, at least, there will be some discussion of this process in the final assessment of the programme. The fact that this expectation is rarely met indicates a further need for clarification of the purposes and content of the examination itself.

Examining the doctorate

There is significant variation in processes of doctoral examination across the UK (Powell and Green 2003; Powell and McCauley 2002, 2003) some of which may not necessarily be problematic. And we are being recommended by QAA to make changes such as the introduction of independent chairs for vivas. However, there is a need for principles to underpin the way in which universities operate their examination processes at the doctoral level if we are to be confident of parity of standards across the sector and across disciplines. We give three examples of such principles here. (i) The sole purpose of the examination should be to enable judgement to be made on whether or not the candidate has produced satisfactory evidence to demonstrate that the criteria for the award have been met. Examiners are employed only to measure the candidate's achievement against the published criteria. (ii) Processes and procedures of the examination should be driven solely by the candidate's need to be able to demonstrate his/her abilities in relation to the university's set criteria. (iii) Universities need to be assured that doctoral awards are made only when the candidate has demonstrated that the criteria for the award have been met, and they need to assure that those criteria relate to a level that is comparable with the sector as a whole and relate to the QAA's qualifications framework.

The notion of disciplinary tradition may be an acceptable explanation for the different approaches to research, but it must not be allowed to legitimize the diversity of approaches to the examination where that diversity creates lack of parity in the treatment of submitted work.

A consistent framework for the doctoral award

The various demands made on the doctorate through time have led to adjustments at the margins. The pressures for training of a generic kind within doctoral programmes, the demands of longer programmes, the apparently differing requirements of the professions and of the arts and humanities and the emergence of new research areas have all led to the invention of supposed new routes to a doctoral level of achievement as already noted. It is therefore time to ask what the doctorate is – rather than who or what is it for with the inevitable constant redefinition according to the perceived needs of the ever-shifting audiences it is attempting to satisfy. It is only recently that there has been an understanding that most successful doctorate candidates in the UK do not go on to teach in universities, that not all are studying full-time, nor are they all under the age of 25 and destined to complete within four years. The increasing diversity that is a feature of the current postgraduate research scene in the UK (and elsewhere – see Powell and Green 2007) requires a common framework within which to define the award. We suggest below some common themes that build towards a consistent framework for *all* doctoral study.

- *Contribution to an area of research:* The doctoral award is based on research that makes a contribution to knowledge and/or to practice in a defined area(s). The assessment process should address the need for a level of contribution that is significant enough for the award to be made – where significance needs to be determined at the level of the specific discipline(s). What should be common in doctoral study is a contribution to the area concerned, which means that, after the thesis is made public, the area is better informed than it was before.
- *Viability and accessibility of the contribution:* The contribution must be in a form that is viable enough to be sustained over a period of time and

readily accessible throughout that time. Lack of such viability and accessibility denies the whole purpose of 'contribution' in that others cannot make use of the new understandings. Theses should never be kept confidential because to do so would be to deny the key purpose of doctoral study. The only exception here might be a limited time embargo on some information within the submission in order to protect commercial sensitivity such as a pending patent. Confidentiality should never be used to protect participants – there are perfectly legitimate ways of anonymizing data within research reports to offer such protection.

- *Professional and academic knowledge:* The precedence, and occasional exclusionary status, given to so-called academic knowledge is no longer sustainable. Understandings necessary to advance the professions and knowledge within non-traditional, practice-based domains are valid where it can be determined that the basic criteria for what counts as worthwhile 'knowledge' can be met. Again, the notion of what is a significant enough contribution to warrant a doctoral award may differ across areas other than the traditionally 'academic', but nevertheless contribution in the terms of the specific area is what is required.

- *Differing nomenclature and commonality of level:* In our view there is strong argument for using the title of PhD (with no elaboration) for all doctoral awards regardless of the discipline or profession in which they are awarded. However, given the pragmatic need to denote the area in which the studies have fallen for the sake of marketing and for professional status reasons, it seems that there may be an argument that it is reasonable to use titles such as EdD and EngD sparingly. Nomenclature in this sense is, for us, not the prime issue. What is of import, however, is the treatment within institutions of these differing awards in terms of their quality control and regulatory organization.

All doctoral awards should be treated in these respects as being of a kind. Criteria for the awards will differ but they should only differ within parameters and will make reference to the same (doctoral) standard. In essence, there may be different ways to reach the same level – to us route and process are not the issues – what matters is that the doctoral standard can be seen to have been attained.

In pragmatic terms the range of doctorates within a university should be described within a common frame, organized within a common administrative structure and related to criteria that can be readily compared and that are thus transparently of a level or standard. Similarly, the way in which step-off awards are used should have parity across the different doctoral awards. If the MPhil can be used as a step-off award after two years of study on a PhD programme, then there would need to be a clear justification for it *not* similarly being available after two years of an EdD programme. Separating out some doctoral awards for different treatment in any of these respects potentially diminishes them.

- *The place of published work as evidence in doctoral submissions:* In the UK many universities have a separate set of regulations for the 'PhD by Published Work' (Powell 2004). This notion of a distinct award with particular processes and procedures is somewhat anachronistic when much of the rest of Europe works within a model where doctoral submissions comprise previously published works. Indeed, the anachronism is compounded by the fact that many UK universities work to doctoral criteria that explicitly state that the thesis should contain material of 'publishable quality'. Universities offering the separate award to a limited group (typically, staff and alumni – see Powell 2004) risk accusations of insularity.

  The time is right therefore for a reconsideration of regulatory frameworks that at present separate out prior publications with the intention of finding ways of breaking down the barriers between these two separate awards (the PhD and the PhD by Published Work). Published and non-published work should be seen as parts of the same continuum; after all the latter is work not published but judged to be of 'publishable quality'. Again, we refer to what we see as the bedrock of doctoral awards – the criteria. To our understanding, where a judgement is made that the criteria for an award have been met by a candidate, then prior publication of part or all of the evidence that he/she used to demonstrate that this is so is not of concern. Candidates should be supervised in such a way as to help them establish an intellectual position and defend it with appropriate evidence. Whether that evidence is wholly or partially published is not an issue. This is one area of doctoral education – and there are very few – in which the UK can learn to its advantage from some of its European partners.

- *A doctoral award signifying doctoral standard:* Examination at the doctoral level should be solely a matter of judging whether or not the candidate has produced a thesis and sufficient supporting evidence to satisfy the criteria set down for the award. In this interpretation there can be no interim assessments that contribute to the final judgement-making, though there might be assessments that permit progression through phases of study (or facilitate exit with a different award). There cannot be partial doctoral qualifications; it is an all or nothing award.

  Similarly, there cannot be any marks of distinction within the singular category of doctoral award. The award is one of excellence and there cannot be gradations of this superlative. When an institution awards a doctorate with distinction – as a small minority in the UK do – this gives rise to the implausible notion of a doctorate without distinction, a second-rate order of excellence. A doctorate *is* a distinction and to confound this in any way will lead to the kind of difficulty faced in France (see Powell and Green 2007) where to get an 'ordinary' doctorate is seen as a failure by some. In short, the award equates to a level; once a candidate has reached the level it does not matter how far above it they were because the criterion is solely to demonstrate that it has been reached.

- *Transparency of the oral examination:* The oral examination is the context in which the examiners can test out the candidate's intellectual position – his/her thesis – in terms of its contribution to knowledge. The examiners must judge the candidate's ability in marshalling evidence that supports the thesis and his/her understanding of that thesis within the broader intellectual context. The substance of questions in the oral should be constrained by what is included in the criteria for the award; this is not the time to ask questions that relate to matters that are not part of those criteria. Neither is this an opportunity for a final, fine-tuning of the literary presentation of the submission or the reworking of some parts of the research. The thesis should stand or fall on its merits – without amendment except for that which the candidate may offer by way of last minute adjustments *before* the oral examination takes place.

The kind of testing out that we have in mind is best done in as public a forum as possible. Conducting the examination behind closed doors with Byzantine restrictions on who may attend and how attendees may contribute to the examination is counterproductive to its sole aim. Making the oral examination an openly public event will lead to transparency of the process and is more likely to be both fair and rigorous. Such an approach also enhances the general dissemination of research findings.

It is worth noting here that in some countries such as Australia there is no oral examination and that in some parts of Europe it is a very public event designed as a rite of passage rather than an examination in the UK sense of the term, with the outcome firmly established *before* the examination commences. Indeed, the situation with regard to the openness of the doctoral examination in the UK to public scrutiny is distinctive in the world context and in some senses may be seen as idiosyncratic.

- *Doctoral learning and skills:* Coming to operate at the doctoral level within an intellectual discipline(s) is, in part at least, a matter of learning about that discipline(s) by practising research methods that are appropriate to it. Learning from one's own practice in this way is a kind of intellectual behaviour that those operating at the doctoral level will necessarily continue to develop. It is an irrevocable part of being a 'doctor'. Given the critical importance of this continuing sense of learning through practice and thus of self-improvement, the criteria for a doctoral award need to address this kind of continuity of independent, self-developing learning.

It is relatively straightforward to define subject-specific skills with respect to research methods, but it is less so in the case of generic skills. Discussion about how best to develop generic skills programmes is premature and ultimately unsatisfactory if the relationship between them and the doctoral level remains unclear. A generic skill may well be worth having but it is not necessarily a part of doctoral study unless it can be related demonstrably to how an individual may be judged to be operating at a doctoral level within the relevant discipline. As we have suggested earlier, if the skill is not reflected in the criteria for the award, then it should not be part of a programme of study and it should not be part of the doctoral assessment. On the other hand if it is part of the criteria, then the converse applies and it should be part of both the programme and the final assessment. We are suggesting here that much of what is subsumed under the collective term 'generic skills' is not in fact a necessary part of the concept of the doctoral level and therefore should not be a necessary part of the process of doctoral study.

The constant demands for more skills training within the doctorate from various quarters highlight the lack of understanding of the nature, structure and purpose of the doctorate. As a recent report by the UKCGE notes, 'the result is that while there is widespread agreement – particularly among university managers – about the need for, and generic purposes of doctoral research training, thereby is also widespread unease and scepticism – particularly among students and their supervisors – about the value of what is being provided' (UKCGE 2000: 15).

We might also question whether such generic training can be offered at the doctoral level with any kind of real validity. More fundamentally, however, the doctorate for us is not about teaching students how to build rafts or play management games, important as these skills might be to their subsequent employment. It is about meeting the criteria for the award.

What is required, however, is a more rigorous analysis of which generic skills *are* part of the doctoral level. For example, we need to ask if it is reasonable to suggest that anyone holding a doctoral title ought to be able to communicate their ideas effectively in both written and oral form and engage with others from different disciplines in relation to their ideas. Following from this it becomes a matter of embedding those skills that are part of the doctoral standard in the criteria for the award and in turn of finding ways of assessing the candidate's ability to demonstrate them within the final examination. Neither of these steps is impossible or implausible – but current practices typified by allocating so many hours of study to generic training without considering the above are necessarily flawed.

- *A supervised award:* The global tradition has been that doctoral study involves a supervisor who guides, advises or mentors the student through the necessary research project(s). However, the precise role of that supervisor is rarely clearly defined. The role of the supervisor is unique in higher education in that it involves teaching or leading or advising someone towards a goal within a defined intellectual field that when achieved will necessarily change that field or at least people's understandings about aspects of it; and, of course, the contribution potentially affects other, related fields. The supervisor's responsibility is therefore to start the student off in a particular intellectual direction. This is no small matter because it requires of the supervisor both experience and expertise in order to ensure that the trajectory is reasonable both in research terms and in relation to the criteria for the award. The crux of the relationship between student and supervisor, however, is that the student subsequently needs to demonstrate to that supervisor something that the supervisor did not know at the start of the project. The leader becomes the led; the pupil becomes the master. This then is the major challenge for supervisors and needs to be the critical focus for those who train them. The complexity of research and of the task of supervising demands teams rather than individual supervisors as is reflected in the revised QAA Code of Practice (QAA 2004). We have grave concerns about the role of the supervisor as expressed in the recent European Charter, which seems to us to risk undermining much of the work done in the UK in moving supervision away from a master–apprentice model.

- *The form and media of doctoral evidence:* In providing satisfactory evidence to demonstrate that doctoral criteria have been met, the outcomes of the research will be evidenced in a form and media most appropriate to the subject under consideration. All doctoral submissions should involve the development of an intellectual argument that in its questions and conclusions contributes to knowledge, though the evidence that this argument draws upon will vary according to discipline. The kinds of evidence used to support such an argument and the way they are presented for examination may involve words, formulae, artefacts, actions and may be cast as hypotheses and/or interpretive, non-deductive analyses and so on. Within these variations, what is constant is that the research questions are appropriately matched by type of analysis and kind of presentational format and media. Following from the above, questions over the format of submission, that is, traditional thesis or portfolio, are misleading. What is important is that the candidate marshals evidence to defend his/her position – if a portfolio is an appropriate way of presenting evidence then it must be acceptable. It is for the candidate ultimately to choose, and subsequently defend, the mode of presentation of evidence. In so choosing, the candidate must be clear that because of the need for the examiners to assess his/her development as a researcher, the submission must make overt that development; that is, the process as well as the outcomes must be available for scrutiny.

- *What counts as a doctorate:* There is clear guidance on what counts as a doctorate at the national level in the UK. The level of doctoral outcomes must relate to the national guidelines as set out in the Framework for Higher Education Qualifications (FHEQ). There it is stated, 'Doctorates are awarded for the creation and interpretation of knowledge, which extends the forefront of a discipline, usually through original research. Holders of doctorates will be able to conceptualise, design and implement projects for the generation of significant new knowledge and/or understanding' (QAA 2001a). It is worth noting in relation to some of our earlier discussion that this statement does not distinguish between kinds of doctorate (that is, there is no separate description for professional doctorates or for the 'PhD by Published Work'); this is the UK doctoral standard and therefore applies to all doctoral awards in the UK. An award where the candidate does not have to give evidence of a continuing ability to contribute to the field in question is at a lesser standard and should not carry the title of doctor. Any diminishing of this principle is likely to lead to an underevaluation of the UK doctorate as a whole by those from overseas.

Conclusion

In this chapter we have tried to set down observations about the PhD as it exists in the UK today and some analyses of related current issues, such as generic skills training. Following our attempts to better understand the current position of the UK doctorate, we are left unsure about the underpinning of its status. This may be unwarranted, as the doctoral award has changed over time and clearly it will change further in the future.

But it is clear to us that the issues facing the award (and however one argues about the detail, it does seem indisputable that issues of significance do exist) need to be addressed in a coherent, unifying way if the UK is to retain a system of doctoral education that can sustain its position in the increasingly competitive global context. Other countries are facing a similar dilemma and we need in the first instance to look at the models of review they are adopting (see Powell and Green 2007). But who has the authority to undertake this work? The last thing that we would wish to encourage is another group tinkering at the margins with little or no authority in relationship to students, sponsors, universities or funders.

14

The Impact of the Changing European Higher Education Landscape on Doctoral Studies

Tim Birtwistle

Introduction

Some might be tempted to believe that a national system of higher education will continue to exist untainted by foreign influences or unchallenged by foreign systems. However, the reality of globalization exists for higher education just as much as it does for other sectors and certainly just as much, if not in some ways more, for doctoral studies.

The landscape of higher education in the United Kingdom is more open to external policies and influences than at any time in its history. The forces of global competition for funds, staff and students are increasingly apparent. The competence of the European Union (EU) in higher education is felt as is the less structured but in many ways more pervasive participation by all parts of the United Kingdom in the development of the European Higher Education Area (EHEA) (the Bologna Process). The European Commission communication 'Delivering on the Modernisation Agenda' (2006) regarding education, research and innovation sets the agenda, whilst highlighting that within the EU there are 4000 institutions, over 17 million students, 1.5 million staff of whom 435,000 are researchers. Given that the PhD as a research degree had its origins in Europe (Park 2005a), it is not surprising that it is included in the European change agenda. The title 'doctor' dates back to the late twelfth century when the University of Bologna granted the title Doctor in Civil Law, but the notion of the research degree probably emerged as late as the nineteenth century in Germany with a swifter adoption of its principles in the US than across Europe. With competition, mobility and the calls for transparency (to enable a like to like comparison) complacency is misplaced.

The world is smaller now in terms of ease of mobility, and those who have transferable skills may well seek to earn their living in different places, driven by money, research resources, academic freedom, lifestyle and so on. People will also seek to gain the skills necessary to achieve their career goals from the best possible place (Avveduto 2000). According to the OECD (2003) non-nationals make up a substantial proportion of doctoral candidates in many countries; for the UK it is more than 33 per cent of the 25,000 plus total number, for the US it is 27 per cent of a total of 79,000 registrations. Mobility is an issue with a push-and-pull effect, and a loss of intellectual capacity acts to the detriment of any economy.

The Bologna Process context

On 25 May 1998 the ministers responsible for higher education in France, Germany, Italy and the UK signed the Sorbonne Joint Declaration. It is this that opened the Pandora's Box now known as the Bologna Process (Bologna 2005), leading to the creation of the EHEA by 2010. This is a pan-European initiative based on ministerial meetings with no treaty structure and each country implementing the proposals in their own particular way, some with legislation (for example, Italy) and others without (for example, the UK, although devolution has made the landscape of higher education more intricate and less uniform, if it ever were uniform).

The text of Sorbonne is much less frequently quoted or referred to than subsequent communiqués of ministerial meetings that have set the strategy and marked down the milestones for the journey to achieve the EHEA. However, there are some essential points noted by Sorbonne, including reference to a system based on two cycles using credits and structured around semesters. The second cycle is the graduate one and includes a 'shorter master's degree and a longer doctor's degree' with an emphasis on 'research and autonomous work'. So we have a reference to doctoral studies at this early point in the Bologna Process; however, after this came the Bologna Declaration of 19 June 1999 with 29 signatory states and a greater emphasis on broader issues whilst still including the two cycles and credits. This introduction of new and wider aims, for example, the social dimension and higher education as a public good, was continued with the Prague Ministerial conference in May 2001 (plus four new signatory states).

In September 2003 the Berlin Ministerial Conference took place. The number of signatory states increased to 40 (Scotland having its own seat at the table for the first time) and a much greater emphasis came to the fore on research and links to the European Research Area (ERA). The 'third cycle' was created with an overt reference to doctoral studies.

Participants in Bologna now include the Council of Europe, European Student Union Body (ESIB) and the European University Association (EUA). All, in their different ways, stress the twin focal points of teaching and research in higher education with, for example, the Council of Europe's project on The Heritage of European Universities and the recommendation of the Council of Europe's Council of Ministers on the Research Mission of the Universities. The Berlin Communiqué states:

> Conscious of the need to promote closer links between the EHEA and the ERA in a Europe of Knowledge, and of the importance of research as an integral part of higher education across Europe, Ministers consider it necessary to go beyond the present focus on two main cycles of higher education to include the doctoral level as the third cycle in the Bologna Process. They emphasise the importance of research and research training and the promotion of interdisciplinarity in maintaining and improving the quality of higher education and in enhancing the competitiveness of European higher education more generally. Ministers call for increased mobility at the doctoral and postdoctoral levels and encourage the institutions concerned to increase their cooperation in doctoral studies and the training of young researchers.
>
> Ministers will make the necessary effort to make European Higher Education Institutions an even more attractive and efficient partner. Therefore Ministers ask Higher Education Institutions to increase the role and relevance of research to technological, social and cultural evolution and to the needs of society.
>
> Ministers understand that there are obstacles inhibiting the achievement of these goals and these cannot be resolved by Higher Education Institutions alone. It requires strong support, including financial and appropriate decisions from national Governments and European Bodies.
>
> Finally, Ministers state that networks at doctoral level should be given support to stimulate the development of excellence and to become one of the hallmarks of the European Higher Education Area . . .
>
> Berlin Communiqué (2003)

The central importance of research and the pivotal role of doctoral candidates in forming a core of young researchers to enable Europe to achieve the objectives of the Lisbon Agenda regarding a knowledge-based economy were recognized. What was needed next was the investment of GDP necessary to match that of the US to allow these objectives a chance to succeed. Words, one might say, are cheap; the investment of a total of 3 per cent of GDP into research is without doubt expensive (especially when moving from a figure barely above 1 per cent in many cases). Nonetheless, the stated aim is 3 per cent of GDP – time will tell, but progress to date does not raise expectations.

In May 2005 the Bergen ministerial meeting confirmed the objectives, increased the number of signatory states to 45 and set specific implementation targets for London 2007. A major goal is the adoption of an overarching framework of qualifications for the EHEA coupled with a commitment to the development of national qualifications frameworks by 2010. In 'A Framework for Qualifications of The European Higher Education Area'

(February 2005), the third cycle is clearly defined in terms of outcomes with no credit attached. In England the Burgess Consultation Paper (March 2006) recommends that Level D in the English Framework be numbered Level 8; this is to increase transparency and to make mapping across to the European Qualifications Framework easier.

The third cycle is firmly on the agenda for the Bologna Process. It is also a feature on all the qualifications frameworks, articulated in terms of learning outcomes but normally without credit attached to it, although some systems do allocate credit, as does Burgess for Level D (8) with taught elements (for example, a DBA, but not for PhD or DPhil). The EUA has undertaken a major investigation into doctoral programmes (EUA 2005) and Eurodoc (2004) has gathered evidence regarding supervision and training.

Analysis of the varied provision that falls under the banner of the third cycle is taking place. Mobility of researchers and research funds demands greater transparency of doctoral and postdoctoral provision. The potential for being misled by what appears to be something familiar, the title 'doctor', is immense. The knowledge of the diverse range of provision that is the capstone element of studies is required, as is participating in the moves to transparency. It is essential to help shape the future rather than having to react to what the future brings.

The Lisbon Agenda

In March 2000, the EU heads of state and governments agreed to make the EU 'the most competitive and dynamic knowledge-driven economy by 2010'. This is the so-called Lisbon Agenda (also known as the Lisbon Strategy, Lisbon Process and the Lisbon Objectives). The realization that such an objective could only be achieved by investment in research that in turn would lead to 'growth and jobs' was apparent.

Whether the objectives can be met by 2010 is increasingly in doubt. As Commission President Barroso (2005) said: 'the future has changed. It is time to rethink the Lisbon strategy . . . Creating . . . [a] "Europe of Opportunities" is what I think the Lisbon Agenda should be about'.

A mid-term review of the Lisbon Agenda took place in March 2005 focusing on the speed of progress (or rather lack of it) and the causes of this. 'The Lisbon Scorecard V – Can Europe compete?' (Murray and Wanlin 2005) is one analysis of the different speeds at which different member states are moving.

The Lisbon Agenda has been a force behind the Bologna Process, and in line with the Lisbon Strategy one of the aims of Bologna is to increase the attractiveness of European higher education and research and thus foster competitiveness of the European knowledge economy. This further strengthens the links between the EU and the Bologna Process. Investment in research and development is needed and for this to take place the prerequisite is investment in cerebral capital and research capability.

The European Research Area

For the EU there is the link between the Lisbon Agenda and the European Research Area (ERA).

In June 2004 the commission adopted the communication 'Science and technology: the key to Europe's future' which, amongst many other things, recommended a doubling of the EU research budget to around € 10 billion a year from 2007 to 2013. As with the pledge to increase investment in R&D to 3 per cent of GDP, there is a gap between rhetoric and reality. Once again the link between the principles, objectives and strategy of the EU and Bologna is made apparent. However, the stark fact is that the EU lags behind both Japan and the US by, at a conservative estimate, at least one percentage point of GDP. On top of this there is the rapidly emerging challenge from, amongst others, China and India.

The links

The macro context within which higher education is operating for universities based in the EU is set by national policies sitting within EU policies including the ERA. Overarching this EU dimension is the Bologna Process. The EU is a major player in Bologna in terms of having 25 (28 counting the European Economic Area) of the 45 signatory states and contributing to the strategic development. The EUA participates in all areas of policy analysis and acts as a pressure group/lobbyist for its members.

The EUA Graz Declaration (2003) stated:

> Universities advocate a Europe of knowledge, based on a strong research capacity and research-based education in universities – singly and in partnership – across the continent.

> European universities are active on a global scale, contributing to innovation and sustainable economic development.

The Salzburg Seminar (2005) on 'Doctoral Programmes for the European Knowledge Society' established a set of ten basic principles for the third cycle set within the fundamental recognition of the need for a link between the EHEA and the ERA. The headlines of these principles are:

1   The core component of doctoral training is the advancement of knowledge through original research
2   Embedding in institutional strategies and policies
3   The importance of diversity
4   Doctoral candidates as early stage researchers
5   The crucial role of supervision and assessment
6   Achieving critical mass
7   Duration
8   The promotion of innovative structures

9   Increasing mobility
10 Ensuring appropriate funding

This shows the complete commitment to research as a fundamental component of the very essence of being a university; this is not always the case in practice (Birtwistle 2003). However, the EUA established the Doctoral Programmes Project (2005), acknowledging the growing significance of the third cycle in Bologna after the Berlin Communiqué (2003); the purpose of the report is to provide 'a broad view of the current landscape of doctoral programmes in Europe'. To this end the findings of the project, albeit based on 48 institutions in a very varied landscape, provide a rich source of information. Alongside this can be viewed the evidence put forward in the Eurodoc paper (2004) and then the European Commission recommendation (2005) on the Charter for Researchers.

Doctoral programmes for the European Knowledge Society (EUA 2005)

The introduction to this chapter firmly places its context within Bologna post-Berlin whilst at the same time emphasizing that doctoral studies are the 'first phase of the young researcher's career'. The road to the 2007 London Ministerial Meeting clearly follows the direction laid down by the Bergen communiqué with the 'ten basic principles' for the third cycle. Forty-eight universities (including seven from England and one from Scotland) from 22 countries participated in the study for the project which had three core strands to it, namely: the structure and organisation of doctoral studies; supervision, monitoring and assessment; and mobility, European collaboration and joint doctoral degrees.

Doctoral programmes follow many different paths, but perhaps can be broadly categorized as either:

- an individual study programme based on an informal to formal working alliance between a supervisor and a doctoral candidate (an apprenticeship model, sometimes described as 'master–slave' relationship) with no structured coursework phase;

or

- a structured programme organized within research groups or research/graduate/doctoral schools with two phases: a taught phase (mandatory and voluntary courses or modules) and a research phase.

The report then questions the validity and appropriateness of the individual doctoral programme 'to meet the new multiple challenges of research training' whilst acknowledging that, especially in some disciplines, it is still the dominant model. That is certainly the case in the UK and other

Bologna signatory states, for example, Germany (Thaller 2006). The report cites good practice at University College London (UCL) with its use of a Graduate School and the 'offer' of training in, *inter alia*, transferable skills. The importance of the provision of training in core research skills as well as generic personal and professional skills is emphasized. The notion of the point of transition from MPhil to PhD does not seem to be recognized except in the context of part-time doctoral studies. In the analysis of recruitment it is recognized that it is an 'increasing trend' for research Masters programmes to act as an entry point – however, the idea of registration after study and after the point of transition is not mentioned.

The case studies used to evidence good practice (including UCL above) might highlight the fact that the evidence base for the report is provided by a self-assessment through the use of strengths, weaknesses, opportunities, and threats (SWOT) analysis rather than an external audit of systems, procedures and policy. Could the proximity of the assessor to their own operating circumstances affect the perception and final analysis?

The use of the Doctoral Contract is suggested as good practice. It seems that this is in effect a tripartite agreement between the candidate, the supervisor and the university (sometimes represented by the head of the home department, sometimes the director of the graduate school and sometimes both). The purpose of the agreement is to define the rights and obligations of the parties in terms of intellectual property rights, provision of infrastructure and services, any taught course requirements, the rules of the thesis and so on. Would this ensure a minimization of disputes? Main areas of dispute include a falling out between supervisor and candidate and the requirement for the university to ensure continuity of supervision in the event of the original supervisor, for whatever reason, becoming unavailable. Certainly, in recent times, first, the visitor, then Office of the Independent Adjudicator, and the courts, have been involved in such disputes.

Given the context of the report (Bologna), it is not surprising that notions of mobility, mobility of funding, joint degrees and ultimately a 'European doctorate' emerge. Straightforward mobility (horizontal mobility, spending a period of research time at a host university) does not pose too many problems that are outside the normal reference points of obligations and liability for mobility. The problem is a logistical one for the part-time candidate requiring leave of absence from the workplace to undertake the period at the host university. Mobility of funding causes greater problems, especially if this is in terms of research grants and also in terms of supervision. Joint degrees pose a problem to some legal jurisdictions (possibly to many UK universities because their charter may well not specifically permit such activity), although joint certification of the activity may well be possible, but does it really add value? In any case details of study will be shown on the Diploma Supplement.

The notion of an overarching qualification that is supranational has been mooted at various levels and times. In this context the proposal for a Doctor Europaeus dates back to 1991. The concept has developed so that a minimum set of criteria does exist, including that the thesis is reviewed by a professor from the home university plus two professors from two other universities from two other countries; at least one member of the jury shall come from a different European country than that of the home institution; a part of the thesis defence must be made in one of the official EU languages other than that of the country of the home institution; and at least one trimester of study must have taken place in another European country. Will this idea become a reality in any meaningful way? This will depend upon a number of things, which include any legal impediments (who will give the title?); and whether there is a market demand for such a rather complex and expensive commodity (both demand from candidates and from employers).

The report continues to analyse the doctoral process and to attempt to identify good practice from the 48 universities.

On 11 March 2005 the European Commission published its Recommendation on the European Charter for Researchers and on a Code of Conduct for the Recruitment of Researchers under its competence from Article 165 EC Treaty. This is firmly within the Lisbon Agenda and the objectives of research and development. The possible conflation of the EUA report and the Commission recommendation may lead to changes to the third cycle and may also lead to some uncomfortable collisions between national norms and traditions and what is viewed as the way to the future. Are doctoral candidates employees, or are they candidates who may have a contract of employment for, for example, teaching duties? What is the future of the individual study programme? Can single-country third cycle awards continue to provide what the market wants? What is the career outlet that doctoral candidates perceive as their natural destination (academe or industry/commerce)? (Ackers 2005)

The view of the European Council of PhD candidates and junior researchers (Eurodoc)

Not surprisingly, Eurodoc has a view about the management, structure, supervision, cost and future of the third cycle. In the recommendations for the organization of Core Research Career Structures in academia (2006) the position is put forth that researchers are professionals and therefore need a career structure with 'defined requirement profiles and clear duties'. This builds on the gathering of evidence undertaken by Eurodoc (2004), which again links into the EUA work and the EU Commission Charter. The evidence unfortunately groups the UK as a single educational system but clearly reaches the conclusion that the third cycle is not rude with health and needs to address issues such as supervision and better training for the candidates in research methods and transferable skills. This perhaps ignores the changes that have been put into place (Roberts 2002). The problem of critical mass for the delivery of training and the cost to the university for providing it is looked at by the EUA with illustrations of partnerships and regional consortia. However, there is the underlying problem of rivalry and competing for a limited number of candidates both internationally and regionally (Reichert 2005).

Conclusion

The microscope is focused on higher education and its role and value to society. The Bologna Process continues to move forward and the third cycle (doctoral cycle) is (post-Berlin 2003) firmly a part of the qualifications framework. Other areas of the world are also reviewing their provision, aims, outcomes and costs. The Australian March 2005 'Framework for Best Practice in Doctoral Education in Australia' stated that 'Research is the fundamental substance of a doctorate and any person who has earned a doctorate should be expected to have undertaken a period of research education leading to the successful design, implementation, analysis, theorizing and writing of research that makes a significant and original contribution to knowledge' (DDOGS 2005). The match between the 10 Salzburg Principles and the 16 headings in the Australian Best Practice grid is great.

A similar exercise has been ongoing in the US since 1995 with the National Research Council (National Research Council 1995) analysing the changing size and structure of research-doctorates in the US. In 1999 the University of Washington undertook 're-envisioning the PhD'.[1] In 1990 the Carnegie Institute initiated a longitudinal study and analysis of US doctoral programmes (Carnegie 1990 and updaters); this is ongoing.

Will the independent study programme survive? This is the dominant method for undertaking doctoral studies in universities in the UK, yet most commentaries cast doubt about its wider acceptance. In an age of transparency with an agenda apparently led by rights, the opportunity for a misuse of power and abuse of authority plus a perceived lack of training in core skills leads to a strong possibility that this mode will be marginalized. The academic world is global: perhaps more global than the commercial world, and as such a high level of acceptance of the capstone academic award must be a requirement of those undertaking such research. If the drive around the world is for doctoral candidates to undertake some more formal training (more formal than suggested by Roberts), then this will drive change. Those who obtain a doctorate will seek careers across a broad range of geographic and sectoral opportunities; the market will demand global acceptance. Bologna, the EU, the Lisbon Agenda and global competitive forces will impact all systems. To ignore these forces would be foolhardy.

Note

1 http://www.grad.washington.edu/envision/index.html (accessed 15th May 2007).

15

The Challenges Ahead

Richard Hinchcliffe, Tony Bromley and Steve Hutchinson

Market forces

This book has tried to raise debate over a number of key areas that influence well beyond the politics and practice of research training. Much of the debate concerns, at its heart, the PhD itself and how the research degree is a crucial entry gate into all sorts of elites, including, of course, academia itself. Within a buoyant economy but with high levels of student debt, potential research students must ask themselves the question: 'Is it still worthwhile to do a research degree?' The answer to this question is surely life changing for the individual, but it is also a crucial question that the sector urgently needs to address. Four years after *Set for Success* the concerns around recruitment are becoming increasingly critical: 'In addition to losing quality people to other sectors there is growing concern that the UK is failing to generate its own recruitment pool as the volume and quality of "home grown" students making the transition into doctoral and post-doctoral research is perceived to be in decline' (Ackers et al. 2006).

The intrinsic value of a PhD could be financial in terms of increased salary after the PhD which would outweigh the costs of studying for an extra three years. Pay, both for the PhD and after in terms of a research career, is a factor, but Ackers et al. have identified that this is associated not just with competitiveness but also with 'adequacy' (Ackers et al. 2006: 7). In other words, early career researchers are concerned with the quality of life they may experience in their early career. They must question the vocational aspect: 'will the skills I get from this process make me more employable?', or consider their status: 'will being a *Doctor* make me more employable?'. It is therefore time for the sector to unilaterally engage with a series of questions relating to what a PhD *actually* offers. Thus, are the knowledge, skills, behaviours and attitudes of a PhD graduate truly fit for purpose? Is the current form of the British PhD (regardless of the skills training components) sufficient to compete on a global playing field? Even ignoring the employability agenda, is the current form of the PhD and associated skills training truly sufficient preparation for the forthcoming generations of academics? Is the Joint Skills Statement still fit for purpose, less than five years after it was agreed? Do our researchers truly come up to scratch in the knowledge economy-focussed employability climate?

The universities, Research Councils and OST believe that this agenda has moved quickly forward, but we have far to go. Rosie Sotillo, chief European recruiter for Barclays Bank, has said that they no longer sought PhD recruits from Britain with the necessary high computational and mathematical skills but instead preferred American research graduates (*Profiting from Postgraduate Talent*, the UK GRAD National Conference, September 2006). Ackers et al. also note that some PIs (though not all – it depends on the subject area) are noting the lack of talent coming through to do PhDs. This is perhaps a consequence of UK research degrees being unsuited to a strong economy. Postgraduate degrees of all kinds have traditionally been seen by graduates as a means by which they can increase their employability while there is an economic downturn. In the past decade of continuous economic growth universities have begun to see a downturn in UK domiciled students going on to do a PhD (about 3 per cent over the past 3 years). While this has been offset by numbers of international candidates, such a trend is clearly unsustainable as developing countries create their own higher degree infrastructure and other factors have now seen a downturn in international postgraduate numbers. Rather than seeing a decline in the quality of UK graduates coming through to do postgraduate or postdoctoral work, Ackers et al. suggest that 'it might not be that UK applicants are declining per se, but that the pool of UK applicants prepared to accept the risks of an insecure and poorly paid research career is declining' (Ackers et al. 2006: 27).

Beyond these questions there are other fundamental areas to address, particularly in terms of part-time research degrees. In an increasingly debt ridden age, for many a part-time PhD is the only viable alternative, and as Alistair McCulloch and Peter Stokes (Chapter 4) point out the part-time PhD for those who have retired is losing its lustre and appeal when they are forced through the quality bureaucracy and training that is aimed towards the average young researcher full-time science PhD. Given all these factors, universities have to re-think the PhD as a commodity for a world where the use of traditional definitions and vague cultural assumptions as to what constitutes a research degree can no longer suffice as a marketing tool.

The next generation of academics

Currently, the skills agenda is arguably central to postgraduate 'thinking' from the policy makers and governmental funding bodies. However (in spite of all of the good practice highlighted in this book), at the grass roots of the faculty and departmental committees, research group meetings and supervisory conversations – is the skills agenda *really* key to academic thinking and policy making? Many of those involved in implementing and developing the skills agenda within universities would argue that it is not. Why should a committee of academics – highly successful within their field – and never 'trained' outside their own discipline research specific techniques (and then perhaps only as an 'apprentice' to their own supervisor) – opt for an institution to truly engage with the skills development agenda? However, committees at all levels are engaging with the skills agenda for research students and postdocs due to the incentives created by the Roberts report and beyond. As these reasons for engagement filter through to supervisor level, hearts and minds are being obliged to change. These reasons often have much to do with the securing of future research funding, and colleagues are used to jumping through the hoops required by grant funding of research.

In order to consider the likelihood of change within the sector at all levels, has there been any change in the newest young crop of academics that have been exposed to formal and professional training and development? This is a distinctly difficult concept to measure – but it is not an issue that the sector seems desperate to engage with.

So, will the next generation of academics empathize more with a developmental agenda? If their experience today of skills training is a positive one, and current research students realize a positive benefit of training, then the development agenda can expect ongoing and continued support. If their current experience is poor and they deem no value to have come from the time they may see as being 'away from the research', then no amount of policy directives will change the realities at the coalface. As such, today's developers carry a huge responsibility.

So, let us assume for a moment that the training of today has a positive impact on the academics of tomorrow. This change may of course manifest itself in the form of increased research and professional skills. However, in order for there to be a true cultural shift, can we see any evidence of changes in behaviour, viewpoints and attitudes generally? (And how would we measure and quantify these changes?)

As a framework to build our training programmes, perhaps a useful starting exercise might be to speculate and consider the successful academic of tomorrow and their various required strengths and attributes:

- External, rather than internal focus
- Full involvement in the knowledge transfer agenda
- Carry out interdisciplinary research or researching on the cusps of their discipline where traditionally separate areas of research meet
- Able to pursue a more diverse careers and cross borders and divides into industry/public sector/private sector and (most vitally) back to academia again
- Fully embracing communications technology to facilitate cross-institutional/multinational research
- Working 'for' a university, rather than 'at' one
- Competent people managers, able to lead and properly support their research teams

- Engagement with continued professional development with a mentor and personal development plan
- Overlapping duties include supporting so-called academic related areas
- Critically minded, with good understanding of the epistemological basis of the subject discipline and its place in the history of knowledge as a whole.

Many of today's academics may tick these boxes and be rewarded for their plurality and professional approach. However, for many academics, to achieve these strengths and attributes will require more than a single step. It will require involvement and the effective implementation of management resources at all levels. In this regard, skills training for research students has a vital role to play for the twenty-first century university in that not only does it directly attempt to align those who enter into academia, but it also helps to pump prime future university partners from industry and bridge the divide.

If institutions want to engage with, and retain, their academic staff, it is perhaps incumbent on them that they foster a different level of commitment than that which is currently driven by subject loyalty. While colleagues are being asked to engage with training initiatives on teamwork, mentoring and good people management as part of the Roberts agenda, perhaps it is incumbent upon institutions to look at their own human resource processes. What should be important here is to emphasize the communal aspect of the university as a place where colleagues can feel a sense of belonging, where teamwork is not only valued but consciously recognized; only then perhaps will the issues over training hit home with the academic community. As Archer notes, '[f]rom gardener to governor, each university is home to a very diverse group of people. Interviewees [for Archer's report] described how, in the past, people joined a university as a conscious alternative to the world outside. Today's universities we are told are client-focused, customer-centric, outward-facing. Everybody matters' (Archer 2005: 17). Does the Joint Skills Statement address these matters or does it require reformulating to take into account the future needs of academia in the information age? This is a question that is now starting to exercise the minds of all those involved in the research degree process.

Research student developers, being the principal part of an initiative that is designed to change the research environment, need to reflect the attributes and skills of the best academics. Their academic related posts are often filled by PhD researchers who have moved away from the pure research path but who recognized that fulfilment and job satisfaction rewards can be gained whilst continuing to contribute to the research environment. Many of them are externally focused, embrace the knowledge transfer agenda and are highly skilled in the interpersonal elements required to lead a department or group. Yet, within the sector they are often not valued in the same way as colleagues who are 'pure' academics.

Given the kudos derived from contributions to the research assessment exercise, this attitude is not surprising; however, it is beginning to change in the face of skills programmes for research students making a significant difference to the likelihood of successful research funding applications. Research student developers, we surmise, have a crucial role to play in determining the future make-up of academic culture. The major tool organizations use in order to change effectively is through their recruitment of staff. We are not gatekeepers in the same way as heads of department when appointing staff, but we contribute strongly through alerting individuals to the make-up of the academic environment, the skills that are required to survive and thrive within it and, importantly, the skills required to change it.

In order to effect change therefore we must first remove the veil from our own eyes. Maybe the key to winning the hearts and minds of the cynics is by ensuring that an essential facet of a training and development professional within higher education is that we remain research active. Is training content right? Do we need to think again?

Bibliography

Ackers, L., Oliver, L., Gill, B. and Guth, J. (2005) The Role of the Doctorate in the Junior Research Career – Developments in the UK, Paper delivered at Doctoral Programmes for the European Knowledge Society, EUA Bologna Seminar, Salzburg, February.

Ackers, H. L., Gill, B., Groves K. and Oliver, E. (2006) Assessing the Impact of the Roberts' Review Enhanced Stipends and Salaries on Postgraduate and Postdoctoral Positions, Reports for RCUK. Available at http://www.rcuk.ac.uk/cmsweb/downloads/rcuk/researchcareers/salariesstipends.pdf (accessed 15th May 2007).

AHRC (Arts and Humanities Research Council) (2007) Postgraduate Career Tracking. Available at http://www.ahrc.ac.uk/about/ke/evaluation/pg_career_tracking.asp (accessed 4 April 2007).

Alliger, G. and Janak, E. (1989) Kirkpatrick's levels of training criteria: thirty years later, *Personal Psychology*, 42(2): 331–42.

Archer, W. (2005) *Mission Critical? Modernising Human Resource Management in Higher Education*. Oxford: Higher Education Policy Institute.

Aronson, J., Fried, C. B. and Good, C. (2002) Reducing the effects of stereotype threat on African American students by shaping theories of intelligence, *Journal of Experimental Social Psychology*, 38: 113–25.

Aspin, L. and Aspin, S. (2006) Embedded value in postgraduate training. Unpublished paper, University of East Anglia.

Avveduto, S. (2000) International mobility of PhDs. Available at www.oecd.org/dataoecd/33/49/2096794.pdf (accessed 20 October 2006).

Bandura, A. (1986) *Social Foundations of Thought and Action*. Englewood Cliffs, NJ: Prentice Hall.

Bandura, A. (1997) *Self-Efficacy: The Exercise of Control*. New York: Freeman.

Barnett, R. (2000) University knowledge in an age of supercomplexity, *Higher Education*, 40(4): 409–22.

Barnett, R. and Temple, P. (2006) *Impact on Space of Future Changes in Higher Education*. London: UK Higher Education Space Management Group.

Barroso, M. (2005) The 2005 Robert Schuman Lecture for the Lisbon Council, Brussels, 14 March.

Barry, C. (1997) Information skills for an electronic world: training doctoral research students, *Journal of Information Science*, 23(3): 225–38.

Becher, T., Henkel, M. and Kogan, M. (1994) *Graduate Education in Britain.* London: Jessica Kingsley.

Bee, F. and Bee, R. (1994) *Training Needs Analysis.* London: IPD.

Berlin Communiqué (2003) Realising the European Higher Education Area. http://www.bologna-berlin2003.de/pdf/Communique1.pdf (accessed 9th May 2007)

Biggs, M. (2002) The role of artefact in art and design research, *International Journal of Design Sciences and Technology*, 10(2): 19–24.

Birtwistle, T. (2003) What is a university?, *The English Patient Journal of Education and the Law*, 15(3): 227–37.

Blaxter, L., Hughes, C. and Tight, M. (1998) Telling it how it is: accounts of academic life, *Higher Education Quarterly*, 52(3): 300–15.

Bologna (2005) U.K. presidency website and full documentation. Available at www.dfes.gov.uk/bologna/

Boud, D. and Walker, D. (1993) Barriers to reflection on experience, in D. Boud, R. Cohen and D. Walker (eds) *Using Experience for Learning.* Buckingham: Open University Press.

Boud, D., Keogh, R. and Walker, D. (eds) (1985) *Reflection: Turning Experience into Learning.* London: Kogan Page.

Boud, D., Keogh, R. and Walker, D. (1996) Promoting reflection in learning, in R. Edwards, A. Hanson and P. Raggatt (eds) *Boundaries of Adult Learning.* London: Routledge.

Bourner, T., Bowden, R. and Laing, S. (1999) A national profile of research degree awards: innovation, clarity and coherence, *Higher Education Quarterly*, 53(3): 264–80.

Bourner, T., Bowden, R. and Laing, S. (2001) Professional doctorates in England, *Studies in Higher Education*, 26(1): 65–83.

Bradbury, M. (1975) *The History Man.* London: Secker & Warburg.

Bramley, P. (2003) *Evaluating Training*, 2nd edn. London: Chartered Institute of Personnel and Development.

Bromley, A. P., Boran, J. R. and Myddleton, W. A. (2007) Investigating the baseline skills of research students using a competency based self-assessment method, *Active Learning in Higher Education*, 8(2): 117–37.

Brookfield, S. (1986) *Understanding and Facilitating Adult Learning.* Milton Keynes: Open University Press.

Burgess, R. G., Band, S. and Pole, C. J. (1998) Developments in postgraduate education and training in the UK, *European Journal of Education*, 33(2): 145–59.

Chiang, Kuang-Hsu (2003) Learning experiences of doctoral students in UK universities, *International Journal of Sociology and Social Policy*, 23(1) and (2): 4–32.

CIRGE (Center for Innovation and Research in Graduate education) (2005) Forces and forms of change in doctoral education internationally. Proceedings of Conference on Innovations in Doctoral Education, CIRGE, University of Washington, Seattle. Available at http://www.depts.washington.edu/cirgecon/ (accessed 14 September 2006).

Coate, K., Barnett, R. and Williams, G. (2001) Relationships between teaching and research in higher education in England, *Higher Education Quarterly*, 55: 158 ff.

Coffield, F., Moseley, D., Hall, E. and Ecclestone, K. (2004) *Should We Be Using Learning Styles? What Research Has to Say to Practice.* London: Learning and Skills Research Centre.

Collinson, J. A. (2005) Artistry and balance: student experiences of UK practice-based doctorates in art and design, *International Journal of Qualitative Studies in Education*, 18(6): 713–28.

Combe, C. (2005) Developing and implementing an online doctoral programme, *International Journal of Educational Management*, 19(2): 118–27.

Council of the European Union (1999) Council Directive 1999/70/EC of 28 June 1999 concerning the framework agreement on fixed-term work concluded by ETUC, UNICE and CEEP, *Official Journal of the European Communities*, L 175, 10/07/1999: 43–8.

Crace, J. (2005) Punch the clock, *The Guardian*, Tuesday 24 May. Available at http://education.guardian.co.uk/specialreports/lecturerspay/story/0,,1490462,00.html (accessed 1 October 2006).

CROS (Careers in Research Online Survey) (2005) Available at www.cros.ac.uk (accessed 15 October 2006).

CROS (2006) *Careers in Research On-line Survey*. Bristol: ILRT Survey Unit. Available at www.cros.ac.uk (accessed 9 August 2006).

Cryer, P. (1998) Transferable skills, marketability and lifelong learning: the particular case of postgraduate research students, *Studies in Higher Education*, 23(2): 207–16.

Cryer, P. (2000) *The Research Student's Guide to Success*, 2nd edn. Buckingham: Open University Press.

Daines, J., Daines, C. and Graham, B. (2002). *Adult Learning, Adult Teaching*, 3rd edn. Cardiff: Welsh Academic Press.

Daudelin, M. W. (1996) Learning from experience through reflection, *Organizational Dynamics*, 24(3): 36–48.

DDOGS (Council of Deans and Directors of Graduate Studies in Australia) (2005) Framework for Best Practice in Doctoral Education in Australia. Available at http://www.ddogs.edu.au/cgi-bin/papers.pl?cmd=d&fid=33422 (accessed 20 October 2006).

Dearing, R. (1997) *Higher Education in the Learning Society*. London: National Committee of Enquiry into Higher Education. Available at http://www.leeds.ac.uk/educol/ncihe/ (accessed 15 October 2006).

Deem, R. (1998) 'New managerialism' and higher education: the management of performances and cultures in universities in the United Kingdom, *International Studies in Sociology of Education*, 8(1): 47–70.

Deem, R. (2004) The knowledge worker, the manager-academic and the contemporary UK university: new and old forms of public management?, *Financial Accountability & Management*, 20(2): 107–28.

Deem, R. and Brehony, K. (2000) Doctoral students' access to research cultures: are some more unequal than others?, *Studies in Higher Education*, 25(2): 149–65.

Delamont, S., Atkinson, P. and Parry, O. (1997) Critical mass and doctoral research: reflections on the Harris report, *Studies in Higher Education*, 22(3): 319–31.

Delamont, S., Atkinson, P. and Parry, O. (2004) *Supervising the Doctorate: A Guide to Success*, 2nd edn. Maidenhead: Open University Press.

Denicolo, P. (2003) Assessing the PhD: a constructive view of criteria, *Quality Assurance in Education*, 11(2): 84–91.

DfES (Department for Education and Skills) (2003) The Future of Higher Education. Available at http://www.dfes.gov.uk/hegateway/strategy/hestrategy (accessed 30 October 2006).

Dinham, S. and Scott, C. (1999) *The Doctorate: Talking About the Degree.* Kingswood, New South Wales: University of Western Sydney.

Draper, S. W. (2005) The Hawthorne, Pygmalion, placebo and other expectancy effects: some notes. Available at http://www.psy.gla.ac.uk/~steve/hawth.html (accessed May 2006).

Duke, C. (1997) Lifelong, postexperience, postgraduate – symphony or dichotomy?, in R. G. Burgess (ed.) *Beyond the First Degree: Graduate Education, Lifelong Learning and Careers.* Buckingham: SRHE/Open University Press.

Dweck, C. S. (2000) *Self-Theories: Their Role in Motivation, Personality, and Development.* Hove, UK: Psychology Press (Taylor and Francis Group).

Elias, P., Purcell, K., Durbin, S. et al. (2006) *The Employment of Social Science PhDs in Academic and Non-academic Jobs.* Swindon: Economic and Social Research Council.

Eraut, M. (1994) *Developing Professional Knowledge and Competence.* London: Falmer Press.

ESRC (Economic and Social Research Council) (2005) *Postgraduate Training Guidelines*, 4th edn. Available at http://www.esrc.ac.uk/ESRCInfoCentre/Images/Section_A_Introduction_to_the_ESRC_Postgraduate_Training_Guidelines_tcm6-9064.pdf (accessed 16 October 2006).

ESRC (Economic and Social Research Council) (2006) The employment of social science PhDs in academic and non-academic jobs: research skills and postgraduate training. Available at http://www.esrc.ac.uk/ESRCInfoCentre/Images/employment_of_soc_sci_ phds_tcm6-15385.pdf (accessed 3 January 2007).

EUA (European Universities Association) (2003) Statement on the Research Role of Europe's Universities. Available at http://www.eua.be/eua/jsp/en/upload/Research_Liege_conf_23042004.1083058845634.pdf (accessed 20 October 2006).

EUA (European Universities Association) (2005) *Doctoral Programmes for the European Knowledge Society.* Report on the EUA Doctoral Programmes Project 2004–2005. Available at http://www.eua.be/eua/jsp/en/upload/Doctoral_Programmes_Project_Report.1129285328581.pdf (accessed 20 October 2006).

Eurodoc (2004) Gathering of Evidence and Development of a European Supervision and Training Charter, T. Brown (ed.). Available at www.eurodoc.net/workgroups/supervision/Eurodocsuptrain.pdf

European Commission (2005) Commission Recommendation on the European Charter for Researchers and on a Code of Conduct for the Recruitment of Researchers. Available at http://www.fnrs-mobility.be/doc/am509774CEE_EN_E4.pdf (accessed 30 October 2006).

European Commission (2006) Delivering on the Modernisation Agenda for Universities: Education, Research and Innovation. Available at http://www.madrimasd.org/proyectoseuropeos/documentos/doc/education_research_and_innovation.pdf (accessed 30 October 2006).

Forsyth, I., Joliffe, A. and Stevens, D. (1995) *Evaluating a Course: Practical Strategies for Teachers, Lecturers and Trainers.* Abingdon: Routledge Falmer.

Gilbert, R. (2004) A framework for evaluating the doctoral curriculum, *Assessment & Evaluation in Higher Education*, 29(3): 299–309.

Gilbert, R., Balatti, J., Turner, P. and Whitehouse, H. (2004) The generic skills debate in research higher degrees, *Higher Education Research and Development*, 23(3): 375–88.

Gilligan, C. (1982) *In a Different Voice: Psychological Theory and Women's Development.* Cambridge, MA: Harvard University Press.

Goodchild, L. and Miller, M. M. (1997) The American doctorate and dissertation: six developmental stages, *New Directions for Higher Education*, 25(3): 17–32.

Green, Bill, (2005) Unfinished business: subjectivity and supervision, *Higher Education Research and Development*, 24(2): 151–63.

Green, H. (2005) Doctoral education in the UK: trends and challenges. Review paper prepared for Forces and Forms of Change in Doctoral Education International Conference. CIRGE, University of Washington, September.

Green, D. H. and Powell, S. D. (2004) The high price of good quality, *The Independent* (Education: Graduate Options), 13 October.

Green, H. and Powell, S. (2005) *Doctoral Study in Contemporary Higher Education*. Maidenhead: Open University Press.

Hamblin, A. (1974) *Evaluation and the Control of Training*. London: McGraw-Hill.

Harman, K. M. (2004) Producing 'industry-ready' doctorates: Australian Cooperative Research Centre approaches to doctoral education, *Studies in Continuing Education*, 26(3): 387–404.

Harris, M. (1996) *Review of Postgraduate Education*. Bristol: HEFCE, May. Available at http://www. hefce.ac.uk/Pubs/hefce/1996/m14_96.htm (accessed 21 July 2006).

HEFCE (Higher Education Funding Council for England) (2001) Improving standards in postgraduate research degree programmes. Available at http:// www. hefce.ac.uk/news/HEFCE/2001/supply.htm (accessed 2007).

HEFCE (Higher Education Funding Council for England) (2002) Improving standards in postgraduate research degree programmes. Available at http://www.hefce.ac.uk/pubs/rdreports/2002/rd11_02/rd11_02.doc (accessed 30 October 2006).

HEFCE (Higher Education Funding Council for England) (2003a) Improving standards in postgraduate research degree programmes: informal consultation. Available at http://www.hefce.ac.uk/pubs/hefce/2003/03_01.htm (accessed 30 October 2006).

HEFCE (Higher Education Funding Council for England) (2003b) Improving standards in postgraduate research degree programmes: formal consultation. Available at http://www.hefce.ac.uk/pubs/hefce/2003/03_23.htm (accessed 30 October 2006).

HEFCE (Higher Education Funding Council for England) (2003c) Research capability fund: request for strategies. Available at http://www.hefce.ac.uk/pubs/circlets/2003/cl10_03.htm (accessed 30 October 2006).

HEFCE (Higher Education Funding Council for England) (2004) Funding for research degree programmes (RDPs). Available at www.hefce.ac.uk/research/postgrad/rdpfund.htm (accessed 14 September 2006).

HESA (Higher Education Statistics Agency) (2004) *Destination of Leavers from Higher Education 2004/05*. Available at http://www.hesa.ac.uk/manuals/04018/dlhe0405.htm (accessed 15 October 2006).

HM Treasury (2002) *Investing in Innovation: A Strategy for Science, Engineering and Technology*. London: HMSO.

HM Treasury (2003) Lambert Review of Business-University Collaboration. Available at http://www.hm-treasury.gov.uk/media/DDE/65/lambert_review _final_450.pdf

Hogg, M. A. and Vaughan, G. M. (1998) *Social Psychology*, 2nd edn. Glasgow: Prentice Hall.

Honey, P. (1998) *The Learning Experience*. London: BBC Worldwide.

Honey, P. and Mumford, A. (1992). *The Manual of Learning Styles.* Maidenhead: P. Honey.

Huczynski, A. and Buchanan, D. (2001) *Organisational Behaviour: An Introductory Text,* 4th edn. Harlow: Prentice Hall.

Industrial Society (2000) *Managing Best Practice: Training Evaluation.* London.

Institutional Management in Higher Education (2003) Sticks and carrots: the effectiveness of government policy on higher education in England since 1979, *Higher Education Management and Policy,* 15(1): 119–37.

J M Consulting (2005) *Costs of Training and Supervising Postgraduate Research Students.* A report to HEFCE. Bristol: J M Consulting Ltd.

Jagger, N., Davis, S., Lain, D., Sinclair, E. and Sinclair, T. (2001) *Employers Views of Postgraduate Physicists.* Report by the Institute for Employment Studies for the Engineering and Physical Sciences Research Council.

James, P. (1998) Progressive development of deep learning skills through undergraduate and postgraduate dissertations, *Educational Studies,* 24(1): 95–105.

Jarvis, J. (2000) The changing university: meeting a need and needing to change, *Higher Education Quarterly,* 54(1): 43–67.

Johnson, L., Lee, A. and Green, B. (2000) The PhD and the autonomous self: gender, rationality and postgraduate pedagogy, *Studies in Higher Education,* 25(2): 135–47.

Kane, E. (2005) The European Charter for Researchers and the Code of Conduct for Their Recruitment: Report of Conference Proceedings. UK Research Office, Brussels.

Kearns, P. and Miller, T. (1997) Measuring the impact of training and development of the bottom line. FT Management Briefings. London: Pitman Publishing.

Kirk, R. F. (1987) *Learning in Action: Activities for Personal and Group Development.* Oxford: Basil Blackwell.

Knowles, M. (1996) Andragogy, in R. Edwards, A. Hanson and P. Raggatt (eds) *Boundaries of Adult Learning.* London. Routledge.

Kolb, D. A. (1984) *Experiential Learning: Experience as the Source of Learning and Development.* New Jersey: Prentice Hall.

Kuhn, T. (1962) *The Structure of Scientific Revolutions.* Chicago, IL: University of Chicago Press.

Leonard, D. (2001) *A Woman's Guide to Doctoral Studies.* Buckingham: Open University Press.

Leonard, R. and Barber, K. (1998) Postgraduate training & research in collaboration with industry (twenty years of experience in the UK). Manchester: UMIST. Available at http://www.ctc.puc-rio.br/icee-98/icee/papers/340.pdf (accessed 31 October 2006).

Lindner, J. R., Dooley, K. E. and Murphy, T. H. (2001) Differences in competencies between doctoral students on-campus and at a distance, *American Journal of Distance Education,* 15(2): 25–40.

Lindsay, R., Breen, R. and Jenkins, A. (2002) Academic Research and Teaching Quality: the views of undergraduate and postgraduate students. *Studies in Higher Education* 27(3): 309–327.

Lodge, D. (1989) *Nice Work.* Harmondsworth: Penguin.

Lorimer, H. and Philip, L. J. (2005) Advanced research training in geography: the Scottish experience, *Journal of Geography in Higher Education,* 29(2): 279–92.

Lowndes, B. (1998) Evaluating the evaluation of training. MBA Dissertation. University of Nottingham.

Lucas, W. A. and Cooper, S. Y. (2006) Measuring entrepreneurial self-efficacy (personal communication).

Lucas, W., Cooper, S., Ward, A. and Cave, F. D. (2006) Developing self-efficacy and entrepreneurial intent for technology entrepreneurship: the role of work experience. Paper presented at the 3rd AGSE International Entrepreneurship Research Exchange, Auckland, New Zealand, February.

Lyotard, J.-F. (1984) *The Post-Modern Condition: A Report on Knowledge*. Manchester: Manchester University Press.

Marsh, H. W., Rowe, K. J. and Martin, A. (2002) Ph.D. students' evaluations of research supervision: issues, complexities, and challenges in a nationwide Australian experiment in benchmarking universities, *Journal of Higher Education*, 73(3): 313–48.

Mau, W.-C. (2003) Factors that influence persistence in science and engineering career aspirations, *The Career Development Quarterly*, 51(3): 234–43.

McCormack, C. (2004) Tensions between student and institutional conceptions of postgraduate research, *Studies in Higher Education*, 29(3): 319–34.

McCulloch, A. (2004) Part-time majority, *Times Higher Education Supplement*, 10 September.

McFarlane, B. (2005) The disengaged academic: the retreat from citizenship, *Higher Education Quarterly*, 59(4): 296–312.

Metcalfe, J., Thompson, Q. and Green, H. (2002) Improving standards in post-graduate research degree programmes: a report to the Higher Education Funding Councils of England, Scotland and Wales. Bristol: Higher Education Council for England. Available at http://www.hefce.ac.uk/pubs/rdreports/ 2002/

Metz, M. H. (2001) Intellectual border crossing in graduate education: a report from the field, *Educational Researcher*, 30(5): 12–18.

Moon, J. (1999) *Reflection in Learning and Professional Development: Theory and Practice*. London: Kogan Page.

Morley, L., Leonard, D. and David, M. (2002) Variations in vivas: quality and equality in British PhD assessments, *Studies in Higher Education*, 27(3): 263–73.

Moynagh, M. and Worsley, R. (2005) *Working in the Twenty-First Century*. Leeds: ESRC Future of Work Programme and King's Lynn The Tomorrow Project.

Murphy, R., Wiesemes, R., Lewis, P. and Sisson, T. (2004) Report on the Research into the Generic Skills Training and Development of Postgraduate Research Students and Contract Research Staff. Available at http://www.nottingham .ac.uk/gradschool/documents/roberts-money/roberts-money-research.doc (accessed 9 August 2006).

Murray, A. and Wanlin, A. (2005) The Lisbon Scorecard V: Can Europe compete? London: CER. See also http://www.euractiv.com/Article?tcmuri=tcm:29-137075 -16&type=News (accessed 30 October 2006).

Musselin, C. (2004) Towards a European academic labour market? Some lessons drawn from empirical studies on academic mobility, *Higher Education*, 48(1): 55–78.

National Research Council (1995) Research-Doctorate Programs in the United States: Continuity and Change, Washington. Available at http://newton.nap.edu/ html/researchdoc/.

Neumann, R. (2001) Disciplinary differences and university teaching, *Studies in Higher Education*, 26(2): 135–146.

Neumann, R. (2005) Doctoral differences: professional doctorates and PhDs compared, *Journal of Higher Education Policy and Management*, 27(2): 173–88.

Newby, A. (1992) *Training Evaluation Handbook*. London: Gower.

Noble, K. A. (1994) *Changing Doctoral Degrees: An International Perspective*. Buckingham: Society for Research into Higher Education and Open University Press.

OECD (2003) *Science, Technology and Industry Scoreboard 2003 – Towards a Knowledge-Based Economy*. Paris: OECD.

OST (Office of Science and Technology) (1994) *Consultative Document: A New Structure for Postgraduate Research Trainings,* Supported by Research Councils. London: Cabinet Office.

OST (Office of Science and Technology) (1997) Survey of postgraduates funded by the research councils. Available at http://www.ost.gov.uk/research/funding/postgrad_survey/index.htm (now removed).

Park, C. C. (2003) Levelling the playing field: towards best practice in the doctoral viva, *Higher Education Review*, 36(1): 47–67.

Park, C. C. (2004) The graduate teaching assistant (GTA): lessons from North American experience, *Teaching in Higher Education*, 9(3): 349–61.

Park, C. C. (2005a) New Variant PhD: the changing nature of the doctorate in the UK, *Journal of Higher Education Policy and Management*, 27(2): 189–207.

Park, C. C. (2005b) War of attrition: patterns of non-completion amongst postgraduate research students, *Higher Education Review*, 38(1): 48–53.

Park, C. C. (2007) Redefining the Doctorate. Discussion paper, The Higher Education Academy, ISBN 978-1-905788-29-3.

Pearson, M. (2005) Framing research on doctoral education in Australia in a global context, *Higher Education Research and Development*, 24(2): 119–34.

Pearson, M. and Brew, A. (2002) Research training and supervision development, *Studies in Education*, 27(2): 135–50.

Pedler, M., Burgoyne, J. and Boydell, T. (1997) *The Learning Company: A Strategy for Sustainable Development*. London: McGraw-Hill.

Phillips, E. M. and Pugh, D. S. (2000) *How to Get a PhD*, 3rd edn. Buckingham: Open University Press.

Pole, C. (2000) Technicians and scholars in pursuit of the PhD: some reflections on doctoral study, *Research Papers in Education*, 15(1): 95–111.

Powell, S. D. (2004) *The Award of PhD by Published Work in the UK*. Lichfield: UK Council for Graduate Education.

Powell, S. D. and Green, H. (2003) Research degree examining: quality issues of principle and practice, *Quality Assurance in Education* (Special edition 'Assessing and Examining Research Awards'), 11(2): 55–64.

Powell, S. D. and Green, H. (2007) *The Doctorate Worldwide*. Buckingham: Open University Press (forthcoming).

Powell, S. D. and Long, E. (2005) *Professional Doctorate Awards in the UK*. Lichfield: UK Council for Graduate Education.

Powell, S. D. and McCauley, C. (2002) Research degree examining – common principles and divergent practices, *Quality Assurance in Education* (Special edition 'Standards and the Doctoral Award'), 10(2): 104–16.

Powell, S. D. and McCauley, C. (2003) The process of examining research degrees: some issues of quality, *Quality Assurance in Education* (Special edition 'Assessing and Examining Research Awards'), 11(2): 73–84.

Pratt, J. (1997) *The Polytechnic Experiment: 1965–92*. Milton Keynes: Open University Press.

PRES (2006) *Postgraduate Researcher Experience Survey*. Available at www.grad.ac.uk/news (accessed 8 August 2006).

QAA (Quality Assurance Agency) (2001a) The framework for higher education qualifications in England, Wales and Northern Ireland. Available at http://www.qaa.ac.uk/academicinfrastructure/FHEQ/EWNI/default.asp#an nex1 (accessed 30 October 2006).

QAA (Quality Assurance Agency) (2001b) Guidelines for HE Progress Files. Available at http://www.qaa.ac.uk/academicinfrastructure/progressfiles/guidelines/ progfile2001.pdf (accessed May 2007).

QAA (Quality Assurance Agency) (2004) Code of practice for the assurance of academic quality and standards in higher education. Section 1: Postgraduate research programmes. Available at http://www.qaa.ac.uk/academicinfrastructure/ codeOfPractice/section1/postgrad2004.pdf (accessed 21 July 2006).

Rae, L. (1983) *The Skills of Training* Aldershot: Wildwood House.

Rae, L. (1997) *How to Measure Training Effectiveness.* London: Gower.

RCUK (Research Councils UK) (2001a) Joint Statement of Skills Training Requirements of Research Postgraduates. London: RCUK. Available at www.grad.ac.uk/jss

RCUK (Research Councils UK) (2001b) Joint Statement of the Research Councils'/AHRB's Skills Training Requirements for Research Students. Available at http://www.bbsrc.ac.uk/funding/training/skill_train_req.pdf (accessed 21 July 2006).

RCUK (Research Councils UK) (2005) *Career Development and Skills (Roberts) Reporting 2005.* London: RCUK. Available at www.grad.ac.uk (accessed 8 August 2006).

Reichert, Sybille (2005) Bergen Conference of Ministers, May 2005 – Short Summary of the Parallel Session on Doctoral Training and the Synergy between Higher Education and Research.

Roberts, S. G. (2002) *SET for Success – The supply of people with science, technology, engineering and mathematics skills.* The report of Sir Gareth Roberts' Review, Higher Education Funding Councils of England, Scotland and Wales. London: HM Treasury. Available at http://www.hm-treasury.gov.uk/documents/enterprise _and_productivity/research_and_enterprise/ent_res_roberts.cfm (accessed 15 October 2006).

Rogers, J. (2001) *Adults Learning,* 4th edn. Buckingham: Open University Press.

Rose, G (2002) Group differences in graduate students' concepts of the ideal mentor. *Research In Higher Education,* 46(1): 53–80.

Rowe, G. and Wright, G. (1999) The Delphi technique as a forecasting tool: issues and analysis, *International Journal of Forecasting,* 15: 353–75.

Rugby Team (2006) Evaluation of skills development of early career researchers – a strategy paper from the Rugby Team. Report to the UK GRAD Roberts Policy Forum, January 2006. Available at http://www.grad.ac.uk/rugbyteam (accessed 15 October 2006).

Rugg, G. and Petre, M. (2004) *The Unwritten Rules of PhD Research.* Maidenhead: Open University Press.

Salas, E. and Cannon-Bowers, J. (2001) The science of training: a decade of progress, *Annual Review of Psychology,* 52: 471–99.

Salmon, P. (1992) *Achieving a PhD: Ten Students' Experience.* Stoke-on-Trent: Trentham Books.

Salzburg (2005) Bologna Seminar on Doctoral Programmes for the European Knowledge Society. Available at www.bologna-bergen2005.no/EN/Bol_sem/ Seminars/050203-05Salzburg/050203-05_Conclusions.pdf; this was followed up by the March 2006 Brussels Seminar, the October 2006 Brussels II Seminar and the December 2006 Nice Seminar.

Schön, D. A. (1983) *The Reflective Practitioner: How Professionals Think in Action.* New York: Basic Books.

Schön, D. A. (1987) *Educating the Reflective Practitioner: Toward a New Design for Teaching and Learning in the Professions.* San Francisco: Jossey Bass.

Senge, P. (1990) *The Fifth Discipline: The Art and Practice of Learning Organisations.* London: Random House.

Shaw, M. (2005) 2005 Autumn update on emerging practice on the use of personal development planning (PDP) for postgraduate researchers (PGRs). Cambridge: The UK GRAD Programme. See also http://www.grad.ac.uk/cms/ShowPage/ Home_page/Publications/Publications_intro/p!ebfaepa (accessed May 2006).

Shaw, M., Brown, T. and Pearce, E. (2004) A national review of emerging practice on the use of personal development planning for postgraduate researchers. Cambridge: The UK GRAD Programme. See also http://www.grad.ac.uk/cms/ ShowPage/Home_page/Publications/Publications_intro/p!ebfaepa (accessed May 2006).

Shepherd, J. and Davis, C. (2005) 'Criminal' PhD cuts trigger job fears, *Times Higher Education Supplement*, 30 September, No. 1711, p. 6.

Shinton, S. (2004) *What Do PhDs Do?* UK GRAD Programme. Available at http://www.grad.ac.uk/cms/ShowPage/Home_page/Resources/What_Do _PhDs_Do_/p!eXeccLa#62566 (accessed 15 October 2006).

Simmonds, D. (2003/2006) *Designing and Delivering Training.* London, Chartered Institute of Personnel and Development.

Simpson, R. (1983) *How the PhD Came to Britain: A Century of Struggle for Postgraduate Education.* Guildford: Society of Research into Higher Education.

Souter, C. (2005) *EMPRESS (Employers' Perceptions of Recruiting Research Staff and Students).* Available at http://careerweb.leeds.ac.uk/downloads/Empress _LR_000.pdf

Spensley, F. (2002) Taking horses to water (paper posted on the Internet but now removed).

Stajkovic, A. and Luthans, F. (1998) Self-efficacy and work-related performance: a meta-analysis, *Psychological Bulletin*, 124(2): 240–61.

Stiles, D. R. (2000) Higher education funding patterns since 1990: a new perspective, *Public Money & Management*, 20(4): 51–7.

Taylor, J. (2002) Changes in teaching and learning in the period to 2005: the case of postgraduate higher education in the UK, *Journal of Higher Education Policy and Management*, 24(1): 53–73.

TDLB (Training and Development Lead Body) (2002) *Occupational Standards for Training.* London: Institute of Personnel and Development.

Thaller, Nicole (2006) Standards for Doctoral Programmes. Are there Organizational Determinants to successfully support Doctoral Candidates? IAAEG, University of Trier. Available at www.iaaeg.de/documents/

The Independent (2005) A blow to the heart of research, 17 November.

Thorne, L. E. and Francis, J. C. (2001) PhD and Professional Doctorate experience: the problematics of the National Framework, *Higher Education Review*, 33(3): 13–29.

Tight, M. (2003) *Researching Higher Education.* Maidenhead: SRHE/Open University Press.

Trigwell, K. and Dunbar-Goddet, H. (2005) *The Research Experience of Postgraduate Students at the University of Oxford*. Oxford: Institute for the Advancement of University Learning.

UKCGE (UK Council for Graduate Education) (1998) *Gradate Schools Survey*. Warwick, UKCGE. Available at http://www.ukcge.ac.uk/report_downloads .html (accessed 14 September 2006).

UKCGE (UK Council for Graduate Education) (2000) Research Training for Humanities Postgraduate Students. Lichfield, UKCGE. Available at http://www.ukcge.ac.uk/report_downloads.html (accessed 14 September 2006).

UKCGE (UK Council for Graduate Education) (2001) Research Training in the Creative and Performing Arts and Design. Lichfield, UKCGE. Available at http://www.ukcge.ac.uk/report_downloads.html (accessed 20 January 2005).

UK GRAD (2006) *Guide to Gradschools*. Example timetable for a day on a GRADschool, p. 2, and Statistics from GRADschool appraisals in 2005, p. 5.

UK GRAD Regional Hub Coordinators (2006) What will the environment be like to researchers in 2012? Briefing note for Research Councils Strategy Forum (24 March). Cambridge: UK GRAD.

University of Nottingham (2006) Available at www.nottingham.ac.uk/gradschool/ robertsmoney.

Walters, M. (1996) *Employee Attitudes and Opinion Surveys*. London: Institute of Personnel and Development.

Warr, P., Allan, C. and Birdi, K. (1999) Predicting three levels of training outcome. *Journal of Occupational and Organisational Psychology*, 72: 351–75.

Wikeley, F. and Muschamp, Y. (2004) Pedagogical implications of working with doctoral students at a distance, *Distance Education*, 25(1): 125–42.

Wildman, T. and Niles, J. (1987) Reflective teachers: tensions between abstractions and realities, *Journal of Teacher Education*, 3: 25–31.

Wisker, G., Robinson, G., Trafford, V., Creighton, E. and Warnes, M. (2003) Recognising and overcoming dissonance in postgraduate student research; *Studies in Higher Education*, 28(1): 91–105.

Wu, S. (2002) Filling the pot or lighting the fire? Cultural variations in conceptions of pedagogy, *Teaching in Higher Education*, 7(4): 387–95.

Wyatt, J. (1998) 'The lengthening shadow of one man': the public intellectual and the founding of universities, *Higher Education Review*, 30(2): 29–49.

Index